Slavery and Essentialism in Highland Madagascar

This book explores the prejudice against slave descendants in highland Madagascar and its persistence more than a century after the official abolition of slavery.

'Unclean people' is a widespread expression in the southern highlands of Madagascar, and refers to people of alleged slave descent who are discriminated against on a daily basis and in a variety of ways. Denis Regnier shows that prejudice is rooted in a strong case of psychological essentialism: free descendants think that 'slaves' have a 'dirty' essence that is impossible to cleanse. Regnier's field experiments question the widely accepted idea that the social stigma against slavery is a legacy of pre-colonial society. He argues, to the contrary, that the essentialist construal of 'slaves' is the outcome of the historical process triggered by the colonial abolition of slavery: whereas in pre-abolition times slaves could be cleansed through ritual means, the abolition of slavery meant that slaves were transformed only superficially into free persons, while their inner essence remained unchanged and became progressively constructed as 'forever unchangeable'.

Based on detailed fieldwork, this volume will be of interest to scholars of anthropology, African studies, development studies, cultural psychology and those looking at the legacy of slavery.

Denis Regnier is Assistant Professor and Head of Humanities and Social Sciences at the University of Global Health Equity in Rwanda. He gained his PhD in anthropology from the London School of Economics, UK.

London School of Economics Monographs on Social Anthropology

Managing Editor: Laura Bear

The Monographs on Social Anthropology were established in 1940 and aim to publish results of modern anthropological research of primary interest to specialists. The continuation of the series was made possible by a grant in aid from the Wenner-Gren Foundation for Anthropological Research, and more recently by a further grant from the Governors of the London School of Economics and Political Science. Income from sales is returned to a revolving fund to assist further publications. The Monographs are under the direction of an Editorial Board associated with the Department of Anthropology of the London School of Economics and Political Science.

Titles include:

Affective Encounters
Everyday Life among Chinese Migrants in Zambia
Di Wu

Slavery and Essentialism in Highland Madagascar
Ethnography, History, Cognition
Denis Regnier

https://www.routledge.com/LSE-Monographs-on-Social-Anthropology/book-series/BLANTLSEMSA

Slavery and Essentialism in Highland Madagascar

Ethnography, History, Cognition

Denis Regnier

Routledge
Taylor & Francis Group

LONDON AND NEW YORK

First published 2021
by Routledge
2 Park Square, Milton Park, Abingdon, Oxon OX14 4RN

and by Routledge
52 Vanderbilt Avenue, New York, NY 10017

Routledge is an imprint of the Taylor & Francis Group, an informa business

British Library Cataloguing in Publication Data
A catalogue record for this book is available from the British Library

Library of Congress Cataloging-in-Publication Data
Names: Regnier, Denis, author.
Title: Slavery and essentialism in highland Madagascar : ethnography,
history, cognition / Denis Regnier.
Description: Abingdon, Oxon ; New York : Routledge, 2020. |
Series: London
school of economics monographs on social anthropology | Includes
bibliographical references and index.
Identifiers: LCCN 2020028683 (print) | LCCN 2020028684 (ebook)
|ISBN 9781350102477 (hardback) | ISBN 9781003086697 (ebook)
Subjects: LCSH: Slavery–Madagascar–History. | Race
discrimination–Madagascar–History. | Essentialism
(Philosophy)–Madagascar. | Social psychology–Madagascar.
Classification: LCC HT1399.M28 R44 2020 (print) | LCC HT1399.
M28 (ebook)
| DDC 305.5/6809691–dc23
LC record available at https://lccn.loc.gov/2020028683
LC ebook record available at https://lccn.loc.gov/2020028684

ISBN: 978-1-350-10247-7 (hbk)
ISBN: 978-1-003-08669-7 (ebk)

Typeset in Times New Roman
by Taylor & Francis Books

MIX
Paper from
responsible sources
FSC
www.fsc.org   FSC™ C013985

Printed in the United Kingdom
by Henry Ling Limited

To the memory of my mother, Monique Donnay

Contents

List of illustrations

Figures

Tables

Acknowledgements

My first thanks are for all the villagers in Beparasy who let me live among them and who opened their homes to me: *Misaotra indrindra anareo aby!* In particular, my research could not have been successful without the steady support and assistance of the two friends I have named in the book, Redison and Naina. Redison hosted me from my very first day in Beparasy. During my stay, villagers considered me as a member of his family and he always introduced me as his *rahalahy* (brother). Redison, his wife Raely, his mother Ramarcelline and the inhabitants of the small hamlet of Soatanana made me feel we were kinsmen, and I thank them for that. Naina, Redison's brother-in-law, accompanied me on many of my journeys and proved a humorous and reliable companion. *Ramose* and *Monsieur le maire*, while not figuring as well-identified characters in this book, were also immensely instrumental to the success of my fieldwork. *Ramose* honoured me with his friendship and never tired of sharing his knowledge of local customs and family stories. *Monsieur le maire*'s benevolence and support through his extensive networks facilitated many encounters and interviews.

Without the hospitality and kindness of the Berosaiña, the people who are at the centre of this book, it would have been impossible to carry out this research. My gratitude goes particularly to those who appear here under the names of Ramarcel, Vohangy, Raboba and Randriatsoa. They agreed to answer questions which were sometimes difficult and in some cases clearly embarrassing. Ramarcel certainly got the greatest share of this – since we had become good friends it was to him that I turned whenever I had a difficult question to ask. However, neither Ramarcel, the other Berosaiña nor the villagers of Beparasy ever took offence at my careful but nonetheless obstinate inquiries into sensitive issues. I deeply thank all of them for their tolerance.

In Ambalavao, Redison and Raely's relatives kindly provided us with a place to stay for a night or two when we were waiting for uncertain lifts to leave in the direction of Beparasy. Since I regularly used their services, I became friends with the few drivers in Ambalavao who dared to bring their cars on the difficult track leading to Beparasy. I thank them for the safe driving and for the good moments we spent together. I am equally grateful to the managers of one of Ambalavao's hotels, who kindly offered me discount rates for a room whenever I felt the need for a hot shower or a bit of intimacy. In Fianarantsoa I met the scholars Clarisse Rasoamampionona, Fulgence Rasolonjatovo, Henry Rasamoelina and François Noiret, with whom I discussed the anthropology of the Betsileo. Olivia Legrip-Randriambelo was also carrying out fieldwork in the southern Betsileo region, and on regular occasions we shared our observations over a rice dish in a small *hôtely* of Ampasambazaha. In Antananarivo, Michel Razafiarivony helped me secure a research visa. I thank him and all the members of the Musée d'Art et d'Archéologie for inviting me to present my research upon arrival as well as hosting an end-of-fieldwork report. At a later stage, Tana-based researchers Lolona Razafindralambo and Juvence Ramasy became good friends and I greatly benefited from conversations with them.

The largest part of the research upon which this book is based was initially carried out for a PhD at the London School of Economics. In London, Vao Brown wittily taught me the rudiments of the Malagasy language before I went to the field. At the LSE my PhD supervisors, Rita Astuti and Maurice Bloch, deserve gratitude far beyond what I can offer. They have been incredibly supportive all the way through, and readers familiar with their thinking will easily understand my intellectual debt. I still have fond memories of the highly constructive supervision sessions with Rita, while walking her dog Dapple in the streets of London, and with Maurice in his Parisian study. The LSE anthropology department formed a supportive and engaging intellectual environment where my research project could grow smoothly. The administrative staff was tremendously efficient and friendly. I wish to thank in particular Yanina Hinrichsen, the departmental manager, for her amazing ability to help people in all circumstances. The LSE writing-up seminar provided a wonderful opportunity to discuss my first writings with other post-fieldwork PhD students and departmental staff. My cohort of PhD students, as well as some people who were a bit ahead or behind me, formed a bunch of incredibly smart colleagues: Gustavo Barbosa, Max Bolt, Tom Boylston, Natalia Buitrón Arias, Alanna Cant, Kimberly Chong, Ankur Datta, I-Chieh Fang, Elizabeth

Frantz, Catherine Furberg Moe, Ana Gutierrez Garza, Tamara Hale, Agnes Hann, Michael Hoffmann, Daniela Kraemer, Giulia Liberatore, Dina Makram Ebeid, Aude Michelet, Xandra Miguel-Lorenzo, Luca Pes, Sitna Quiroz, Dave Robinson, George St Clair, Miranda Sheild Johansson and Matt Wilde. I thank all of them for having been humourful and intellectually stimulating companions, and I wish to warmly thank Gustavo, Michael, Daniela and Aude for offering me a bed or a couch whenever I had to spend nights in London. I am incredibly grateful to all the LSE academic staff for their exemplarity and mentorship, both as teachers and researchers, with special thanks to Catherine Allerton, Rita Astuti, Laura Bear, Maurice Bloch, Fenella Cannell, Matthew Engelke, Stephan Feuchtwang, Chris Fuller, Deborah James, Martha Mundy, Michael Scott, Charles Stafford and the late Olivia Harris. I also thank my PhD examiners, Michael Lambek and Jonathan Parry, for their sharp and insightful comments on my thesis; I have kept them constantly in mind while writing this book. In London I started long discussions with Dominique Somda, then a visiting scholar at the LSE, about our respective fieldwork in Madagascar. These still ongoing discussions have helped sharpen the ideas and arguments I am presenting here, but above all I thank her for her friendship. Dan Sperber initially helped me to settle in at the LSE and has encouraged my anthropological training from its very beginnings – I am very grateful to him for that.

Over the years, since I first embarked on this research, I have met a great number of scholars. Through their work and/or our discussions, interactions and exchanges they have all, to various degrees, contributed to shaping the anthropologist I have become. These people include, in addition to those I have already mentioned: Sander Adelaar, Richard Allen, Nicolas Argenti, Aurélien Baroiller, Loïs Bastide, Nicolas Baumard, Laurent Berger, David Berliner, Benoît Beucher, Randall Bird, Sophie Blanchy, Delphine Burguet, Gwyn Campbell, Solange Chatelard, Liana Chua, Fabrice Clément, Jennifer Cole, Grégory Delaplace, Stéphanie Demoulin, Marco Di Nunzio, Barry Ferguson, Martin Fortier, James Fox, Luke Freeman, Peggy Froerer, Sébastien Galliot, Marco Gardini, Denis Gay, Susan Gelman, Liza Gezon, Thomas Gibson, Mathilde Gingembre, Sarah Gould, the late David Graeber, Hannah Höchner, Amber Huff, Eva Keller, Peter Kneitz, Gabriella Körling, Conrad Kottak, Antonie Kraemer, Kun-hui Ku, the late Pier Larson, Samuel Lempereur, Jerome Lewis, Laurent Licata, Karen Middleton, Olivier Morin, Frank Muttenzer, Joël Noret, Sarah Osterhoudt, Seth Palmer, Mike Parker Pearson, Pierre Petit, Jacques Pollini, Joëlle Proust, Roland Rakotovao, Gabriel

Rantoandro, Benedetta Rossi, Benjamin Rubbers, Samuel Sanchez, Bruno Saura, Marlene Schäfers, Aurore Schmitt, Caroline Seagle, Genese Sodikoff, Hans Steinmüller, Bram Tucker, Radu Umbres, Annabel Vallard, Iain Walker, Andrew Walsh and Vincent Yzerbyt. I would like to close this list by heartily thanking Laurent Legrain and Maïté Maskens for being two great friends in addition to being wonderful anthropologists.

My PhD fieldwork in Madagascar was funded by a grant from the Central Research Fund of the University of London and a Dissertation Fieldwork Grant from the Wenner-Gren Foundation. The LSE and the LSE Department of Anthropology provided financial help during the pre- and post-fieldwork phases. Postdoctoral fellowships at the École normale supérieure de Paris and at the Université libre de Bruxelles, funded respectively by the European Research Council and the Fonds de la Recherche Scientifique (F.R.S.-FNRS), allowed me to go back several times to Madagascar and undertake further research. I am grateful to all these institutions for their support.

Sections of Chapters 7 and 8 have appeared in *Social Anthropology* (volume 23, issue 2) and *Anthropological Forum* (volume 29, issue 3). I thank the publishers for granting me permission to reproduce this work here. I wish to express my gratitude to Laura Bear, the editor of the LSE Monographs on Social Anthropology, and the committee for the LSE Monographs Competition for giving me the opportunity to publish in such a distinguished series. The great Malagasy photographer Pierrot Men granted me the right to use one of his wonderful pictures of the Malagasy highlands for the book cover – I am extremely grateful to him for this. The book's manuscript was completed at the Maison des Sciences de l'Homme du Pacifique in Tahiti. *Mauruuru roa* to its director, Eric Conte, and its secretary, Elisabeth Lance, for offering me comfortable office space, great coffees and pleasant company during several periods of intense writing.

My deepest thanks, finally, go to my wife Anjasoa, our children Camille and Léo, my son David, my siblings Valérie and Stéphane and their partners Benoît and Marie, my father Yvon and my mother Monique, who unfortunately did not live long enough to see this book published. Without their love, support and patience during all these years it would have been much more difficult for me to go through all the obstacles standing in the way.

Note on language

The official language of Madagascar is spoken, written and understood throughout the island since it is used in schools, the administration and the media. Oral language, however, shows a great deal of regional variation. The southern Betsileo way of speaking has a number of distinctive features, which are too numerous to be summarised here. Among these is the fact that the final syllable '-na', frequent in official Malagasy words, is most of the time inexistent in the southern Betsileo vocabulary. Thus the southern Betsileo equivalents of *razana* (dead, ancestors), *fasana* (tomb), *olona* (people) and *fianakaviana* (family) are respectively *raza, fasa, olo* and *fianakavy*. To take another example, the equivalent of the final syllable '-tra' in official Malagasy is '-tse' in the southern Betsileo language, as in *fototse* and *saotse*, the local variants of *fototra* (root) and *saotra* (thanking). In the book I will often switch between these linguistic forms, depending on whether I am referring to pan-Malagasy concepts – such as *tanindrazana* (ancestral land) – or transcribing words or sentences from interviews in the vernacular language.

Map of Madagascar

1 An encounter with southern Betsileo 'slaves'

The people known today as the Betsileo occupy a large territory of the southern highlands of Madagascar.[1] Administratively speaking, the Betsileo homeland is situated in Amoron'i Mania and Matsiatra Ambony, the two *faritra* (regions) that were parts of the former *faritany* (province) of Fianarantsoa. In geographic terms, Betsileo territory is roughly situated between the Mania River to the north and the Andringitra chain and the Zomandao River to the south. The eastern side of Betsileo territory ends approximately when the rainforest starts, while the western part extends into vast areas that are only scarcely populated until one reaches the region inhabited by the Sakalava. The immediate neighbours of the Betsileo are the Merina (north), the Betsimisaraka (north-east), the Zafimaniry (north-east), the Tanala (east), the Bara (south) and the Sakalava (west).

The use of the name 'Betsileo' for the people living in the southern highlands is recent and dates back to the creation of a Betsileo province by King Radama I (1793–1828) after his conquests in the early nineteenth century. Prior to being subjected to Merina rule, the region that was going to be known as Betsileo comprised many petty kingdoms. The kingdoms of Isandra and Lalangina are usually seen as the most important of these polities since they had a state-like organisation (Kottak 1977; 1980: 66–87). To the north of Isandra and Lalangina was the kingdom of Manandriana; to the south was the region constituted of separate kingdoms (Tsienimparihy, Vohibato, Alananindro and Homatsazo) and which came to be known as Arindrano after its 'unification' by Radama I.[2]

Most scholars draw a distinction between the north and the south of Betsileo country because of their different histories. North Betsileo includes today the regions of Manandriana, Ambositra and Fisakana, which are located north of the Matsiatra River. This area was once part of the sixth division of Imerina before being annexed to the

Betsileo province and administrated by the Merina governor of Fianarantsoa. Except for the region of Manandriana, which has a long history, the area now called North Betsileo became densely populated and politically organised only under Merina rule in the nineteenth century (Kottak 1980: 304–305; Freeman 2001: Chapter 2). As a result, its inhabitants are something of a mix between Merina and Betsileo. The region south of the Matsiatra River, by contrast, had an important political and economic history long before Merina annexation. The Merina kings called this region *andafy atsimon'i Matsiatra* ('south across the Matsiatra'). In the literature, it is sometimes called for this reason the 'historical' Betsileo. Yet, although the Betsileo as an ethnic group is by and large an invention of Merina administration that was subsequently taken on by French colonial rulers, today all the people from the northern and southern parts of the territory call themselves Betsileo. It is nonetheless important to bear in mind that the people I studied, who live in the extreme south of the Betsileo region, acknowledge that their *fombandrazana* (ancestral customs) differ from the Betsileo who live further north. This is true even though, as we shall see, many of my informants claimed that their ancestors came from northern Betsileo. Such differences and awareness make it difficult to give an encapsulated description of Betsileo society that would unambiguously apply to the north and the south.[3]

Today, the majority of southern Betsileo are rice-growing peasants living in villages and hamlets in the vicinity of their rice fields. People also raise cattle (*omby*, i.e. zebus), especially in the extreme southern region, but they do so in a much smaller proportion than their southern neighbours, the pastoral Bara. In the fairly recent past, cattle-raising was more important and rice cultivation did not occupy the central place that it has now in the southern Betsileo economy. The local economy shifted to an intensive rice-growing agriculture under Merina rule during the nineteenth century, not least because the Merina directly encouraged its cultivation. Local peasants had to grow rice because of fiscal pressure: they had to cultivate it intensively in order to make a surplus to generate income. This income was required in order to pay the heavy taxes imposed by Merina rulers (Ralaikoa 1987: 34).

This transformation of the economy also deeply modified the rural settlement patterns of the southern Betsileo. During the eighteenth century and until the second half of the nineteenth, people mostly lived in fortified villages on hilltops. It was important to protect oneself in fortified sites because wars between local lords and raids from outsiders were frequent. In wars, as in raids, captives were taken to be sold as slaves. When the risk of inter-polity war decreased under Merina rule and when southern Betsileo had to become wet-rice cultivators in order to pay their taxes, things changed rapidly: the fortified village on a hilltop was no longer seen as the most desirable mode of settlement. Land was allocated to people, and families established themselves close to their rice fields, forming small hamlets protected by a circular hedge of thorny trees and cactuses. These hamlets were named *vala* (cattle pen) since they were organised around a corral (see Figure 1.1). Manure was transported down to the rice fields thanks to a canal passing through the pen. This ingenious and efficient technique allowed peasants to increase their production of rice.[4] At the same time, however, the move to the *vala* and the general impoverishment of the population because of heavy fiscal pressure meant that the numbers of cattle owned by southern Betsileo peasants significantly decreased, in particular in the region of Ambalavao (Ralaikoa 1987: 299).

The basic units of southern Betsileo social organisation are the tomb-centred, named local descent groups, which are called *foko* or *firazanana*. Membership to these groups is cognatic, optative and non-exclusive, but shows a strong patrilineal bias since most people prefer patrilocal post-marital residence and they are most often buried in their father's tomb than in others (Kottak 1971; 1980), even though they have the right to be buried in a number of tombs built by the descent groups to which they belong. Ancient Betsileo society was made up of three endogamous status groups: *hova* (nobles), *olompotsy* (commoners) and *andevo* (slaves). As the present book will show in some detail, this division of all Betsileo into three categories continues to be relevant.

Figure 1.1 A descent group gathering around their cattle corral (*vala*)

Until the Merina conquest, Betsileo polities were independent, state-like formations organised around a *mpanjaka* (ruler) of noble descent.[5] They had capitals which were fortified hilltop villages with a *lapa* (royal residence) and a number of people surrounding the rulers; i.e., advisers, servants, soldiers and slaves. Inter-polity wars were endemic in the southern highlands but were stopped by Merina rule, which became effective in the southern part of Betsileo country only after the conquests of Radama I between 1810 and 1820. Nonetheless, a climate of general insecurity continued to exist in these regions, since, on the fringes of the kingdom, Merina garrisons could only exert loose control and could not prevent raids by outsiders, especially the Bara neigh-bours.[6] In the south of Arindrano, the Merina established in 1852 a garrison in Ambohimandroso which became the administrative and economic centre of the area, headed by a Merina *komandy* (governor). It is also in Ambohimandroso that the Christian missions first estab-lished themselves in the region (Raherisoanjato 1982b). In 1899, how-ever, the French colonial administrator, General Joseph Gallieni, decided to make the then small village of Ambalavao the new admin-istrative and economic centre. Since then, Ambalavao has remained the main town in the extreme south of the Betsileo homeland, with a current population of around 30,000 inhabitants.

A brief historical sketch of Beparasy

The region of Beparasy where I conducted most of the research dis-cussed in this book is located in the south of Arindrano, between the basin of Ambalavao and the Andringitra chain, a mountain range forming a natural frontier between Betsileo and Bara areas. Because of the region's altitude, its proximity to high, rocky mountains and its exposure to the winds, its climate is pleasantly mild during the hot season but can be relatively cold for the rest of the year. Considering the high level of insecurity that existed in the southern highlands until the end of the nineteenth century, one may find it somewhat surprising that people decided to make this cold, remote and somewhat risky corner their home. In this section I want to explain why they chose to do so and the particular circumstances through which this happened. My account is mostly based on oral histories that I collected in Beparasy and Ambalavao.[7]

Beparasy is located in the former territory of a polity that was part of Arindrano. This polity was divided in the early nineteenth century by Radama I, as part of his political strategy after the relative failure of trying to unite the polities of Arindrano under the authority of

Rarivoarindrano (Raherisoanjato 1984b: 230). The polity was then split into a northern and a southern part, with two different rulers. The ruler of one of these two halves established his *lapa* (royal residence) on the top of a hill that I shall call here Ambatofotsy.[8]

The hilltop village with the royal residence in Ambatofotsy was abandoned a long time ago and the *fanjakana* (government) is to be found today in the village which is the seat of the *kaominina* (commune). It is situated in a valley close to Ambatofotsy hill, and descendants of the former rulers still live in the village. Their house stands at its centre, besides a large *kianja* (gathering place) with a massive *vatolahy* (standing stone), and is still called *lapa* by villagers. A few other descendants of *hova* (nobles) live in the area around the village. Oral traditions recall that the polity governed by the rulers of Ambatofotsy was sparsely populated until the beginning of the nineteenth century, with the arrival of many people fleeing Radama's wars, most notably after the massacres committed by his army at Ifandana and the enslavement of part of the population (on this tragic episode, see Dubois 1938: 223–226).

The region of Beparasy, located a few hours' walk from Ambatofotsy and the seat of the commune, remained unoccupied until an even more recent date. I was told that only *mpiarakandro* ('those who go with the day', i.e. cattle herders) went up seasonally to let their zebus graze on the banks of the river meandering through its valleys. These herders came mainly from the north, but also occasionally from the west. Beparasy elders tell stories about the *vakirà* (blood bond) that a Betsileo noble once contracted with a Bara ruler to strengthen their agreement on the sharing of pasture. The agreement stipulated that the Bara would drive their zebus to the west, whereas the Betsileo would lead theirs to Beparasy. Local historians also explain that in a much more distant past the region was inhabited by *Vazimba*, whose presence is testified, they say, by the ancient tombs and megaliths found in the nearby mountains.[9] Contemporary Beparasy villagers thus see themselves as the third wave of inhabitants of the region, after the *Vazimba* and the seasonal herders.

It was only towards 1880 that people started to intensively cultivate land in Beparasy. According to my informants, *mitady tany malalake* ('looking for free, spacious land') was the principal reason for their ancestors' arrival. As I have explained, since the transformation of the Betsileo economy into an intensive rice-growing agriculture, people have been continuously forced to migrate to find new cultivable land. A few people also recalled that their forebears fled the heavy burden of *fanompoana* (royal service) and *hetra* (taxes) imposed by Merina administration in northern Betsileo, where these obligations were probably more easily enforced than in the recently conquered and less administered south. Another possible factor encouraging the move towards the less populated and remote southern regions, although it was never mentioned to me, may have been the many epidemics that plagued the more densely populated Betsileo areas during the nineteenth century (Campbell 2005: Chapter 6). Whatever the reasons, it seems that most of these settlers came from parts of the southern highlands that are now considered Betsileo. While some arrived from other parts of Arindrano, many came from much further north, sometimes from regions located to the north of Fianarantsoa.

What made the region of Beparasy particularly attractive to newcomers in spite of its cold climate and remoteness was the abundance of water (see Figure 1.2). Sources coming from the nearby mountains provide water during most of the year, and the river that passes through the region never dries up, even during the most severe droughts. By comparison, permanent water sources are rare in the basin of Ambalavao, where only two of the basin's numerous rivers never dry up (Portais 1974: 17). Above all, any peasant wanting to cultivate wet rice needs to find a site that allows a good and easy management of water supply. The region of Beparasy offered good opportunities for such endeavours.

According to oral histories, the first people to arrive were four men named Rainibao, Raikalatsara, Rakamisy and Rainidama. Three of these four (Rainibao, Raikalatsara and Rakamisy) occupied the top of a strategically located hill that I shall call Vatobe. From its summit

Figure 1.2 Landscape of the southern highlands during the dry season

they had a very good overview of the whole area. Since Rainidama, the fourth man, was in charge of supervising a somewhat remote place, he founded a village on a separate hilltop. With their kinsmen and affiliates, these men worked hard to lay out *farihy* (i.e., rice fields in wet valley bottoms) on the river banks. Since the land was at that time partly covered by a forest, the first settlers had to clear it in order to build their rice fields. Later, when the population increased and the well-irrigated fields in the valley bottoms were not enough to feed everyone, Beparasy villagers had to carve out *kipaha* – i.e., terraced rice fields on the hills' slopes – which required an elaborate hydraulic system of reservoirs and canals in order to make use of the water flowing from the mountains.

Insecurity prevented these new settlers from leaving their hilltop villages during the last two decades of the nineteenth century. In the evening, after a day of labour in the rice fields and gardens, they always had to return to villages fortified with stones and trenches, and guarded at night. Elders told me that at that time it was not only cattle that needed protection. As is still the case today (Rasamoelina 2007), cattle rustling was a serious problem, but people too were at risk since *mpangalatr'olo* (literally 'thieves of people', raiders who took captives for enslavement) were not uncommon in the region. Villages on hilltops such as these were called *afo* (fires), because the fires lit up at night were visible from a long distance.

Soon after they arrived in Beparasy, the four men were joined by other migrants. Until the turn of the century the ancestors of most families of present day Beparasy lived together in the two *afo* (i.e., the two fortified villages on hilltops). All these people were allocated land upon their arrival by the four men, who had been charged by the ruler of Ambatofotsy with administering four separate areas. Rakamisy and Rainibao allocated land and oversaw people on the eastern side of Vatobe, in the basin that provided the largest stretches of land suitable for rice cultivation. Raikalatsara did the same for the people who started to grow rice on the other side of the hill, while Rainidama was responsible for the families farming land further west.

In the years 1900–1902, following annexation of Madagascar by the French in 1895–1896, the so-called *campagne de pacification* (pacification campaign) in the south significantly decreased the risk of raids in the southern highlands.[10] The fortified hilltop villages were progressively abandoned and families built independent *vala* close to their rice fields. Towards the turn of the century, eight families who were living on Vatobe founded the eight *vala* that are the most ancient villages of the *fokontany* of Beparasy-I and Beparasy-II.[11]

These villages increased in size after the implementation of the French *politique de villagisation* ('villagisation' policy), which obliged people to move in together to form villages of at least *dimiambinifolo tafo* ('fifteen roofs', i.e. fifteen houses). In Beparasy, many families who lived in small *vala* had to form larger villages, although some apparently decided to ignore the law or perhaps already had fifteen houses in their *vala*. This explains the distribution of the population today. Some of the oldest villages are still inhabited by only one local descent group, while others are home to several descent groups. The highest number of inhabitants and descent groups today is found in the village of Beparasy-I, commonly referred to as the region's *tanambe* (big village), where I counted sixty-four houses accommodating members of five descent groups and their affiliates. After the villagisation policy lost its obligatory character, a large number of *vala* reappeared, as people tended to relocate, once again, closer to their rice fields. In consequence, the current population of the five *fokontany* of Beparasy – around 5,000 people, according to the figures provided by the commune and my own estimate – lives scattered in more than 100 villages and hamlets.

As we will see, not everyone in Beparasy tells the settlement history I have just sketched in exactly the same manner. Crucially, differences emerge depending on whether the *mpitantara* (historian) is a free or a slave descendant.

Settling down in Soatanana

When my wife, Anjasoa, and I first arrived in Beparasy after a long journey from Ambalavao in an old Peugeot 504, the vehicle's driver led us to a small set of houses. I had told him that we wanted to visit my friend Redison. He knew very well where to find him. I was surprised, however, when we arrived at our destination. It seemed that many things had changed since my first visit three years earlier, the most obvious being that Redison had built his own house. A fairly nice one by local standards, Redison had chosen a place some distance from the already existing hamlets and villages. Two other houses had also been built to the north of Redison's home. Clearly a new hamlet had been founded in Beparasy. Redison had named it Soatanana.

During my earlier visit, Redison was living in a two-room house in the 'big village', less than one kilometre south of Soatanana. Now he had a nice two-storey house on a relatively large piece of land, and I could see that it was being gardened. Upon arrival we were given a separate room on the ground floor of Redison's new house.

We soon realised that Soatanana, in spite of its limited size, was a lively hamlet. Many people were passing by and there was always something going on. A significant part of this regular movement was due to the teaching positions at the local Catholic school of two of the hamlet's inhabitants: Raely, Redison's wife, and Vaofara, her sister-in-law. After her arrival in Soatanana as Raely's brother's wife, Vaofara had been recruited by Raely, who was heading the school. As a consequence, groups of schoolchildren were often hanging around in Soatanana, doing whatever they had been told to do by Raely or Vaofara, while the two teachers were busy with other tasks. Raely and Vaofara's colleagues, as well as the pupils' parents, were often seen in Soatanana too. In many respects, the hamlet was a sort of extension of the Catholic school, which was located besides the Catholic Church, not far from the 'big village'.

Many of the frequent visitors to Soatanana also came to see Redison, either to ask him for advice or help on a particular issue, to inform him about a forthcoming event or, more simply, to pay him a courtesy visit. I had not realised it during my first visit but now I could see that Redison was an important figure in Beparasy, and there seemed to be several reasons for this. First of all, although he was only in his early forties, he was the main leader of the local Catholic community. His position was not due so much to his wife's leadership of the Catholic school as to his own education. After his *baccalauréat* (i.e., his school leaving certificate), Redison had studied in Antsirabe and Fianarantsoa at the Catholic seminary with the aim of becoming a priest. His career as a Catholic priest was short-lived, however, since, while doing an internship in the south of Madagascar, he fell in love with Raely, at that time a young teacher at the Catholic school under Redison's supervision. When Raely fell pregnant, Redison decided to give up priesthood because he realised he wanted to marry and have children. Given their background and their numerous commitments in Catholic activities, which include schools and youth associations, Redison and Raely are unanimously recognised as leading figures in the Catholic community of Beparasy.

Redison has also imposed himself as a locally influential man because of his political activities and ambitions. Since his arrival in Beparasy he has been tirelessly involved in local politics, taking up multiple responsibilities and positions such as *conseiller* (advisor) at the commune, vice-president of the *fokontany* of Beparasy-I and president, secretary or treasurer of various other associations, especially those devoted to environmental protection and health promotion. The year before my stay in Beparasy he had even run to become mayor of the commune, only to be beaten by someone who had then offered him an office as advisor at the *mairie* immediately after the elections. Redison was also a privileged contact person for all the NGO workers who came to Beparasy with the goal of developing a region they often considered *un peu arriérée* (a bit backward), as one of them once put it to me.

The presumed backwardness of the region did not prevent Redison and Raely from moving to Beparasy when they were in their mid-twenties. After their marriage they had tried for a while to make a living in Ambalavao, but, as Redison recalled, these were very difficult times as they were poor and life in town was expensive. They then decided to move to Redison's mother's village in Beparasy. The initial plan was that Raely would teach at the Catholic school and Redison would cultivate rice and open a small grocery, since there were none at that time in Beparasy. As Redison's older brother was already living on their mother's land, Redison used the money that the Catholic Church had given him when he gave up the priesthood to buy a rice field from one of his uncles. The uncle had left Beparasy for the east coast a long time before and had no interest in keeping his share of the land.

While they were living in Ambalabe, Redison and Raely got into trouble with some members of Redison's family. The reasons for the disputes were never clearly explained to me, but it was indirectly suggested that the problem had to do with the relationships that Redison and Raely maintained with a family of slave descent, which strongly displeased Redison's maternal kinsmen. Following the disputes, Raely and Redison decided to leave the *vala* and to rent a small house in the 'big village', until they built their own house and founded Soatanana

In Soatanana, Redison and Raely did not live with their children. Their three boys studied at a private primary school in Ambalavao, where they lived with their grandmother Ramarcelline, Redison's mother. Redison and Raely fostered two teenagers, a girl and a boy, to compensate for the absence of children in their household – a common practice among the Betsileo (Kottak 1986). The girl, in her early teens, was one of Redison's cousins from his mother's village. Redison told me that when he asked her parents whether he could take her with him to Soatanana they quickly accepted because they were too old and too poor to take good care of the girl. The other child in Redison's house was a slightly older boy, whose parents had both died and who had lived with one of his relatives until Redison and Raely moved to their new house in Soatanana. From that moment on the boy was often in Soatanana to help in the garden or in building works. At some point he had asked Redison whether he could stay and live with them. As in the girl's case, the boy's relatives readily accepted this arrangement, mainly because Redison had offered to take charge of everything, from school fees to clothes and food.

At the time of our arrival, in addition to that of Redison and Raely, the small hamlet of Soatanana was comprised of the house of Raely's brother, Naina, and his wife, Vaofara, and a third house which looked like hardly more than a tiny hut. A second hut was in construction, with assembled wooden sticks partly covered by a roof of dried grass. The hut was Raboba's house, where he lived with his wife, Ravao, and three of their children and grandchildren (see Figure 1.3).

Meeting 'slaves'

I had come to the southern highlands of Madagascar with the idea of studying slave descendants who were independent, land-owning peasants, unlike the migrants of unknown origins described by Evers (2002) or the share-croppers described by Kottak (1980) and Freeman (2001). My original plan was to visit my friend Redison in Beparasy, spend a bit of time with him and his family, and then ask him whether there were such slave descendants in his region. I thought that, if this was the case, Redison might be able to help me get in touch with them and settle down in their village. Before asking Redison such a question, however, I first had to make sure that my friend was not himself of slave descent. But how was I going to find out, if this was precisely the kind of question that one cannot ask directly? Moreover, since I was rapidly identified in Beparasy as Redison's *vahiny* (guest) and *havana*

Figure 1.3 Raboba's tiny hut (left) and Naina's house (right) in Soatanana

(relative), it was out of the question to start asking around about Redison's social status. In any case, in the beginning I had no clue about how to ask these kinds of questions in an appropriate way, and neither did I know who I could turn to and discuss these issues without acquiring a reputation for being a *vazaha* (white foreigner) who asked rude, inappropriate or even insulting questions.

Given these initial difficulties, acquiring consistent and reliable knowledge of the stories of (and about) the slave descendants of Beparasy took a very long time. In fact, this process lasted for the two years I stayed, and even in the last few months of my fieldwork I was still learning important fragments of information about them. At first, because of my reluctance to ask direct questions that could have put people off and endangered my research, the answers I received to my prudent questions did not get me very far. When talking about local history and past slavery, for example, people would sometimes acknowledge the existence of slave descendants in Beparasy without telling me who they were or where they lived, and I would not dare to push them further. My inquiry at the beginning was like trying to assemble a jigsaw puzzle without knowing where to find the pieces. In spite of being Malagasy, my wife was no better equipped than me, since she also did not know how to ask these questions without being rude. And being Malagasy, she was even more concerned than I was about not offending people. As a result, during the first four or five months of our stay in Soatanana we did not even know that our neighbour, Raboba, who lived in the tiny hut, was considered to be of slave descent. It was only after we had learned how to ask the right questions – as well as how to understand the most euphemistic answers – and only after we established more trusting friendships with people that we were able to establish with some certainty that while our host Redison was not considered to be of slave descent, our neighbour Raboba was. We were told that Raboba was a Berosaiña and that the Berosaiña were *olo tsy madio* (unclean people) because they were *andevo* (slaves).

When I learned that Raboba was considered a slave descendant I thought that this explained his living conditions in Soatanana. Recalling Kottak's, Evers' and Freeman's accounts, I inferred that Raboba, Ravao and their children were a poor, slave descent family. I then hypothesised that it was because of Redison's and Raely's Catholic background that they had allowed Raboba and his family to live with them in Soatanana, in spite of their slave, 'unclean' ancestry. As documented by the confident tone of my field notes, this explanation seemed to me obvious at that time. But it was deeply wrong. The story of the foundation of Soatanana and of Raboba's position in it turned out to be completely different to what I had imagined. Of course, it took me a significant amount of time to figure this out.

Little by little I learned that the land where Redison had built his house and founded Soatanana was actually part of a relatively large estate of *tanety* (hilly plains), *tanim-bary* (rice fields) and *ala* (forest) that belonged to one of the three branches of the Berosaiña in Beparasy. First Redison, and then his brother-in-law Naina, had bought small plots of this land from Raboba, who had acted as the *tompontany* ('master of the land', i.e. landowner) for these transactions, which were officialised at the *fokontany*.[12] Redison's stepfather, Rasamuel, had once suggested that he build his house on this land, saying 'You see, Redison, all this land belongs to us. If you want, you can build your house here.' Rasamuel had been married to Redison's mother for several decades and he had raised Redison, whom he considered his son. He was a Berosaiña and one of Raboba's kinsmen in Beparasy, and therefore also a slave descendant. Since Rasamuel was Raboba's 'father' in the classificatory sense, he had some authority over him and could have 'asked' him to give a plot of this land to Redison (see Figure 3.1 in Chapter 3).

Unfortunately, shortly after he had made this offer to Redison, Rasamuel passed away. In the following year, Redison went to see Raboba, his neighbour in the 'big village' at that time, to explain what Rasamuel had suggested to him. Redison asked Raboba whether he would give him permission to build his house on the piece of land identified by Rasamuel. To increase his chances, he proposed that Raboba should move as well, pointing out that his rice fields were located right below the piece of land, which would made it a very convenient place to live. Raboba was seduced by the proposition and accepted, on condition that Redison buy him the piece of land where he wanted to build his house. Redison bought it, and shortly after started the construction of his house. A few months later Raboba also started to build the first of his two tiny huts.

Thus, by settling down in Soatanana, we unwittingly found ourselves living on land that belonged to the slave descendants of Beparasy. We also found ourselves in the middle of stories involving free descent families and the Berosaiña. As I gradually discovered these stories I decided to stay in Soatanana and abandoned my initial plan of finding a slave descent village to live in. In any case, it appeared that there was no village inhabited only by slave descendants in Beparasy. But since I had kinship connections with the Berosaiña through Redison and Raboba, and since I ended up building my own house on land that formerly belonged to the Berosaiña, a slave descent group, Soatanana was a good place to stay and to conduct my research.

Notes

1 Extensive accounts on Betsileo society can be found in the massive mono-graph written by a French missionary-turned-ethnographer (Dubois 1938), in the oral traditions collected by a Betsileo protestant pastor (Rainihifina 1956, 1975) and in Kottak's ethnography (Kottak 1980). Earlier accounts by missionaries and French officials include Besson (1897), Haile (1899, 1900), Johnson (1900), Moss (1900), Richardson (1875), Shaw (1877, 1878) and Sibree (1898).

2 Before the nineteenth century there were more petty kingdoms in Arindrano than those I have cited, and there were smaller polities that were not yet part of Lalangina and Isandra. I omit these details here for the sake of clarity. On the history of the southern Betsileo region, see in particular Dubois (1938), Rainihifina (1956), Kottak (1980), Raherisoanjato (1984a) and Solondraibe (1994).

3 I am stressing the existence of north–south differences only because I found that often scholars tend to generalise about 'the Betsileo' in spite of the fact that cultural homogeneity is sometimes problematic.

4 See Dubois (1938: 76–77) and Raherisoanjato (1988) for a more precise description and drawings of a *vala*. Raherisoanjato argues that some *vala* had already appeared before Merina occupation, probably in the eighteenth century.

5 The Betsileo are well-known for the long and elaborated funerals of their 'sacred' rulers (Hertz 1907; Edholm 1971; Razafintsalama 1983; Rahamefy 1997). Genealogies seem to indicate that the ancestors of those who established themselves as 'nobles' (*hova*) and the ruling class of the small polities in the southern highlands came from the eastern coast in the early eighteenth century (Raherisoanjato 1984a, 1984b).

6 A missionary from the London Missionary Society, travelling in the region in 1895, reported that the Bara from the west had lifted 500 heads of cattle and carried off 300 men and women into captivity a few days before his visit (Knight, quoted in Portais 1974: 19–20).

7 As in the rest of the book, names of places and individuals have been changed, or sometimes omitted, to protect anonymity.

8 A *lapa* is the house of a sovereign or a noble (Richardson 1885). Southern Betsileo *lapa* were built with wooden planks, whereas most other houses were made of plaited bamboo on a wooden architecture. The houses made of mud and bricks which are now found everywhere in the Betsileo countryside only appeared in the late nineteenth century. On traditional architecture in Madagascar, see Acquier (1997).

9 In oral histories, *Vazimba* is a generic term for the people who, presumably, inhabited Madagascar before the arrival of the people to whom contemporary Malagasy refer as their ancestors. They are portrayed in various ways but are often considered as having rudimentary ways of life and customs (e.g., they lived in caves). The historical existence, beyond the myths, of such a population has been (and, to a certain extent, still is) discussed by

archaeologists, historians and anthropologists (Randrianja and Ellis 2009). On the cultural importance of the Vazimba, see in particular Bloch (1986), and, for the Betsileo more specifically, Raherisoanjato (1982a).

10 For an account of this campaign from the point of view of the 'pacifica-tors', see Lyautey (1903). The pacification campaign was in fact a war to conquer the parts of the island that were not under Merina rule when the French annexed the island as a colony in 1896.

11 *Fokontany* are the smallest administrative divisions of the Malagasy state. Other villages were, of course, founded on the other side of Vatobe and further west, and these villages came to form five separate *fokontany*. I only mention the *fokontany* of Beparasy-I and Beparasy-II because they are the most densely populated and because I carried out most of my fieldwork on this side of Vatobe.

12 The president of the *fokontany* testified with his signature that the seller and the buyer agreed on the transaction. Since land disputes were very frequent in Beparasy, people increasingly sought to secure their contract with an officialisation by the *fokontany*.

2 Three lenses: ethnography, history and cognition

Before further describing and analysing the relations between free and slave descendants I discovered in Beparasy, let me take a step back in order to explain the focus of the book and make a few remarks on methodology, ethics and terminology. To speak of the focus of a book is a common metaphor, but here I want to push the optic trope a bit further than usual. Schematically, the book can be thought of as the outcome of my inquiry into three questions and of my use of three different types of 'photographic lenses' to answer them.

The overall aim of the book is to contribute to the study of the condition of slave descendants in Madagascar. The existing literature suggests there is, in some societies of the island, a strong pattern of discriminatory practices towards slave descendants, and that in the southern Betsileo highlands this kind of discrimination is particularly strong.[1] The question I ask is: why is there such strong discrimination among the southern Betsileo, the people studied in this book? To frame and try to answer this question I use a wide-angle lens. By this I mean that I place my ethnographic data in the light of what is known about local history, past slavery, its abolition and the trajectories of freed slaves and their descendants after the abolition. Using a wide-angle lens thus means I engage in some historical forays.

I take off the wide-angle and use instead a normal lens when I address a more narrowly framed question. Since my free descent informants told me that the only problem they have with slave descendants is that it is forbidden to marry them, and since I could see that senior members of free descent groups indeed make every effort to prevent their relatives from marrying slave descendants, the question I ask is: why is this so? Why do free descendants categorically refuse to marry slave descendants? Approaching this second question with a normal lens lets me give a descriptive–interpretative account of what I could understand of the relations existing between people of free and slave descent in the small community of people I lived with, with specific attention to the question of marriage.

My use of a third type of lens is motivated by a particular aspect of the answers I received when I asked my free descent informants why they could not marry slave descendants. These answers led me to think that free descendants essentialise slave descendants and that this essentialisation is crucial to explain the existing prejudice and discrimination against slave descendants. Thus the third question I ask is: why do free descendants essentialise slave descendants? To answer it, I take off the normal lens and put on a long-focus lens. With this I try to look into my free descent informants' minds, so to speak. I make some educated guesses about the extent to which they hold essentialised representations of slave descendants, and how these representations develop in individuals. These guesses draw on the knowledge I acquired through long-term fieldwork and also on several decades of research on psychological essentialism in cognitive, developmental and social psychology.

For a photographer, each type of lenses has its own merits. The great merit of the normal lens – the 50mm lens for an SLR camera – is that it is the closest to the human eye. It produces the photographs that look the most natural to us, whereas the wide-angle and long-focus lenses produce pictures significantly different from those forming on the retina through the natural lenses of our eyes. It is the reason why the normal lens is called normal and why it is the standard lens for photographers. I believe that something similar can be said about the merit of the descriptive–interpretative approach in anthropology. Interpretative descriptions are highly valuable because they are experience-near accounts – they provide accounts that are the closest to human experience.

However, just as photographers do not only use the normal lens on the grounds that it produces the pictures that are the closest to human vision, there is no reason to think that ethnographers should limit themselves to experience-near interpretative descriptions when they conduct fieldwork and write ethnographies. Photographers use lenses other than the normal lens for various reasons, which can be technical, aesthetic or practical. In anthropology, what I called here the wide-angle lens – i.e., the historical approach – is now frequently used and recognised as a legitimate part of the ethnographer's camera bag. The addition of a long-focus lens – i.e., a 'cognitive' lens – in the bag is less frequent and more controversial.

Why would anthropologists use a cognitive lens in ethnography? One possible answer is Jon Elster's (2007) idea that social scientists need to resort to a toolbox – a large collection of theoretical tools – rather than to a unified or narrowly defined set of methods or theories. In order to explain social phenomena, Elster contends, it is necessary for investigators to have recourse to the greatest possible variety of concepts and theories because the utility of a toolbox comes precisely from the diversity of the tools it contains. Elster's theoretical pluralism unsurprisingly includes the concepts and theories of cognitive psychology, since he considers them useful to account for the mechanisms underlying various social phenomena.

Another possible answer is that the addition of the cognitive lens is necessary if anthropologists want to produce explanations that are more sophisticated than those they have achieved so far: 'It would be preferable, for the sake of simplicity, if a sophisticated understanding of social phenomena could be achieved with little or no psychology, but [...] this is as implausible as achieving a deep understanding of epidemiological phenomena without a serious interest in pathology' (Sperber and Mercier 2012: 368; see also Sperber 1996).

A third answer is that anthropologists, since they study culture, have to deal with cognitive issues such as, for example, memory or categorisation (Bloch 1991, 2012). If they leave these notions unexamined and refer to cognitive processes in only vague terms, Bloch argues, they are doomed to produce accounts that are only naïve or, worse, blatantly false. Bloch stresses that sheer ignorance of cognition is one of the main reasons why anthropologists tend towards extreme forms of cognitive relativism. Focusing on rituals and other non-ordinary contexts, they take what is said during these events as a reliable guide to how people think. But what people say during the specific occasion of a ritual does not necessarily correspond to how they think in ordinary life. By mistaking ritual communication for ordinary communication, anthropologists are inclined to exaggerate the idea that others do not think like us (Bloch 1977).

A fourth reason why anthropologists might consider adding a cognitive lens to their fieldwork equipment and theoretical toolkit is that it is long overdue. 'For too long,' writes Matthew Engelke in *Think Like an Anthropologist*, 'anthropologists have at best ignored, and at worst disavowed, findings and approaches in the cognitive sciences. That's beginning to change in some quarters' (Engelke 2017: 49)[2]

Fieldwork conditions and methodology

Participant observation fieldwork in Madagascar was conducted during twenty-five months from February 2008 to March 2010, and then during shorter visits between 2012 and 2015. Most of the research took place in Beparasy, the region I introduced in the previous chapter, which is located south of the nearest town, Ambalavao, capital of the Ambalavao District in the Matsiatra Ambony region (see general map).

Almost all of the people living in Beparasy identify themselves as Betsileo. The region is, by local standards, very rural and poor. The vast majority of villagers make a living as rice-growing peasants. The wealthiest families raise cattle that they can sell at the Ambalavao market in case of hardship or special needs. Beparasy has remained fairly remote and isolated until today because it is difficult to access by car, especially during the rainy season. There is no power supply and peasants do not use powered machinery to work their fields. At the time of my fieldwork, not a single villager owned a car or motorcycle. Most people walked when they needed to go to Ambalavao, except those who owned a bike. The journey on foot took an entire day.

Throughout my fieldwork I was accompanied by my wife, Anjasoa, who is Malagasy but not Betsileo. Since most interviews were conducted in the Malagasy language, her help was invaluable, from the formulation of my questions to the translation of my informants' answers. We first lived in a room at our hosts, and then we spent some time in another house in the hamlet before eventually moving to the house that we built with the help of our neighbours and friends. By doing so we gradually moved from our initial status of *vahiny* – a word meaning 'guests' but also 'people who are estranged to the place' – to that of villagers belonging to the local community. '*Nareo tsa vahiny koa*' ('you are not guests anymore') was the main compliment that people addressed to us after we had moved to our newly built house. Our local status also significantly changed with the birth of our daughter, Camille, in November 2009. Thereafter, people used almost exclusively the teknonymic *papan'i Camille* and *maman'i Camille* as terms of address and reference. After we had become parents, built our house and established our own hearth, people seemed to view our presence differently. Many clearly changed their behaviour towards us, for the most part in a positive way. While until then we had been the guests of a local family, we gained independence as a separate household and received our share of courtesy visits. Our visitors in turn often invited us to come and visit them in their village. At one point it almost looked as if we were on our way towards becoming local *raia-mandreny* – 'mothers and fathers' – an expression used for the senior members of a local descent group but also, by extension, for the notables in a particular place.

Yet the building of trust was no easy task at first. Conrad Kottak, who wanted to do fieldwork in a place close to Beparasy in 1966–1967, recalls in his book how he finally decided to choose another field site because of the hostility and suspicion that he faced in the region, compared with another village further north where people were wealthier, more educated and more used to the presence of foreigners (Kottak 1980: 22–23). Although in 2008–2010 the situation in this respect was probably better than in 1966–1967, many Beparasy villagers still considered the presence of a *vazaha* (white foreigner) among them as a potential threat. I regularly heard that some people thought I was there to steal people's land – expressing fears inherited from the French colonial period – or the bones of their ancestors, since a persistent rumour in Madagascar has it that foreigners export these bones to make powerful medicine. Our dog was not spared and earned the rather unfair reputation of eating small children.

I considered people's suspicions seriously and took care not to do anything that could worsen them. I avoided, for example, approaching the tombs when I was walking alone. The initial mistrust prevented me from collecting systematic data, such as genealogies and kinship networks, until I had reached an advanced stage in my fieldwork. The suspicious reactions I encountered when I started a census of the small village of Ivondro, which was close to the hamlet where I had arrived just a few months earlier, served as a reminder of Kottak's difficulties. The first young mother who I asked for the names and the ages of her children refused to answer. Accepting finally – but reluctantly – on the insistence of a friend, she asserted: 'If something bad happens to my children, I will hold you responsible.'

During the first six months my fieldwork benefited from the cheerful support of Naina, a young man in his mid-twenties and the brother of our host's wife. Since he was our neighbour and could speak some French, I had recruited him as a part-time field assistant and interpreter. He facilitated my first meetings with local families, accompanied me on the long walks that I undertook to familiarise myself with the topography of the region and helped me to draw a map of Beparasy. In order to do this we visited more than 100 villages and hamlets on foot. During this initial period my main goal was to acquire some autonomy in the Malagasy language and in developing contacts with people. Villagers became increasingly accustomed to my presence and soon identified me as 'the *vazaha* who is the guest of Redison in Soatanana'. It was during this period that I started to participate in agricultural work or other tasks at the invitation of some families, and I continued to answer positively to their invitations throughout my fieldwork. In consequence I was regularly in the fields working the land, in the forest fetching firewood or in villages helping with house building. I attended meetings of a political or religious nature, including Christian ceremonies, as well as various kinds of family gatherings. I did not record any of the informal conversations I had with people on a daily basis, but I used a digital recorder to keep trace of the lengthy, more formal interviews that I conducted at a later stage.

Since I made a case above for the value of a cognitive lens in the ethnographer's camera bag, I probably need to make clear from the outset that during my 2008–2010 fieldwork I did not conduct any field experiment in Beparasy. Yet I certainly had a cognitive lens with me, since during my pre-fieldwork time at the London School of Economics I had become acquainted with research in developmental and cognitive psychology that was directly relevant to anthropological questions in broad terms and to the kind of questions that I am addressing here. This background provided me with a number of conceptual tools that I carried with me in the field and made me particularly attentive to ethnographic–cognitive issues. Later on, on the occasion of a postdoctoral fellowship, I came back to Beparasy and implemented the experimental tasks that I will present in Chapter 8.

Ethical concerns

Conducting research on slave descendants in the southern highlands of Madagascar poses specific ethical problems because of the nature of the discrimination that exists against them. As we shall see, prejudice and discrimination are principally based on knowledge of people's 'origins'; that is, on the knowledge of the places where people's forebears came from and on the knowledge of descent. Researchers need to be aware that disclosing genealogical, geographical or historical data about individuals or families can therefore contribute to their discrimination.

I witnessed forms of prejudice and discrimination existing against a local descent group because, it was alleged, this group was of slave descent. These people, however, denied having slaves among their ancestors. Since I wanted to disentangle this issue I had to form my own opinion as to whether they were really of slave descent or whether there might be other reasons for the discrimination they faced and the ascription of an inferior status to them. Eventually I came to the conclusion that they most probably did have slaves who were freed by the colonial abolition in 1896 among their ancestors. But would it be right,

I asked myself, to write this in my ethnography? Would it not mean, in practice, taking the side of the free descendants and writing 'against' those who deny having a slave ancestry? After all, even though I became convinced that they probably are slave descendants, I have of course no indisputable evidence for that. To make things worse, the topic of slave ancestry is a very sensitive issue in the region, to the point that people can be fined an ox if they say or only imply that someone is of slave descent. In this book I will deal with this issue as follows: I will explain in detail how I came to form my opinion about these people's alleged slave ancestry and how I came to better understand the difficult problem of being of slave descent, hoping that the 'positive' effect of giving a precise account of the reasons for the discrimination will counterbalance the 'negative' effect of confirming their slave origins in spite of what they say.

Another related dilemma I encountered was whether it is ethical to write that some of my slave descent friends probably lied to me, or at least purposely dissimulated the truth. In the book I will sometimes make it apparent that some people probably did so. It is an important point, since lying and dissimulating are some of the slave descendants' few means of resisting the peculiar kind of discrimination they face. I therefore consider this behaviour as a strategy of resistance, even though in some instances it also looks like a kind of self-deception. Ethnographers are sometimes forced, for good reasons, to lie to their informants. They should also be ready to explain that well-disposed informants have sometimes little choice other than to lie to them. However uncomfortable we feel about this, it is certainly an important part of the practice of ethnography (Metcalf 2002).

As a way to offset these decisions, names of persons and places – except for a few places and some historical figures – have been changed, to ensure that people cannot be too easily identified. Some specific aspects of the region of Beparasy – including parts of its history – and of the lives of my main informants will be omitted as well, since their inclusion would make it too easy to identify them. These precautions are taken at the cost of historical and ethnographic accuracy, but they are very important given the current situation of slave descendants.

Terminological issues: marriage, slavery and caste

In the book I shall make extensive use of the words 'marriage' and 'slavery' but refrain from using 'caste', even though it is sometimes employed by scholars of Madagascar. Since each of these three terms has been the subject of important anthropological debates, some preliminary remarks need to be made.

Marriage as an anthropological concept has been famously discussed by Leach (1961) and Needham (1971), and both have argued that it is not possible to define it universally. For Leach, a marriage consists of a 'bundle of rights' and thus there cannot be a universal definition for it since some rights can be present and others absent in different cases of marriage. Carrying Leach's argument forward, Needham argued that 'marriage' is a polythetic term. Anthropologists use it on the basis of the family resemblance that the social relationships they observe have with those that have been previously called 'marriage'. As I will show, traditional forms of marital union in highland Madagascar significantly differ from the usual conceptions of marriage in the West. But unlike some early scholars of Madagascar, who wondered whether these unions could be called 'marriage' at all (e.g., Grandidier 1913), I will not refrain from using the term in this book.

Leach's and Needham's arguments about marriage apply to the concept of slavery. Whereas early anthropologists were all interested in kinship and marriage, anthropological interest in slavery only began in the 1970s under the lead of Marxist anthropologists (Kopytoff 1982). As with marriage, when cases of slavery found in various societies became increasingly documented, social scientists were tempted to try to find a definition of slavery because the cases reported significantly differed from those that were the most familiar to Western scholars, i.e. domestic slavery in classical antiquity and plantation slavery in the New World. The debates between Africanists on whether there is a continuum between slavery and kinship (Miers and Kopytoff 1977), or whether slavery is, on the contrary, 'the antithesis of kinship' (Meillassoux 1986: 86), can be viewed as yet another illustration of the pitfalls of thinking in terms of universal definitions and 'interpretive generalizations' (Sperber 1996: Chapter 2), since it is always possible to find cases that fit either of the two arguments well.

Yet scholars working on slavery often worry about a universal definition (e.g., Testart 1998). Since various forms of exploitation (e.g., human trafficking, debt bondage or child soldiers) are now called 'new slavery' (Bales 2004) or 'modern-day slavery' (Sage and Kasten 2008), some have argued for the need of a new reconceptualisation, either to narrow the meaning of the term for the sake of clarity in scholarly debates (Rossi 2009: 5–7) or to make conventions against abuses more enforceable, because, without clear definitions, courts cannot launch successful prosecutions (Miers 2003). While it is certainly important to agree on a definition of slavery in international law, I consider with Leach and Needham that, from a theoretical point of view, attempts at formulating a universal definition of this concept are pointless.

'Slavery', just like 'marriage', is a word used by scholars to describe particular kinds of social relationships that share a family resemblance with others.

Scholars of Madagascar have also argued over issues of definition. Basing their argument on a careful examination of historical documents, Bakoly Ramiaramanana and Jean-Pierre Domenichini have questioned the translation of *fanandevozana* by the French word *esclavage* (slavery) on the grounds that the Malagasy *fanandevozana* was very different from the Western conception of slavery (Domenichini-Ramiaramanana and Domenichini 2010; Domenichini and Domenichini-Ramiaramanana 1982, 1998). They proposed instead the term *sujétion privée* (private subjection) to stress that the relation of slaves to their owner was similar to that of free subjects to their ruler. Ramiaramanana and Domenichini's proposal was received with hostility by some scholars, who accused them of revisionism (see Rantoandro 2005). People apparently understood their argument as an attempt to attenuate the oppressive nature of the system of slavery in Madagascar. The reasons for this hostile reaction to what could seem otherwise a good point in terms of scholarly research are complex, but it must be kept in mind that the abolition of slavery is, in history and ideology, inseparable from the French colonisation of Madagascar. Anti-slavery ideology played an important role in the French conquest of Madagascar, and the early studies of Malagasy slavery by French officials tended to justify colonisation (e.g., André 1899; Piolet 1896).

These political issues aside, it must be recognised that, since slavery as an anthropological or historical concept was first used to describe the cases of domestic slavery in Greece and Rome, and then later the cases of chattel slavery in the New World, the word is not well-suited to refer to the *fanandevozana* of pre-colonial Madagascar. If no further explanation is provided, the uncritical use of the term 'slavery' can even obscure the understanding of what the *fanandevozana* really consisted of. There is nonetheless enough family resemblance between the Malagasy *fanandevozana* and many other cases that have been described as slavery to use the term 'slavery' in order to give an idea of the kind of phenomena we are dealing with. I shall therefore do so in the present book.

'Caste' is the last theoretical term that I want to discuss briefly. It is often used to describe the different social groups that made up pre-colonial Malagasy society (e.g., nobles, commoners and slaves) and still have importance today. Given that some of these groups were endogamous, descent-based and that ideas of uncleanliness were also sometimes present, they seem indeed to be 'caste-like'. Nonetheless, I prefer to use the term 'status group', proposed by Max Weber (cf.

Gerth and Wright Mills 1948: 186–187), mainly because 'caste' evokes
the South Asian context where a complex hierarchical system of many
castes and sub-castes is based on occupational difference and is justified by
religion. These features are not clearly present in the Malagasy context,
and therefore it seems to me that the use of the term 'caste', while not
entirely irrelevant, would obscure my account rather than illuminate it.[3]

Scope and outline of the book

I conceived this book as a short, readable ethnography and as an original analysis putting forward a few historical and cognitive arguments
that might have some scientific value – at least that is my hope –
beyond the specific social issue I analyse, the local context I describe
and the boundaries of the discipline in which I work. Thinking about
the structure of the book, I wondered for a while whether I should
engage in the discussion of other works on slavery and post-slavery in
Madagascar, precisely because 'using a wide-angle lens' could also
mean adopting such a comparative perspective. After reflection, however, I eventually decided to stay focused on my ethnography and
arguments, and to unfold them without spending too much time discussing other accounts, to which I will thus refer only briefly.[4] The
main rationale behind this decision, in addition to the issue of read-
ability, is that I am writing a companion volume in collaboration with
Dominique Somda and Marco Gardini. Unlike the present mono-
graph, this book will be explicitly comparative and will discuss the
history of Malagasy slavery, its multiple forms and its various legacies,
thereby expanding the work I started with Dominique Somda (Regnier
and Somda 2019).[5] I realise that my decision to not allow space for
discussing extensively the work of other scholars of Madagascar and
the condition of slave descendants elsewhere in the island might be
regarded as a limitation of this monograph, but I ask my readers to be
patient and wait for the next book.

I started Chapter 1 with a sketch of southern Betsileo society and
history, and introduced the region of Beparasy, giving a brief account
on the circumstances of my arrival and my first encounter with people
who are regarded as 'slaves'. The purpose of the next chapter is to
introduce the Berosaiña, the group of alleged slave descent in Beparasy.
I portray a few members of the group, show the diversity of their social
situations and stress their ownership of land and tomb to highlight that
they are, in many aspects, on an equal footing with the other inhabitants of Beparasy. My inquiry into the reasons why the Berosaiña are
considered to be slave descendants starts in Chapter 4. Using the

disputed marriage between a free descent woman and a Berosaiña as a starting point, I explain how the Berosaiña deny having slave ancestry and stress the role of their founding ancestor in the settlement of the region, and contrast their views with other versions of the story offered by local historians. Chapter 5 focuses on the process of customary marriage and the practice of making 'blood bonds', which are essential to understand the condition of the Berosaiña. I provide evidence in Chapter 6 that Beparasy families strictly avoid marrying the Berosaiña and I analyse the three cases of prohibited unions that I could observe. Chapter 7 seeks to answer the following question: why is it so important, for people having commoner status, to avoid marrying the Berosaiña? Chapter 8 argues that free descendants in Beparasy essentialise slave descendants and explores this issue from different perspectives. I present the results of a short field experiment designed to probe essentialist thinking, contend that essentialism started after the colonial abolition of slavery, and discuss its development in individuals and its transmission from one generation to the next.

Notes

1 For previous accounts of the discrimination and stigmatisation of slave descendants among the Betsileo, see Kottak (1980), Rasoamampionona (2000), Freeman (2001, 2013), and Evers (2002).
2 In the last decades a number of anthropologists have discussed and integrated cognitive–scientific developments in their work (see, for example, Hutchins 1995; Hirschfeld 1996; Shore 1996; Sperber 1996; Strauss and Quinn 1997; Boyer 2001; Astuti, Solomon and Carey 2004; Descola 2005; Whitehouse and McCauley 2005; Bloch 2012). For recent debates on how anthropologists can contribute to cognitive science, see Beller, Bender and Medin (2012) and Regnier and Astuti (2015a, 2015b).
3 Dumont briefly discusses the case of Madagascar and concludes that it is not a caste system (Dumont 1970: 215). Bloch (1968a: 132) disagrees with Condominas's choice of using the term 'caste' in a loose sense for the Merina case (Condominas 1961). My decision to not use the term here is driven more by pragmatism than by the reasons given by Dumont or Bloch.
4 For studies on Malagasy post-slavery since the 1990s, see in particular Bloch (1994), Beaujard (1998), Evers (2002), Razafindralambo (2003, 2005, 2008, 2014), Brown (2004), Razafiarivony (2005), Graeber (2007), Somda (2009), Keller (2008), Regnier (2012, 2014a, 2014b, 2015a, 2019), Boyer-Rossol (2015) and Gardini (2015). Older accounts include Bloch (1979, 1980), Ramamonjisoa (1984) and Rakotomalala and Razafimbelo (1985). Regnier and Somda (2019) give an overview of this scholarship.
5 The present book will therefore not discuss the history of slavery and the slave trade in Madagascar either. On these issues, see in particular Deschamps (1972), Filliot (1974), Rakoto (1997), Larson (2000), Rakoto and Mangalaza (2000), Campbell (2005) and Randrianja and Ellis (2009).

3   The Berosaiña

Slave descendants among the Betsileo have so far been described in the ethnographic literature in rather monolithic terms, either as the land-poor clients or share-croppers of their former masters who exploit them while at the same time offering paternalistic support (Kottak 1980; Freeman 2001, 2013), or as landless migrants who provide exploitative *tompontany* ('masters of the land', i.e. land owners) with an easily disposable labour force (Evers 2002). What is lacking in these otherwise important accounts is close attention to the details of the slave descendants' genealogies, kinship practices and various trajectories in life, and to the differences that may exist between them and within slave descent families in terms of success, social status and attitudes towards their ancestral land or tombs.

In what follows I seek to depart from such monolithic descriptions by portraying characters that embody some of the differences I observed among the Berosaiña. The chapter thus focuses on individuals, and how they relate to others inside and outside their descent group. To use the metaphor introduced in Chapter 2, I put the normal lens on my camera and offer an experience-near account of what I have learned about some members of the Berosaiña group. I end the chapter with some remarks on the Berosaiña as a descent group.

Raboba, the indebted peasant

Raboba, the slave descendant who built the two tiny huts I mentioned at the end of Chapter 1 (see Figure 1.3), was the first Berosaiña I met since he was our most immediate neighbour in Soatanana. Soon after our arrival, the second hut had become the household's kitchen and the first one the sleeping room. The two buildings were sufficiently close to each other to allow people to easily circulate between them. The house was peculiarly small by local standards. The huts had only one storey and their roofs were low. The two doors were so small and so narrow that I felt ridiculously tall each time I entered Raboba's home. The reason for such an unusually tiny dwelling was that it was supposed to be temporary. Raboba had built the first hut seven months before we arrived in Beparasy, having followed Redison's suggestion to move out from his house in the 'big village' and live with him in the newly founded hamlet of Soatanana, conveniently located close to Raboba's rice fields. The building of a new house was decided from the start but Raboba lacked funds to buy the materials and start the process, so he first built a temporary hut, which later became the sleeping room, and then a second one, which became the kitchen around the time we arrived in Soatanana. By the end of our stay, Raboba was at last building his new, larger house and the family was preparing to move in. The temporary hut had lasted for almost three years, and in the meantime Raboba's tiny house had become the subject of many jokes.

Raboba had three children from a previous marriage: a daughter, who died shortly after giving birth to Raboba's first granddaughter, and two boys, who were twenty and fourteen years old at the time we arrived in Soatanana. Ravao, Raboba's current wife, also had a daughter and a son from previous unions. Her daughter was already married to a young man from Beparasy and lived in her husband's paternal hamlet with their children. Ravao's son, Raboba's younger son, and one of Ravao's granddaughters lived with Raboba and Ravao for most of the year. When we arrived, the tiny hut was also hosting Ravao's mother, who had come to visit from Ambalavao, where she lived with one of her sons. She stayed a few months in Soatanana and then walked back to Ambalavao, in spite of being more than seventy years old.

Before building the little hut in Soatanana, Raboba and Ravao had been living in a larger house in the 'big village'. Raboba's great grandfather, Rainihosy (see Figure 3.1), arrived in Beparasy towards the end of the nineteenth century. When the 'big village' was created during the French *politique de villagisation*, Rainihosy chose to join the families who accepted to live in an unusually large and 'mixed' settlement.[1] For reasons which will become clear in the next chapter, upon his arrival in Beparasy Rainihosy was given a good and large estate of land where he could cultivate rice. His son, Raboba's grandfather, accompanied one of his brothers to fight with the French in World War I. Raboba often expressed regret that, having lost it, he could not show me a picture of his grandfather in uniform and in the charming company of a *vazaha* woman.

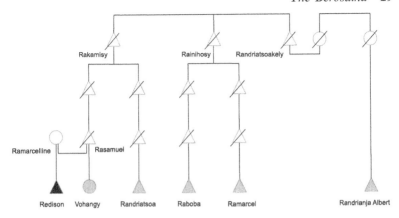

Figure 3.1 Kinship links between Redison and the Berosaiña portrayed in this chapter

When the two brothers returned from World War I they were granted a pension by the French, which provided them with a regular amount of cash, something which was rare at that time and still is for most people of Beparasy today.[2] With this money, Raboba's grandfather was able to pay labourers to work in his field and his life became easier than that of ordinary poor peasants. His two sons were reportedly spoiled and did not learn to work hard in the fields as other young men had to. One of the sons had left Beparasy a long time ago. Now an old man, he lives in Vangaindrano, on the east coast, and has kept very little contact with the family. I was told that Raboba's father was particularly *maditra* (stubborn, disobedient). He led an itinerant life and made a living as a tomb builder. On his death, which occurred early, he was not buried in his father's tomb in Beparasy. Because he had not fulfilled his family duties and had many debts with local people, his relatives found it more appropriate to let his maternal side bury him in one of their tombs. He was buried with his mother in a village located a few dozen kilometres from Beparasy.

While his father was away as an itinerant tomb builder and after his early death, Raboba was raised by his mother in Beparasy under the authority of his grandfather. Like his father, Raboba did not have to learn to work hard in the fields as a young man. People say he was spoiled too. But when his grandfather died, the money from the French pension stopped flowing. Raboba inherited good land but, of course, he had to work on it to make it worth anything. Up to this date, however, Raboba's efforts in managing his estate had not been very successful. In Beparasy he was often described as someone who could be rich, because he owned wide *farihy* (wet rice lands) on the river banks, but who always ran out of rice and money only a few months after the harvest.

Raboba's problems are twofold. The first is that he has been stuck for years in a cycle of debt. When he ran out of rice he borrowed a few *vata* (a measure for rice, equivalent to eight buckets) from whoever agreed to lend to him, at the normal local rate of 200 per cent. At the next harvest, the following year, his lenders came to ask for the *vary maintso* ('green rice', i.e. the payment of a debt of rice at harvest time), leaving Raboba once again with little rice. To reimburse his debts, Raboba was increasingly forced, year after year, to lease parts of the valuable rice fields to his creditors for a derisory rent and renewable three-year contracts. At the time I was in Beparasy, Raboba was cultivating less than one quarter of the almost two hectares of rice land he 'owns' and was leasing the rest. More recently he even decided to sell plots of land. Not only did he sell land to Redison and then to Redison's brother-in-law, Naina, but he also sold a rice field to a school teacher. These sales of ancestral land, as well as the leasing of land for money, intensely irritate Raboba's Berosaiña kinsmen. This is because, according to customs, land belongs corporately to the local descent group and thus any important decision about it should be decided by the senior members of the group. In addition, Raboba's great grandfather, Rainihosy, issued a *fady* (taboo) for his descendants: they should never sell their land and, if they leased it, they should never receive money, only rice. Raboba did not seem to be afraid of breaching this ancestral taboo.[3]

Raboba's second difficulty in managing his estate is a crucial lack of labour force. Rice growing can be labour-intensive at times and requires steady supervision. Raboba usually works alone in his rice fields, although his son and Ravao's son, both in their early teens, helped him when they were not at school. He could not count on his eldest son anymore since a bitter dispute had started between them. The son, as a child and then as a teenager, always had problems living with Ravao, Raboba's current wife. Some time before our stay in Beparasy he left the household and went to live on his own. He therefore asked his father to let him cultivate for his own benefit a part of the family estate. Raboba, because he was heavily indebted and had little land left, refused categorically. The son got very upset and left the house. The dispute was still going on at the time of our departure, with Raboba's son appealing to family authorities on his father's and mother's sides in order to try to collect money that could pay back part of Raboba's debt, cancel the leasing agreements and convince his father to give him a plot of land.

In addition to the recent loss of his eldest son's labour, a few years earlier Raboba's two zebus were stolen by *dahalo* (cattle rustlers). Since then he has only had his spade to plough his rice paddies, although he usually manages to borrow a few zebus for a day from a friend or a neighbour when he needs to do the trampling.

For southern Betsileo peasants, the set of relatives from whom one can usually ask for help, particularly in agricultural work, is the kindred (loosely called *fianakaviana*, i.e. family). Raboba, however, cannot ask for help from his mother's side since they are not from Beparasy and live far away. He cannot count much on his patrilateral relatives either. Although his great grandfather Rainihosy had many descendants, only two men live with their household in Beparasy and these men are much younger than Raboba. One of them was in his early twenties when we arrived. Two years before our stay he had been sent by his mother to Beparasy, where he had never lived before, to work on the family estate of his recently deceased father. Before that he had lived with his parents in Antananarivo and then in Fianarantsoa. He had left school and stayed unemployed for a while, and was often found in bad company, preferring to learn kung fu instead of working or studying. Out of fear that he would soon become a delinquent, his mother decided to send him to his paternal village to work on his father's rice fields. The second of Rainihosy's descendants was in his thirties. He was married and had two young children. Both of them were, like Raboba, working on their own land without asking help from their relatives. I rarely saw them helping each other.

If there is little help available from his kindred, a southern Betsileo man can also turn to his in-laws if they live close enough. But on Ravao's side the prospect of getting help was even worse than on Raboba's. Her siblings did not live in Beparasy, since Beparasy was the *tanindrazana* (ancestral land) of their mother. Her brothers have followed the traditional patri-virilocal pattern of post-marital residence, staying in their father's village, while her sisters married out in distant villages. Ravao chose to go to Beparasy from Ivohibe, where she had grown up, after a few failed marriages and her father's death. She accompanied her mother who, being a widow, wanted to go back to Mahasoa, her paternal village. Both planned to cultivate the small estate of land they were offered by their relatives. While living in Mahasoa, Ravao started an affair with Raboba and then a bit later moved to live with him in the 'big village'.[4]

Ravao is not on good terms with most members of her maternal family. Having learned that Raboba was a Berosaiña and finding out that Ravao was of free descent, I assumed for a while that Ravao's problems with her family were caused by her relationship with an *andevo* (slave). However, I subsequently learned that there were serious disputes about inheritance within the family and that Ravao's choice to live with a Berosaiña was only part of the story. It seems, nonetheless, that this choice prevented the couple from being close to the friendliest of Ravao's relatives – those who, in spite of the problems, continued to pay visits to Ravao and Raboba in Soatanana – and from being engaged in mutual aid practices with them.

Raboba and Ravao are, by local standards, fairly isolated and live much on their own. Twice I observed them harvesting their rice fields with the help of only their children. They did not invite anybody to the harvest because, given their indebtedness, they did not want to give a share of the harvest to each of the participants, as is customary. Raboba and Ravao's rather individualistic mode of harvesting contrasts starkly with the traditional way common in Beparasy, which is based on *haoña* (mutual help). It is normally a happy event to which many relatives and friends are invited to participate, and the success in mobilising people to help at harvest is a good indicator of a family's network of allies.[5]

Because of his poor ways of dealing with land, family and traditional issues, Raboba is not a well-respected man in Beparasy. He is also often criticised among the Berosaiña, his own kinsmen. To make things worse, Raboba has a tendency to drink a good deal of *toaka* (local rum). At the weekly market, whenever he has a bit of money, it is common to find him under the eucalyptus trees, where men and women alike spend the day sitting and sipping until they get heavily inebriated. It is mainly because of Raboba's lack of credibility as a *raiamandreny* (literally 'father and mother', i.e. a notable, respected person) that Ramarcel, to whom I turn next, is considered as the *tale* (head) of the Berosaiña branch of Rainihosy's descendants, in spite of being younger than Raboba and not residing in Beparasy.

Ramarcel, the careful *bizinesy* man

In contrast to Raboba, Ramarcel is an experienced businessman and a much better manager of his rice fields. He has also a better sense of his duties towards his family and his kinsmen. His grandfather, Raboba's grandfather's brother (see Figure 3.1), decided after his return from World War I to go into the *bizinesy* (business) of transporting rice and other local goods from Beparasy to Ambalavao. Most of his descendants have followed in his footsteps. Ramarcel's remaining uncle is in the transport business in Manakara, on the east coast of Madagascar.

Ramarcel's father was instrumental in establishing and organising Beparasy's weekly market. He traded and transported rice, cassava, potatoes, wood and all sorts of goods produced locally. In the second half of his life he moved to Ambalavao but continued to do business with people in Beparasy. Although the house he built in the 'big village' is now unoccupied and in a state of decay, it is still remarkable for its size, its blue-painted *lavarangana* (balcony) and its centrality in the village. Ramarcel and his siblings partly grew up in Ambalavao, where at the time of my first fieldwork they still lived and worked in the business of trading local goods; except the youngest, who in 2009–2010 was studying for his *baccalauréat* at a high school in Ambalavao.

When he was around thirty, Ramarcel decided to leave Ambalavao for the 'big village' in Beparasy to cultivate rice on the land he had inherited from his father. This lasted for a few years, but in the end he decided to go back to Ambalavao, partly because, as he confessed to me, his first wife cheated on him with one of the best friends he had in Beparasy. He separated from his wife and married another woman. Now his Beparasy rice fields are cultivated by a free descendant from the 'big village' on a share-cropping basis, whereby Ramarcel gets fifty per cent of the harvest. Ramarcel says that, unlike Raboba, he will never lease the fields in exchange for money because he wants to observe the *fady* (taboo) issued by his ancestor Rainihosy. His siblings do not claim a share of the harvest since they rarely come to Beparasy and have left Ramarcel to take care of the ancestral estate. The only exception to the relative disinterest shown by Ramarcel's siblings towards their estate in Beparasy is Ramarcel's youngest sister, who on rare occasions shows up at the market to sell goods bought in Ambalavao and to purchase Beparasy products to sell in town. Ramarcel, on the contrary, is often in Beparasy because of his transport business. These frequent visits allow him to keep an eye on the ancestral estate.

In this case, too, I had known Ramarcel for a long time before I learned that he was a Berosaiña. He was the fares collector and often the organiser of one of the two or three *taxibrosy* (bush taxis) bringing passengers and goods to Beparasy's weekly market. I had travelled many times in vans under his management but had no particular contact with him, other than for travelling purposes, until we finally met at a *vadipaisa*, a ceremony held for the transport of the bones of ancestors into a new tomb – an event to which I will return in Chapter 5. Ramarcel's occupation makes him an important person to know because of the relative remoteness of Beparasy and the scarcity of transport opportunities – motorised transport is normally available only one day per week, and much less during the rainy season when the track is often wet and difficult. Ramarcel always knows whether someone in Ambalavao is planning to bring a four-wheel drive, a van or a truck to Beparasy as he is often the middle man in these ventures and must therefore find enough passengers and goods to fill the vehicle up to the load limit, and often much beyond it.

It is well known that the Malagasy devote much care to the place-ment of their dead in *fasandrazana* (ancestral tombs).[6] The Berosaiña are no exception and they have built several tombs in Beparasy. Raboba's and Ramarcel's great grandfather, Rainihosy, prepared his tomb before his death and built a *fasa vodivato* ('bottom-of-a-stone' tomb). These tombs are placed in or under a rock, sometimes in a natural, cave-like hole, sometimes beneath a massive piece of rock under which a hole in the soil is dug so that the rock forms the roof of the tomb. In the smallest of these tombs there is space for only two *farafara* ('beds') consisting of two large flat stones, one for each sex. The tomb is then closed by a wall of piled stones. I was told that in the past the stones were sometimes sealed with mud or lime. Throughout the twentieth century, interior beds and walls have increasingly been built with cement. While to enter ancient *vodivato* tombs people had to remove the wall's stones, contemporary cemented tombs have doors (see Figure 3.2). The tomb built by Rainihosy was of the simplest kind and until 1966 it was used to bury his descendants. During the years 1964–1966, Ramarcel's grandfather used cement to build a new, larger *vodivato* tomb which contains four beds.

Figure 3.2 Cemented *vodivato* tomb in Beparasy

Some of Rainihosy's descendants have yet another tomb in Beparasy. The reason for its existence is that Raboba's grandfather was on such bad terms with his brother (Ramarcel's grandfather) that he decided to be buried with his wife in a separate tomb. He therefore looked for a hole in the rocks on the hills surrounding Beparasy, found a suitable one and started to fit it out. Unfortunately he died before he had found the time and money to finish the tomb. His relatives nevertheless followed his will and buried him in the hole he had chosen, although it had only elementary fittings and no proper entrance wall. He was later joined in the tomb by his wife, another of his brothers, this brother's wife and their daughter.

When a new tomb is built, the general rule for southern Betsileo is that only the descendants of the most remote ancestor in the tomb can be buried in it. Thus, since none of Raboba's grandfather's ancestors were placed in his tomb, only his descendants and his siblings – as well as their spouses (see Regnier 2015b) – have a right to this tomb. By contrast, when his brother (Ramarcel's grandfather) built the 1966 tomb he had done the *vadipaisa*, the ceremony in which the bones of the dead were transported from the old tomb to the new one. The bones of his father, Rainihosy, were placed in the tomb and the old tomb was emptied and abandoned. As a result, all the descendants of Rainihosy are allowed to be buried in this tomb, whereas only Raboba's grandfather's descendants can be buried with him in the unfinished tomb.

Apart from the few individuals mentioned above, the descendants of Raboba's grandfather who were buried in Beparasy have been placed in the tomb built by Ramarcel's grandfather. Prestige was probably a decisive factor here, since a well-fitted, cemented and large tomb is a greater source of pride at funerals than a simple hole in the rocks. It is also remarkable that none of Raboba's grandfather's sons has been buried in his tomb. The fact that all the Berosaiña belonging to this branch are likely to be buried in the tomb built by Ramarcel's grandfather reinforces Ramarcel's power as head of the family, and contributes to diminishing the power and influence of Raboba's grandfather's descendants.[7]

Randrianja Albert, the wealthy foster child

Randrianja Albert is the head of another branch of the Berosaiña who live in Beparasy. Although I never managed to talk to him I often heard people mentioning his name because he is a wealthy man by local standards. Until recently he owned more than thirty zebus.

He had inherited the land of his father, Randriatsoakely, and had lived in Randriatsoakely's house in a 'mixed village' until he had built a larger house beyond his rice fields, close to the Catholic Church and not far from the 'big village'. Randrianja Albert's new house is remarkable for the fact that it is the only one with a tiled roof in Beparasy. Tin and tiled roofs are visible signs of wealth in the region, given that the vast majority of houses have thatched roofs.[8]

Although he was always referred to as Randriatsoakely's son, Ramarcel explained to me that Randrianja Albert was actually not Randriatsoakely's biological son (see Figure 3.1). This fact was later confirmed to me by a free descent friend. Being from the village where Randriatsoakely and Randrianja Albert had lived before the latter constructed his new house, he knew the stories well. After the death of his first wife, who had given him five children, Randriatsoakely married a second, much younger wife. Since his second wife never became pregnant, she decided to foster one of her sister's sons, who was sent to Beparasy from a village south-west of Ambalavao. This child was little Randrianja Albert.

At some point Randriatsoakely's sons from his first marriage moved away from Beparasy. This happened because they were seasonally looking for *karama* (wage labour) and selling *paraky* (tobacco) in the region of Ivohibe, south of Beparasy. One of them decided to stay there and found land to cultivate, and he was soon emulated by his brothers. After the death of Randriatsoakely, his Beparasy estate was left in the hands of his second wife and her sister's son, Randrianja Albert. After the death of his mother, Randrianja Albert inherited the whole estate.

Randriatsoakely's biological children did not wish to cultivate their share of land in Beparasy because they said they had enough in Ivohibe. Yet they are still attached to Beparasy as their *tanindrazana* (ancestral land). In August 2008 I attended a *kiridy* (a festive ancestors-thanking ceremony) at Randrianja Albert's house. Randrianja Albert held the *kiridy* to thank his ancestors because one of his daughters had recovered from a grave illness. Randriatsoakely's sons had come from Ivohibe for the occasion. However, they usually do not come to funerals in Beparasy because they are too far away – it would take too long to send them the invitation and for them to arrive since they would have to walk through the mountains and the journey would take a few days. Despite this fact, their ancestral tomb in Beparasy is still very important for them because it is where their father and two of their siblings are buried. Randrianja Albert also buried one of his daughters who died very young in this tomb. Then, in 1988 – he must have been around forty at that time – Randrianja Albert built a new *vodivato* tomb.

Unlike the case of Raboba's grandfather, however, the rationale for building a new tomb was not dispute or rivalry. It was essentially about securing Randrianja Albert's claims to land ownership. When Randrianja Albert held the *vadipaisa*, he did not only transport the bones of his daughter but emptied out Randriatsoakely's tomb and brought all the bones into his new cemented tomb. By doing so, Ramarcel explained, he strategically prevented the descendants of Randriatsoakely from coming back from Ivohibe one day to reclaim their part of their heritage and, above all, to question Randrianja Albert's rights to monopolise Randriatsoakely's land. Since he is now the *tompompasa* ('master of the tomb') where Randriatsoakely and two of his children are buried, Randriatsoakely's descendants cannot do much in the future to contest his status as head of the local family in Beparasy and his right to cultivate their ancestor's land.

Vohangy, the brave cook

Vohangy is Redison's sister and, like him, she has spent many years away from Beparasy, even though she was born there. Their parents, Rasamuel and Ramarcelline, migrated to the south and lived in Ambovombe and Betroka as petty merchants. Vohangy was married in Betroka and gave birth to her first two children. In 1994 Rasamuel and Ramarcelline decided to go back to Beparasy and live in Rasamuel's house in Mahasoa. In 1997 Vohangy, who had separated from her Tandroy husband, also returned to her *tanindrazana* in Beparasy and occupied one of the two rooms on the ground floor of Rasamuel's house, while her parents lived upstairs. Since then she has given birth four times but never married again. In 2003 her father, Rasamuel, died. Her mother, Ramarcelline, moved out to live in a tiny house in Ambalavao on the insistence of Redison, who wanted to school his three sons in town and asked his mother to take care of them.

Although I introduced Vohangy in the previous paragraph as Redison's sister and Ramarcelline's daughter – this is how all three describe their relationships – it is important to explain that Vohangy is not Ramarcelline's biological daughter (see Figure 3.1). Before getting married to Ramarcelline, Rasamuel had been married to another woman and had three children with her before she died. As I have already explained, Redison is not Rasamuel's biological son either. Ramarcelline already had two children, Redison and his older brother, when she married Rasamuel. Redison, Vohangy and the second daughter of Rasamuel had been raised together by Rasamuel and Ramarcelline while they were in the south.

Vohangy is an energetic and positively minded woman. Since her father's death she has been cultivating his rice fields. She is the only one left among Rasamuel's children, since her brother had been found dead in a field – Ramarcel told me that he was a real *dahalo* (cattle rustler) and was probably murdered – and her younger sister had led an itinerant life with her husband until they recently settled in the region of Sakalalina, to the east of the Route Nationale 7 between Ankaramena and Ihosy. Redison, too, once described this stepsister and her husband as *dahalo* who had made a lot of money with their illegal activities.

In addition to her agricultural work in the rice fields, Vohangy cooks and sells *sakafo* (meals) at the weekly market. In a flimsy shelter made of wooden sticks and rice bags she prepares rice with chicken, beans, fresh-water fish or greens – depending on what is available – as well as take-away food such as banana fritters, boiled fresh-water crabs or crayfish or *mofo gasy* ('Malagasy bread', a sort of crumpet made with rice flour). In the catering business at the market of Beparasy, Vohangy only competes with a free descent old woman whose daily activities involve selling cups of heavily sugared tea and coffee to her regular clients. At the market, she too sells large plates of boiled rice with a tiny side dish.

Vohangy's business ventures at the market have been quite successful but they have also brought her some problems. In 2009 she planned to replace her small wood-and-rice-bags shelter with a more ambitious *hôtely* ('restaurant'). The plan was to erect a mud brick building with a thatched roof, wooden doors and windows, and with a 'kitchen' and 'dining room' for the customers. She hired local people to make the bricks, build the walls, fetch the wood and grass, thatch the roof and fit together doors and windows. The building was almost finished when it was burned down during one night in September. The news spread in Beparasy and people wondered who could have done that. 'Surely it was *fialonana* (jealousy),' many thought.

I heard suggestions that maybe Vohangy's main competitor at the market had paid someone to set fire to the flammable grass roof. Given my keen interest in prejudice and discrimination against slave descendants, I hypothesised that some people in Beparasy did not like the idea of a slave descent woman selling meals at the market, maybe because of issues of uncleanliness and contamination. Ramarcel, for his part, explained to me that it was *fady* (taboo) for the Berosaiña to sell *sakafo masaka* (cooked meals) on their ancestral land and suggested that upset Berosaiña ancestors were somehow behind the fire.

Rakoto Jeannot, a free descent elder from the 'big village' who knew Vohangy very well, suspected that the culprit was one of her kinsmen in Mahasoa. As for Vohangy herself, she rejected the possibility that it could be someone from outside Mahasoa because, she said, she never quarrelled with *olo hafa* ('other people', meaning here people who are not relatives). She explained to me that two of her pigs had already been stolen and that someone had recently defecated in front of her door during the night. She asked the president of the *fokontany* to investigate the case and, a few weeks after the fire, a meeting with the household heads of Mahasoa took place in the *fokontany* office. After long discussion the principal suspect, one of Vohangy's *anadahy* ('brother', i.e. here a cousin) agreed to rebuild the *hôtely* and the issue was settled – even though the young man had refused to publicly acknowledge that he had started the fire.

Randriatsoa, the gifted orator

Randriatsoa, Vohangy's classificatory 'brother' and co-resident in Mahasoa, is renowned as one of the best *mpikabary* (orators) in Beparasy.[9] He is considered as the *tale* (head) of the Berosaiña of Mahasoa, the descendants of Rakamisy (Figure 3.1), despite the fact that he has a brother who is slightly older. Ramarcel explained to me that, although he is himself the *tale* of Rainihosy's descendants and at the same generational level as Randriatsoa, he considers him superior in the Berosaiña hierarchy because he had been named *mpikabary* (orator) by his forebears.[10] Randriatsoa was also in the military for a few years and is viewed as someone who likes commanding people. This led to rivalry between him and one of his *dadatoa* (uncles, but in the classificatory sense – it was his father's father's brother's son) when he was still alive. Being one generation above Randriatsoa, according to custom the uncle should have had authority over him, but Randriatsoa tended to exert and emphasise his privilege as the public voice of the family. As in the case of Rainihosy's children, the regular disputes with Randriatsoa led his uncle to build a new tomb. He did so with the financial backing of some of his children, in particular one of his daughters who had gained some wealth in the rice business in Ambalavao. The construction of the tomb was finished in 2002 and the *vadipaisa* was performed to move the bones of the uncle's father into the new tomb.

The old tomb of Rakamisy and his descendants, from which the uncle's father's bones were removed, was not actually the first family tomb. Rakamisy had first been buried on the Vatobe hill in an earth tomb, another kind of Betsileo tomb where the dead are placed in a cavity a few metres underground.[11] This is achieved by digging a trench steadily downwards until an adequate depth is achieved. Then a cavity of a few cubic metres is carved out and, inside, two beds are made with flat stones. When the deceased has been placed on a bed the cavity is closed by a door consisting of a large flat stone and the trench is refilled with earth. The location of the tomb is indicated by a coarse construction called *aloalo*, which is made of stones piled on the ground above the underground cavity. Other stones are placed on the ground to indicate where the trench was dug and where the entrance to the cavity can be found. The tombs of the first settlers in Beparasy were all of this type. Although most of them have been emptied, the *aloalo* are still important for local families since they provide support for their historical claims on precedence and land in the region.

Rakamisy's descendants, like all the 'old' families of Beparasy, followed the local trends in tomb building. In 1967–1969 a new *vodivato* tomb with cement was built, the bones of Rakamisy and his already deceased descendants were transported and the tomb emptied. The *aloalo* on the hill of Vatobe was left as a memorial to the Berosaiña family history.

The Berosaiña as a descent group

My free descent informants explained to me that 'Berosaiña' was the *anarandrazana* (ancestors' name, i.e. the name of the descent group) of the people I have introduced above. I was also told – and later I could see that this was the case – that the Berosaiña themselves, like any other descent group in Beparasy, used this name to refer to their group at ritual occasions, for example during funerals or *kiridy* (ancestor-thanking ceremonies). These explanations puzzled me, since at the same time I was clearly recalling that the slave descendants mentioned by Kottak belonged to no descent groups (Kottak 1986: 279). How did it happen, I wondered, that slave descendants in Beparasy belonged to tomb-centred groups and had a descent group name, just like any other villagers?

As we shall see in the following chapter, it seems that the name Berosaiña was used in the past to refer to a group of slaves who were owned by a ruler and that, after abolition, this name became viewed as a descent group name for the descendants of these slaves. The practice of naming slave groups was confirmed to me by a local historian in Ambalavao. He explained that, in pre-colonial times in the southern Betsileo region, people who owned many slaves – i.e., mostly rulers and nobles – gave their slaves a collective name. This is different from the usual naming of descent groups, which normally occurs when a head of family, at an important occasion, states that from now on all his descendants will bear a new name. My understanding is that slaves, since they all lived together in small hamlets or parts of villages around their owners' houses, were treated by their masters as if they were a group of kinsmen. Slaves were allowed to marry other slaves and have children, and thus they may have formed, generation after generation, quasi-kin groups into which newcomers – new slaves acquired through wars and raiding or, during the nineteenth century, bought at the slave market – were incorporated. That slaves were given group names is also confirmed by Pastor Rainihifina (1956: 143–144, my translation), a folklorist of the Betsileo, who writes:

> The word *andevo* ('slave') was not used very often, since those who had one master all had an *anarampoko* (group name). As for example: Berovazaha, Beanala, Soarirano, Tsiambala, and so on. They were not called *andevo* but called by these names. That is why there are not many proverbs about slaves in the Betsileo language. The discrimination is visible not so much in the language but in the fact that people do not intermarry with them.[12]

As this quotation makes clear, there are many different group names (*anarampoko*) for slave descendants in the whole Betsileo region. Some of my informants were aware of other names used in the areas neighbouring Beparasy. The words *be* (much/many) and *maro* (numerous) seem to have been often used to name slave groups, probably to stress the wealth of their owners. Yet it would be wrong to infer from this observation that all descent group names with *be* or *maro* indicate slave status. The Bedia and the Maroafo, for example, are large Betsileo groups of free descent and some of their branches are also found in Beparasy. Although for the Betsileo the names of all descent groups have a meaning – and people often know a story about why a particular name was given by one of the group's ancestors – it is impossible to guess by the name whether a descent group is of slave status. It is only through *lovantsofina* ('inheritance of the ears', i.e. local knowledge transmitted orally through generations) that southern Betsileo will come to know that people with a particular group name are of slave descent – an issue to which I will return in Chapter 7.

The inhabitants of Beparasy identify descent groups not only by their name but also by way of their zebus, which have the marks of the local descent groups to which they belong carved on their ears.

A friend told me that the earmark of the Berosaiña's cattle is very famous in the region: the ears are carved in the form of a knife. Cattle earmarking is a widespread and important practice in Madagascar (Hurvitz 1979). Rajaonarimanana (1996: 248–250), writing about the northern Betsileo region of Manandriana, explains that *fofo* (earmarks) are one of the criteria that show the existence of a local descent group, called *akitsanjy* in Manandriana. The other criteria are the *anaran'-akitsanjy* (group name), the corporate ownership of immovable property, the existence of *fady* (taboos) transmitted by the ancestors of the group and the existence of a tomb. We have seen in this chapter that the Berosaiña meet all the criteria, thus we should acknowledge that they form a 'true' descent group. In Beparasy, local descent groups were often referred to as *fañahia* (a word that apparently refers to the lands allocated to the different families during the early settlement of Beparasy – cf. Rainihifina 1975: 10) and my informants explained that the Berosaiña were indeed 'a *fañahia* among the other *fañahia*' of the region. This is crucially important since a lack of a descent group name and organisation, which is paramount to Betsileo kinship (Kottak 1980: 165–172), has been suggested as one of the characteristics of the condition of Betsileo slave descendants (Evers 2002: 36, n. 21, 203; Freeman 2013: 605).

Yet, even though it is used in present-day Beparasy as a descent group name like any other, there is little doubt that the name Berosaiña cannot be casually uttered. I recall a discussion with a man in his thirties at the beginning of my fieldwork, at a time when I still had only a vague idea of who was said to be of slave descent in Beparasy and when I assumed that the name Berosaiña, which I had recorded in my field notes, was a descent group name like any other. Since I had seen him a few times in the company of a man who, I had been told, was a Berosaiña, I asked him whether he was a Berosaiña too. His face froze and he laughed with unease, denying vehemently that he had anything to do with the Berosaiña. This young man had often hung around my place, out of curiosity, apparently because he wanted to make friends with me. He never came back to my house after that day, and clearly avoided crossing my path at the market. I had obviously made a faux pas. From that day on I became more careful in handling the name Berosaiña.

Conclusion: what these stories tell us about the Berosaiña

A Betsileo scholar I met in Fianarantsoa once told me that in his *tanindrazana* the slave descendants lived in the lowest part of the village and that he had known from a very early age that there was an 'invisible line' beyond which he could not marry. In Beparasy, however, I could not find any trace of a clear separation of the Berosaiña from the others. Nor could I find evidence that the Berosaiña had their houses in an unfavourable location following the Malagasy astrological system (Hébert 1965) – aside from the fact that, in a landscape where hamlets and villages are scattered around rice fields, some are always to the west or to the south of others. At first I was concerned that perhaps I was unable to see what my fellow anthropologists working on the Betsileo had seen. I later understood that this absence of a clear geography of power and status was due to the recent history of the region and to the fact that the Berosaiña were not the descendants of local slaves. I was told by elders that in the region only *hova* (nobles) owned slaves in the past and that no *hova* ever lived in Beparasy. Only commoners had been among the first settlers and these had not been rich enough to own slaves. Thus I came to believe that the Berosaiña were former slaves who had arrived in the region shortly after the abolition in order to find free land and start a new life – the third option in Bloch's account of what happened to Zafimaniry and Merina ex-slaves (Bloch 1979, 1980). As it will soon be clear, the history of the Berosaiña is in fact a little more complicated than this.

The ethnographic vignettes I have just provided about the Berosaiña make a number of important points. First, the Berosaiña are *tompontany* ('masters of land', i.e. land owners) whose first presence in the region dates back to several generations and, in terms of their socio-economic situation, they are rather favoured by owning good land, some of them being considered rich by local standards. Second, the Berosaiña have well-established ancestral tombs and belong to the tomb-centred branches of a group that is identified as a 'proper' and recognizable descent group by the other groups. The point about the Berosaiña tombs is significant because in Madagascar ancestral tombs are essential for a group's social status and for the role the group can play in local politics, since they testify to its historical presence on a land. In addition, this is significant because the Betsileo slave descendants described by Kottak (1980) and Freeman (2001) do not seem to have built ancestral tombs that are commensurable, in their use and importance, to those of their former masters, while the Betsileo slave descendants described by Evers (2002) seem to have no ancestral tombs at all.

On this important issue, the slave descendants of Beparasy are in a favourable situation. As explained at the end of Chapter 1, the ancestors of the largest families of Beparasy arrived towards 1880. Because of the great distance between Beparasy and northern Betsileo, the region of origin of many of them, these land-poor settlers all built ancestral tombs and firmly established themselves in Beparasy. As a result, the genealogical depth in the tombs of all Beparasy villagers, whether of free or slave descent, is relatively shallow – it does not exceed five generations of *razana* (dead/ancestors). Thus, it is not only in their outward characteristics that the Berosaiña's tombs look like those of free descendants: they also have a similar number of generations of ancestors in the tomb. On this matter, too, the Berosaiña seem on equal footing with free descendants.

Notes

1 By 'mixed settlement' here I mean that several descent groups lived together, as opposed to the *vala* type of settlement, which often only comprises the descendants of the *vala*'s founding ancestors and their spouses. Later I will use the term 'mixed village' to refer to villages inhabited by free and slave descendants, and 'mixed marriage' to refer to unions between free and slave descendants.

2 The two sons of Rainihosy were not the only inhabitants of Beparasy who fought with the French. For more information on Malagasy soldiers enrolled in the French army during World War I, see Valensky (1995).

3 On the importance of taboos in Madagascar see Van Gennep (1904), Ruud (1960), Lambek (1992), Walsh (2002) and Astuti (2007).

4 For reasons that will soon become clear, Mahasoa is considered as the main slave descent village in Beparasy, even though it is actually a mixed village. Ravao's mother's paternal family is one of the free descent groups who live in Mahasoa.

5 At the very least, according to customs, Raboba and Ravao should have invited their co-villagers in Soatanana; i.e., Redison and Raely, Naina and Voafara, and Anjasoa and me. During the first rice harvest that we witnessed they invited none of us. One year later they invited only Anjasoa and me, feeling forced to do so because we had been joking for a long time that I would harvest with them.

6 Many ethnographies of Madagascar deal, in one way or another, with this crucial issue. See, in particular, Bloch (1971), Mack (1986), Astuti (1995) and Parker Pearson and Regnier (2018).

7 The descendants of Raboba's grandfather have other options than being buried in his unfinished tomb or in the tomb built by Ramarcel's grandfather: they can be buried on the sides of forebears who do not belong to the Berosaiña group, since the choice of the tomb, although negotiated by families, takes into account individual preferences (Parker Pearson and Regnier 2018: 52). Such a preference would mean that they will not be buried in their *tanindrazana* (ancestral land) in Beparasy because, as we shall see in the next chapters, the Berosaiña cannot find spouses locally.

8 It is striking, however, that the two wealthiest heads of family in Beparasy, who have authority over 100 zebus and several hectares of rice land, have a

poorly maintained house with a thatched roof. I was told that they delib-
erately avoid conspicuous signs of wealth out of fear that this will attract
dahalo (cattle rustlers). For the same reason, their large cattle herd is
usually not visible, since it is left in the forest or in the mountains under the
protection of charms.

9 On Malagasy speeches and oratory, see Ochs (1973, 1974a, 1974b), Bloch
(1975), Haring (1992) and Jackson (2013).

10 As we shall see in the next chapter, this difference of status is also the
consequence of the role played by Rakamisy in the early settlement of
Beparasy.

11 For a more extensive discussion of Betsileo tombs, see Dubois (1938),
Rajaonarimanana (1979), Gueunier (1974) and Parker Pearson and Regnier (2018).

12 Rainihifina (1956) also explains that the different categories of people (i.e.,
advisers, servants, soldiers and slaves) who surrounded southern Betsileo
polities' *lapa* (a royal residence) were called by specific names. On
Malagasy naming practices more generally, see Gueunier (2012) and
Regnier (2016).

4   Contested histories

In the preceding chapter I portrayed Berosaiña individuals to highlight the important differences between them and the variety of relations they have with the non-Berosaiña villagers of Beparasy. While Raboba's indebtedness, laziness and tiny house are a source of collective amusement, many villagers are keen to keep good relationships with Ramarcel because of his key role in the local transport business. Randrianja Albert is respected as an important notable, above all because of his wealth. Vohangy's friendly character and hard-working ethos, well appreciated by her customers, boosted her small business so much that in the course of the two years of my stay it had become more popular than that of her free descendant competitor in the catering business at the market. Randriatsoa's rhetorical skills have earned him a solid reputation as an orator and his voice is often heard during *kabary* (speeches) at various occasions. What all this shows is that members of the Berosaiña group have achieved a variety of social statuses and occupy different key roles in the little society of Beparasy.

Yet there is one important aspect that the Berosaiña seemed unable to change by their own efforts: the conviction of the other families of Beparasy that they are *dorian'andevo* or *taranak'andevo* (descendants of slaves). The goal of this chapter is to take a wide-angle lens and explain the history of the Berosaiña as I came to discover it through conversations with some members of the group and other villagers, and start unveiling the reasons why free descendants think that the Berosaiña are 'slaves'.

Meeting Randriatsoa

It was only after I had already learned a good deal about the Berosaiña and become very close to Redison that I dared to ask him direct questions about his mother's marriage with the Berosaiña Rasamuel and the consequences that this relationship had on her life. The opportunity came when we found ourselves walking back together from Ambalavao and had several hours of conversation in front of us. Although Redison was well disposed to tell me what he knew of the story, in truth he knew little, he said, because he was very young when his mother and Rasamuel married one another. He told me that his maternal relatives opposed their marriage because people say that the Berosaiña are *andevo* (slaves). When I asked him why the Berosaiña were considered as *andevo* and why his relatives did not want his mother to marry one of them, he replied that he did not really know. He then suggested that we ask his paternal uncle, Randriatsoa, because, he said, he knew the history of the Berosaiña family very well. He added that we should bring him a bit of money and a bottle of rum, since such gifts are customary when one wants to hear about family history from an elder.

In Chapter 3 I introduced Randriatsoa as a renowned orator, but he is also reputed for his historical knowledge. His grandfather had chosen him for his intellectual capacities when he was a young boy, and charged him with the honour of passing on knowledge within the family about local history, customs, family histories and land owner-ship. Free descendants in Beparasy often recommended him to me when they heard that I was interested in *tantara* (history) and *fomba* (customs): 'You should go to see Randriatsoa, he is very clever and knows a lot about history.' Because of his oratory skills, he was often sent to represent Beparasy at official meetings at the *mairie* and had served for a few years as president of the *fokontany* of Beparasy-I, an office which involves dealing with land disputes, organising protection against *dahalo* and a few other responsibilities.

I had actually interviewed Randriatsoa already, before Redison sug-gested we go to see him. The circumstances surrounding this meeting had been fairly awkward, however. Prior to this interview I had talked to an elder who, unlike many people in Beparasy, seemed largely comfortable discussing issues of slavery and slave descendants – indeed, he even seemed to take pleasure in it. He laughed and replied wittily to some of my questions about the Berosaiña. At the end of our con-versation he suggested that I talk to Randriatsoa. I replied that I would be happy to do so and said I would try to contact him soon. A few days later, to my surprise, the elder knocked on our door accompanied by Randriatsoa. They were both wearing a *lamba* and a hat and car-ried walking sticks – the local men's dress for formal occasions. It turned out that on the same morning the elder had asked a young relative of his to go to Mahasoa to inform Randriatsoa that the *vazaha* (white foreigner) of Soatanana wanted to ask questions about history and customs.

I invited them to enter our house, offered a round of rum and set up my recorder. Before we started the interview, Randriatsoa informed me that he needed to invoke his ancestors before he could talk, and requested a *zinga* (large cup) with a small amount of water. Turning to the eastern wall of the room, he asked his ancestors for blessing and sprinkled water towards the four corners of our house. Although I have interviewed many senior persons in Beparasy, Randriatsoa was the only one who did this systematically before answering my questions.

The interview could now start. We talked about various topics and Randriatsoa answered my questions with enthusiasm. The elder intervened only occasionally while sipping his rum but his presence was preventing me from asking any sensitive questions, since I was concerned that he might intervene and say something controversial. I nonetheless asked a few historical and general questions about slavery, but I did not insist on the topic and the conversation quickly moved on to other issues. After my guests had bidden their farewell I spent the rest of the day wondering whether the elder's unexpected manoeuvre might have been motivated by anything other than the round of rum.

I met Randriatsoa again at various occasions after this interview because he was often attending the funerals in Beparasy. I also paid him a courtesy visit at his house in Mahasoa. In 2009 a son of Randriatsoa's sister died from an unidentified sickness and I attended the funerals. Randriatsoa, as head of the descendants of Rakamisy and of the Berosaiña branch of Mahasoa (cf. Figure 3.1), was the *tompompaty* ('master of the corpse', i.e. head of the funeral). He was happy to see me at the funeral, to which I had come from Soatanana with representatives of Redison's family. I expressed my condolences as best as I could and gave 2,000 ariary as *ranomaso* ('tear'). My name, the name of my village (i.e., Soatanana) and the nature of my gift were written in the family notebook and Randriatsoa asked young men to bring me a good share of *hena ratsy* ('bad meat', i.e. the meat from the zebu killed at funerals). This exchange was a sort of institutionalisation of our being some kind of *havana* (kinsmen).[1]

Since the deceased was only in his teens, the funeral in Mahasoa was not a large event in size or length. Only one zebu was killed and the funeral lasted for only two days.[2] I could see, however, that many free descendants helped with the organisation of the ceremony and the hosting of the guests in the 'mixed village' of Mahasoa. A free descent friend of mine, for example, recalled afterwards that his father's house in Mahasoa had hosted more than fifteen guests of the funerals – most of them would presumably have been considered as slave descendants since they were the Berosaiña's close kinsmen. Many free descent villagers attended the funerals too. I was a bit surprised to see that another of my free descent friends and his siblings were among the *lahy mahery* ('strong men', i.e. the group of men who undertake tasks requiring physical effort, such as fetching firewood, catching and killing zebus, clearing vegetation from the tomb's entrance, or bringing the corpse into the tomb – see Figure 4.1). When I later asked him why he was so actively involved at the funeral in Mahasoa, he told me that the deceased was *havana* (kinsman) for him because he had a *vakirà* (blood bond) with his mother (i.e., Randriatsoa's sister). I learned at this occasion that free descendants had no problem with having blood bonds with slave descendants – an important issue, to which I will return in the next chapter.

Given the young age of the deceased, everyone expected the *kabary* (speeches) at the end of the funeral to be short. This is because, according to custom, long *tetiharana* (genealogical speeches) are held only for *olon-dehibe* ('big persons', i.e. people who are married, have children and have reached an age of maturity). There was indeed no genealogical speech for the boy, but Randriatsoa nonetheless gave a long speech in which he recalled stories and anecdotes from the past, including from the pre-colonial era. In his speech he stressed that Beparasy villagers were *tanana raiky* ('from one village') because they were the descendants of the people who, in the past, lived on the hilltop of Vatobe. People in Beparasy, he insisted, were all *havana* (kinsmen). While speaking, Randriatsoa often pointed at the summit

Figure 4.1 'Strong men' (*lahy mahery*) bringing a deceased to the tomb

of the Vatobe hill, which was close and visible from Mahasoa, and made a lot of expressive gestures. I realised during this event that he definitely deserved his reputation for being a good orator.

Randriatsoa's behaviour during the funeral was also striking as a demonstrative form of grieving. Following a *fomba* (custom) which was described as an old way of expressing grief, he had put on his oldest clothes during the days of the funerals, wearing a torn tee-shirt and ripped trousers. He also walked barefoot. Randriatsoa's way of expressing grief contrasted with that of most villagers of Beparasy. Many attend funerals with their daily clothes, only adding a *lamba* and hat, while others dress up following *vahaza* and Christian influences. Randriatsoa was the only one I could observe grieving in this fashion during the many funerals I attended. When we arrived at the entrance of the tomb he started crying loudly, kneeled and then walked on all four towards the stretcher, which was placed on the ground and had the corpse still attached to it. People around restrained him: *'Mangina, Randriatsoa, mangina!'* ('Calm down, Randriatsoa, calm down!'). After the funeral he also observed a period of traditional mourning, during which he did not shave. I could see on subsequent occasions that Randriatsoa was not only very knowledgeable about ancestral customs but was also very careful in following them.

Talking to the Berosaiña about slavery

Some time after my conversation with Redison I had another chance to talk to the Berosaiña about allegations of slave ancestry. This time it was Ramarcel who offered to facilitate the meetings. He had gradually become one of our best friends and informants, partly because, like most people in Beparasy, we often needed his services to find a lift to or from Ambalavao. During our stays in Ambalavao we were constantly in touch with him via mobile phone, and since we were sometimes stuck for several days in town waiting for a lift we slowly built up a close rapport. He invited us to his place and to his mother's in Ambalavao and we came to know his wife, his children and some of his siblings. In return we invited him to visit us whenever he was in Beparasy, and he did not miss an opportunity to do so. During our meetings in Ambalavao or at our house in Beparasy we held long conversations – he was talkative and liked our company – that were sometimes about his family and the people of Beparasy.

At some point, after we had become very close, I felt it might be possible to have an open discussion with him about the rumoured slave descent of the Berosaiña and the fact that the other families of

Beparasy did not want to marry them. Such a conversation took place one afternoon in Ambalavao. The difficulty was finding a quiet place where we could discuss sensitive issues. Meeting at our friends' or Redison's relatives was out of the question, since there were too many people passing by, and it was also impossible to have such an interview at the small *hôtely* (restaurant) where my wife Anjasoa and I used to stop to eat or drink when we were in town. In agreement with Ramarcel, we therefore decided to set up a meeting in a hotel for tourists run by a Chinese family. Because of the troubled political situation in Madagascar – it was shortly after the 2009 coup – the hotel dining room was empty most of the time.

During the conversation we talked about Redison's mother's marriage to Rasamuel. When we asked Ramarcel why Redison's maternal relatives did not want to let Ramarcelline marry Rasamuel, he replied that Rasamuel was 'someone who dares to say things clearly' (*olona miavonavona resaka*) and this displeased Ramarcelline's family. Redison was also very direct and capable of speaking harshly to people, a rather unusual trait among the southern Betsileo, who prefer not to raise their voices or say things directly. I had sometimes wondered why Redison had this character because I knew his mother and she was very different – easy-going, very polite and patient. Listening to Ramarcel, I thought that Redison had probably inherited his foster father's character. Yet it was nonetheless clear that Ramarcel had not really answered our question and that there was more to say about this marriage refusal. We insisted:

We have heard that when Rasamuel died the people from Ambalabe did not give any zebu or *lamba*. What's the truth on this issue?

The story of Rasamuel and Redison's mother is already twenty years old but it is still very taboo because it is an 'issue of cutting' [of social relations] (*resaka fanapahana*).

What was the reason for this rupture?

Redison's mother's kinsmen have said strong words (*vava*), words that they should never have said.

What were these strong words?

They gave us truly dirty things to eat (*misy tena fampihinana zavatra maloto*). To speak the truth, it was really an insult. And when there is an insult like that things cannot be arranged easily. There must be a zebu killed to cleanse the strong words that had been said.

Is the problem between the two families over now or is it still going on?

It has not been resolved since Rasamuel is dead now, and
Redison's mother's family too is very arrogant (*miavonavona*,
which could be also translated as 'proud'), so we cannot forgive
them and they cannot forgive us. And Ramarcelline's family
abandoned her. They said: 'If there is something that happens to
your husband you will have to sort things out by yourself.' And
that's why Ramarcelline goes alone (*mandeha irery*) and all her
family abandoned her. It's only her children who help her. That's
also why she does her duties on the side of her husband.[3]

Redison explained to us that they said that Rasamuel and
Ramarcelline did not have the same ancestry (*tsy mitovy razana*).

This is so that in the years 1800s, people say, there were rulers
(*mpanjaka*), it was at the times of the lords (*andriana*), Andria-
nampoinimerina, Radama and the others. And those from our
side lived to the east of Ambalavao, in a village called
Mahasoabe. That's where the father of our grandfather was. He
and his wife lived there and they gave birth to seven brothers, it
was a long time ago, in the nineteenth century. And there were
wars between the lords and their allies. Some of them were
defeated and were enslaved. People said: 'They are inferior to us
these people.' And there were people who were neither victorious
nor defeated, they were in the middle.

Immediately after Ramarcel had pronounced these words there was a
long silence. I did not know whether I should push him further on the
topic or leave it at that, since it had clearly been difficult for him to
mention slavery in connection with his family history. The conversation
took another direction but, some time later, when it came back to the
history of his forebears who had come to Beparasy, we dared to ask:

But why did people think that they [implied: your ancestors] were
slaves?

There are some little stories [circulating in the family] that say
that our grandfather was the first to enter in Beparasy and he
acquired a really large piece of land. Then other people came and
our grandfather gave them a place where to live. He said: 'You will
live on this place here' (*Ianareo mipetraka amin'ny ity toerana ity
eto*). Our grandfather gave land to other families coming from the
region of Isandra, from the region of Fianarantsoa and so on.
These people walked and walked and arrived in Beparasy. At the
time we're speaking there are lands [in Beparasy] that our grandfather lent (*nampidramina*) to people. And there are people today

who say to us: 'This land belongs to your grandfather' (*Io tany io an'i dadabenareo*). It's not a land that he sold but that he lent. Our grandfather said: 'You, eat some rice here because this place is quite clean, you're on your way now' (*Ianareo mba mihinam-bary eo fa ity fa mba madiodio, tsy haveriny amin'izao*). But now people don't give it back. And we do not dare to take it back otherwise there would be conflicts. And you see even today on the side of our grandfather we still have a large free land. For example, from the south of Redison's house going back to the river and up to the bridge and the road, and all the western side. And to the east of the bridge, where there is a sort of little island and where people cultivate maize and beans, that's also our grandfather's land. And close to the Catholic Church, there is still free open land there that belonged to our grandfather. Our possession of these three large open lands created jealousy. And so people said: 'They have large lands because they are descendants of people [*taranak'olo*, i.e. implied: of slaves].' And that's how it happened that people in Beparasy did not want to marry our family. There are some senior people (*raiamandreny*) who say weird things about us and people do not marry us. But nowadays it is not at all allowed to say things like that. People told us that these kinds of things did not occur in the past. But there is one of our uncles who can really tell the history of all that. He's in Beparasy, not in Ambalavao. Here in Ambalavao we do not dare to talk about that because our grand-father left [Mahasoabe] for Beparasy. If we say that we will come to ask them the history of our family, it's possible that they will think: 'These guys are going to take some land here' (*Ireto bandy ireto hangalaka tany aty*). We are very careful about this taking of the land. And our uncle in Beparasy … if there is someone who says: 'You are descendants of slaves' (*Ianareo taranak'andevo*), he makes a big speech in front of all the village council (*fokonolo*). People should not talk like that because we all live there, we were all exiled and our home is now in Beparasy.

The story reported by Ramarcel explains the allegations of slave ancestry against the Berosaiña in terms of jealousy because the Berosaiña's ancestors who arrived in the region received a good share of land. After this conversation, however, Ramarcel admitted that he did not know the history of his family particularly well and remained unclear as to why exactly people thought they were slave descendants. The elders among his kinsmen, he said, would know the answer to that. Some days later he proposed, in spite of the reluctance he had expressed above, a meeting with an elder in Ambalavao, who, he said, could perhaps tell us more about the family history and the reasons that people in Beparasy spoke ill about them.

The interview took place but it quickly became clear that the elder was unwilling to talk to us about what we were interested in. Ramarcel attempted to steer the conversation in the right direction on our behalf, and on several occasions he commented on the elder's reticence: 'Here, you see, there is something that he should tell you but he does not dare.' The elder never told us what Ramarcel expected he would and neither did Ramarcel himself. It was quite clear, however, that this unknown piece of the story was closely linked to the reputation of the Berosaiña as slave descendants.

After this disappointing interview, Ramarcel insisted that we see the *mpitantara* (historian) Randriatsoa in order to ask him our questions. I presumed he was doing this in order to help us, but also wondered whether he too wanted to better understand why his family was considered by Beparasy villagers to be of slave descent. I had the impression that he was curious to hear more about these stories and that perhaps our meeting with Randriatsoa would be a good opportunity to learn about things that would otherwise be unlikely to be discussed among the Berosaiña.

When I told him that I had already interviewed Randriatsoa once, Ramarcel replied that it might yield a different outcome if he were to be present at the next interview since, in the family hierarchy, he is at the same level as Randriatsoa because he is the head of his branch among the Berosaiña. This is so, he said, even though Randriatsoa is more senior in the Berosaiña group – i.e., although Randriatsoa is at the same level as Ramarcel in terms of generations, the branch of Rakamisy's descendants is more senior than the two other branches because Rakamisy was the most senior of the three ancestors (see Figure 3.1) – and Ramarcel has to acknowledge his authority as the 'official' historian and orator of the Berosaiña. Were he to attend the interview, he told us, we could ask our difficult questions without problems and Randriatsoa would feel obliged to answer them.

Randriatsoa's account

The meeting with Ramarcel and Randriatsoa did not take place straight away. Ramarcel lived in Ambalavao and did not know in advance when he would be again in Beparasy – his transport business was an unpredictable affair and he spent a good deal of time moving around Ambalavao. Moreover, since it was difficult to communicate with us and Randriatsoa in order to set up a meeting, we saw Ramarcel doing business a few times at the market of Beparasy before we finally managed to fix a date for the meeting. Ramarcel went to see Randriatsoa in Mahasoa to ask whether he would be willing to talk to us again. Randriatsoa accepted, but said that if this was to be a serious event of telling the history of the family he would like us to follow the customs and asked that we offer him a *lamba*. Randriatsoa did not ask for an expensive *lamba arindrano*, as was customary in the past, but for an ordinary *lamba* in addition to a bottle of *toaka vazaha* (industrial rum).[4] Since we did not know what kind of *lamba* would be appropriate, we commissioned Ramarcel to buy one in Ambalavao.

The meeting with Ramarcel and Randriatsoa had to be carefully prepared in order that nothing would interfere with it. While it had been demanded by Ramarcel, I was nonetheless worried that people in Beparasy would think I was investigating the stories of the Berosaiña too specifically. During his visits to our house, Ramarcel was always cautious to avoid going directly to our place. He always paid short visits to Redison and our other neighbours before coming to see us – to make sure, he once explained, that nobody would think he came to Soatanana with the sole purpose of visiting us, although he clearly did so after we became good friends. Indeed, Ramarcel always seemed to be very careful in what he did, either in Beparasy or in Ambalavao, and this was particularly true on the day of the interview. Since he had not enough time to pay his usual visits to the other inhabitants of Soatanana before coming to our house, he came from below the hamlet, through the rice fields and then up on the hill, to avoid meeting people on the dirt road. It was particularly important to do it like this, he told us, because he was carrying the new *lamba* and the bottle of rum for Randriatsoa, and he did not want people to speculate about why he was bringing such items to our house. To make sure that we would not be disturbed during the interview, we asked a teenage girl of Redison's family to stay outside the house so that she could tell people we were busy and ask them to come back another day.

Like Ramarcel, Randriatsoa had come from below our house through the rice fields, but unlike Ramarcel it was not out of discretion but only because it was the shortest way coming from Mahasoa. Randriatsoa wrapped himself in the *lamba* we gave him and, like the first time, asked for a cup with water. He told us to turn to the eastern side of the house and then started a *saotse* (thanking to the ancestors), after first having sprinkled water towards the four sides of the house. While the *saotse* at the beginning of the first interview was short, this one lasted for a few minutes. He explained to the ancestors that, unlike the *vazaha* who came in the past, I was not there to take the land.[5] He told them that I had a Malagasy wife and child, and that if I was going to ask questions it was only for the purpose of my studies, not to steal their land. Randriatsoa ended his thanking by asking his ancestors: 'Give him the degree he is looking for' (*Mba omeo ny diploma tadiaviny*).[6]

I recorded more than four hours of interview on that day, excluding the long break we took for lunch, during which we kept on talking off the record about various issues. It was a rich moment, but for reasons of space I shall limit my account to the answers that Randriatsoa gave to the questions that, encouraged by the presence of Ramarcel, we dared to ask: Why do people in Beparasy refuse to marry the Berosaiña? Why did Redison's mother's family refuse to accept her marriage with Rasamuel? Randriatsoa, who did not seem to be disturbed by the questions, answered them boldly:

> The issue of marriage is this: these people were soldiers and on our side there were soldiers too. Our grandfathers were retired soldiers.[7] These people had a dispute and that's why all this happened. But the origins (*fiavy*) ... each side has its own origins, but the reputation is the same, there is no superior and no inferior (*ny zo mitovy, tsa misy ambony tsa misy ambany*). Nobody was enslaved (*tsa misy olo nandevozina*). The name that was attributed to us was *andevohova*, not *andevo*, it's something different from the *andevo* that existed a long time ago. But when people quarrelled in the past they would curse each other (*mibodro*) and say: 'My descendants will not marry the descendants of so-and-so.' So the reason is that there was a dispute because they were both soldiers, and their grandfather and our grandmother quarrelled with each other. But there are no tabooed people meaning that people cannot marry their descendants (*tsa misy olo voafady hoe tsa mahazo manambady ny dorian'olo*), it's only that people quarrelled. The people who do not quarrel today can marry each other. But we are not of an ancestry that is inferior to these people and these people are not of an ancestry that is inferior to us (*anay tsy ambanin'ny razan'olo io ary olo io tsy ambanin'ny razanay*).
>
> So why do the people from Ramarcelline's village say these things?
>
> It's because their grandfather quarrelled with our grandmother, and they 'shot each other' (*nifampitifitry*). But there was nobody here before we arrived. If we talk about slavery, then we are the ones who have enslaved other people. But we do not say that.

People joined us here. We were not enslaved by others when we arrived. We came here in the past (*taloha*).

And in the past, before people arrived here, there was no history of ... [implied: slavery]?

There was no place where we could have seen each other since everyone has his own land of origin (*samy mana ny tany fiaviny*). A half comes from here, a half comes from there, where could we have seen each other?

It's like a rumour that people circulated ... perhaps because you came from afar?

Nobody knew each other's land of origin (*ny tany fiaviny*) because it's here that we came to know each other's land of origin. Each of us explained where we came from: 'We came from there, we came from there.' But it is here that we came together and we were the first. How could they have seen us? And if we talk about slavery it's us who should have enslaved people, but we did not enslave people and nobody enslaved us. But the land of origin ... No! Each has his own origins but people quarrelled, they quarrelled with us. That's our story, we quarrelled because we were soldiers. And the people who quarrel do not like each other at all. But we marry whoever we want to.

So it is your grandparents who cursed each other?

Yes. But it's not with all people that we quarrelled, it's only with one family. Did someone else give you strange words like that (*Misy manome feo hafahafa nareo tahakan'izany ve*)?

Nobody did, it came only from our observations of what was happening.

If people say that they came before us here they lie. The *Vazimba* came first, but there are no *Vazimba* anymore. And then the cattle herders came but there are no cattle herders anymore. Then the migrants (*mpifindra monina*) came. We were among the migrants and we brought people here. The people who came here were not kinsmen, and they had different lands of origin. So I don't know the origin of so-and-so, because it's here that we learned to know each other. Then people make speeches: 'We came from there, we came from there.' So do I: 'We came from there, we came from there.' Nobody knows each other's land of origin (*Tsy misy mahalala ny tany fiaviny*).

Randriatsoa thus explained that the founding ancestor of the Berosaiña group in Beparasy – the man to whom Ramarcel referred as 'our grandfather' – was one of the four men that I mentioned at the end of

Chapter 1, named Rakamisy, and that he was an *andevohova*. I had already noticed that during the funerals, when he stood up to give one of the closing speeches, Randriatsoa always stressed that he was 'bringing the words' (*mitondra ny teny*) of the *andevohova*, but I could not understand what it really meant. I had also heard Rakamisy being described as one of the *andevohova* in the oral histories that I had collected among free descendants. This was extremely puzzling. How could it be that Rakamisy had been an *andevohova*, with an important role in the settlement history of Beparasy, and that his descendants were today considered to be slave descendants?

At the time of bidding his farewell, Randriatsoa repeated several times before leaving: 'There are people who throw *fotaka* (mud) at us, but we are not *andevo*, we are *andevohova!*' At that moment of my fieldwork I did not understand fully that, in spite of what their name suggests, the *andevohova* were, in ancient Betsileo society, people with relatively high status who held significant political power because they were the local representatives of *mpanjaka* (rulers), mainly in charge of allocating land and solving conflicts. The term *andevohova* is formed with the words *andevo* and *hova*, but in this case *andevo* should be understood in the sense of 'servant'. The *andevohova* were not a kind of royal slave but, rather, high-status commoners (*olompotsy*). In the hierarchy of southern Betsileo polities they constituted the level immediately above the heads of local descent groups (Rainihifina 1975: 95–99; Ralaikoa 1981: 34; Solondraibe 1994: 30). A ruler was assisted by a number of *andevohova* he had chosen to maintain the contact between him and his subjects. According to Raherisoanjato (1984b: 225, my translation), 'an *andevohova* was a man of high influence. He administered people from one or two *foko* [descent groups], depending of the size of the families.' I was told by Beparasy elders that there were twelve *andevohova* in the small polity of Ambatofotsy, including the four of Beparasy.

Writing about the region of Manandriana (north of Betsileo country), Rajaonarimanana (1996: 25–27) provides an account of how commoners could become *andevohova*. If a man desired to become an *andevohova* he had to see the ruler and offer him an ox. Then the ruler would indicate him a region where he could go to try to form a village. Provided he could find other migrants to follow him to this place, the man would then become the *andevohova* for these groups. I was told by a local historian in Ambalavao that the custom of asking the *hova* when one was in search of land to cultivate subsisted long after 1895. The (former) *hova* would then send these people to the *andevohova* of his (former) fief, who would give them land to cultivate like in the past.

In present-day Beparasy, the descendants of the four *andevohova* still have the important function of mediating conflicts between descent groups, in particular *ady tany* (land conflicts). For this purpose they keep notebooks with detailed information about the lands of the different groups of Beparasy.

After the discussion with Randriatsoa I wondered whether he might be correct and that some free descent people confused words that many do not understand any more. It was indeed the case that in casual conversations some people seemed to have only a vague knowledge of the structure of ancient Betsileo society and sometimes confused the word *andevohova* with *andevo* or even *hovavao*.[8] Redison, for example, clearly mistook *andevohova* for *andevo* in some of the discussions we had. That he could make this mistake was not entirely surprising, since he had lived for a long time out of Beparasy and away from Betsileo country, and was not much versed in local history. But what made the hypothesis of confusion rather implausible was that the descendants of the other three *andevohova* – the descendants of Rainibao, Raikalatsara and Rainidama (cf. Chapter 1) – were not considered to be slave descendants.

Rakoto Jeannot's version of the story

It was some time after Randriatsoa's interview that I eventually found a plausible explanation for this puzzle. It came out during a conversation with Rakoto Jeannot, an elder from the 'big village'. I had become good friends with him after I had helped him plant beans and potatoes in one of his fields. I had also participated in his rice harvests and attended the funerals of his sister, which were held in a small hamlet of eastern Beparasy, where she had married. At this occasion the elder had invited me to sit next to him in the *tranon-dahy* (men's house, i.e. the room where male guests gather during funerals). After that event he would always stop by our house on his way to his fields, his spade on his shoulder, to greet us and see whether I would like to work with him. An open and humorous person, he was one of the most respected *raiamandreny* of Beparasy. Redison had told me that the elder had a *vakirà* (blood bond) with his stepfather, Rasamuel, so that, when he was working as a driver and transporting goods to the south of Madagascar, Rakoto Jeannot would often stop his truck in Betroka to spend the night at Ramarcelline and Rasamuel's house. Because of his job he could understand some French and was happy to practise it with me, as much as I was to practise my Malagasy with him while we worked together in the field.

When I learned that Rakoto Jeannot had a blood bond with Rasamuel I thought he might be the right person to ask about the apparent
contradiction that puzzled me so much. I also supposed that, given this
relation, he might have a more balanced view about Rasamuel and the
Berosaiña than most free descendants. And of course, being very close
to a Berosaiña, he could have learned parts of their family history that
were not known by free descendants. I thus asked Rakoto Jeannot
whether we could interview him a bit more formally than usual and
record the conversation. He accepted and said we could come to his
house any day at around 8 a.m. The following week we went to the
'big village'. We offered him a bottle of rum and the interview started
after he had drunk a bit and rubbed his forehead and the back of his
neck with some drops of the beverage. I soon realised that my sensitive
questions would have to wait for another occasion, since the room
quickly filled up with adults and children who had heard that we were
there. At the back of the room a granddaughter of the elder was also
lying on a bed, wrapped in thick blankets with a newborn baby in her
arms. She was there for the *mifana* (postpartum period), during which
a woman must go back to her parents' village, stay in bed with her
baby, keep warm and eat as much as she can. After ten minutes of
interview, the elder said that we could not go on like this because he
was being distracted all the time. He then proposed that we continue
another day in the quieter setting of our house in Soatanana. Since I
had my sensitive questions about the Berosaiña in mind, I was glad
that he took this decision and invited him to come to our place as soon
as he could. He said he would come the following week.

It actually took much longer, since Rakoto Jeannot had to work in
his fields and was busy with other affairs. Two months later the interview resumed where we had left it. I asked the elder what he knew of
the settlement of Beparasy. When he mentioned Rakamisy, Randriatsoa's great grandfather, as one of the first men who came to
Beparasy and one of those in charge of distributing the land to newcomers, I interrupted him:

> But here, you see, there is something that I don't understand. Why
> is Rakamisy always presented as an *andevohova* if everyone says
> that the Berosaiña are *andevo*?
>
> (Laughing and lowering his voice) I don't dare talking about
> that! It's very difficult.
>
> I don't understand why Randriatsoa says during his speeches
> that he is an *andevohova*.
>
> Because Rakamisy was close to the *hova* [i.e., the ruler].

Was Rakamisy a slave of the *andevohova*?

No. He was *andevohova* for himself but not for the others.

Why only for himself? I don't understand. And why are people afraid of talking about that?

People do not dare to talk clearly about that since they are afraid that the persons they mention will hear it. Then these persons will go to the State (*fanjaka*) and will accuse people: 'How come we are slaves?'

People know that Rakamisy was a slave even though they say he was an *andevohova*?

Yes. That's why he gave land only to his relatives and not to everybody.

But did Rakamisy also arrive towards 1870 or later?

Later.

After colonisation?

No, before.

Was he a slave before he arrived?

(Laughing) Yes!

Who was he the slave of?

(Laughing) It's difficult [to talk about that]. (Lowering his voice) To the east of Ambalavao, on the road going to Anjoma, that's where the lord (*andriana*) whom he served lived.

How is this place called?

Vinany.

Why did slaves from Vinany come here?

Because even though they lived at the *hova*'s, they could work for themselves and for the *hova*, and make money. And when they managed to get enough money they could buy themselves back. Rakamisy had bought himself during the times of slavery. He was already free before 1896.

Why did he get the power of dividing land here [i.e., the power of an *andevohova*]? Who gave him this power?

Two men were already here [i.e., Rainibao and Raikalatsara]. Then there was an order of the ruler: 'Here is Rakamisy, he will come with you, give him land so that he can give some to his family.'

But how come he was good friends with Rainibao [i.e., one of the four men]?

Oh yes, they were very good friends!

Did they make a blood bond?

No, they didn't. They were friends (*mpinamana*).

But why did the ruler give him power if he was a former slave?

Because he was free since he had bought himself back. He did not count as a slave anymore.

He got very good land ...

Oh yes!

Because he was among the first to arrive in Beparasy?

Yes, after Rainibao and Raikalatsara.

At this moment I thought that I had finally discovered the reason for the Berosaiña's questionable reputation. They had one ancestor who had been a slave in the past and who could not, in spite of having bought his freedom, rid himself of the stigma of slave status. But it remained strange to me, nonetheless, that he had been accepted as an *andevohova* in such circumstances. In fact, the story of the Berosaiña's reputation as slaves was somewhat different:

But then I wonder why people say that the Berosaiña, for example Raboba here (I made a gesture towards the house of our immediate neighbour in Soatanana) but also the other Berosaiña, are slaves ...

Wait! About Raboba ... (Lowering his voice) They were three brothers who arrived in Beparasy, but two of them had not managed to buy themselves back. Only Rakamisy had. And so in his case one should not say this [i.e., that he is slave], one should say commoner (*olompotsy*). But he could not abandon his relatives, and he always did things for them. If someone died he was involved, because it was his family. So people said: 'Ha, he still belongs to them, they are his friends.'

And so his two relatives were freed only at the time of colonisation?

Yes. These are the grandfathers of Raboba and Randrianja Albert [i.e., Rainihosy and Randriatsoakely – see Figure 3.1].

This discussion was one of the tipping points of my fieldwork since it eventually gave me the key to the Berosaiña's ambivalent status in Beparasy. Without contradiction, free descendants viewed them as both slave descendants and descendants of an *andevohova*. Even though Rakamisy had been among the first to arrive in Beparasy at the end of the nineteenth century and had the function of an *andevohova*, he was also a former slave and some of his kinsmen joined him after being freed at the abolition of slavery. Yet nobody had been able – or, rather, willing – to explain this story to me until I heard it from Rakoto Jeannot.

Putting together Ramarcel's, Randriatsoa's and Rakoto Jeannot's versions of the story with other pieces of local history that I gathered elsewhere, a plausible history of the Berosaiña of Beparasy emerged. Rakamisy and his siblings were the slaves of a ruler in Vinany. As explained by Rakoto Jeannot, Rakamisy managed to buy his freedom before the abolition of slavery in 1896. Since he had become a free man again he could take the lead in going to the uncultivated lands of the polity and he was asked by the ruler of the region to administer, as *andevohova*, a part of the ruler's fief which was not yet – or only sparsely – inhabited and cultivated.[9] Later, when all the slaves in Madagascar were freed by the French abolition decree of 1896, Rakamisy's two 'siblings', Rainihosy and Randriatsoakely, joined him in Beparasy.[10]

Rakoto Jeannot's account was illuminating, but there were still gaps and inconsistencies in the story. In particular, the exact nature of the relationship between Rakamisy and Rainibao, the two *andevohova* who shared responsibility for the land and the people to the eastern side of the Vatobe hill, remained unclear to me for quite a long time after I had talked to Rakoto Jeannot. Randriatsoa had told me that Rakamisy and Rainibao had become *mpivakira* (kinsmen through a blood bond) but the elder denied it, saying that they were only *mpinamama* (friends). I was intrigued by this relation and continued to ask questions about it, though without much success until the very end of my fieldwork.

An explanation for the existence of a 'special relation' between Rakamisy and Rainibao

I eventually obtained an answer to this question from a free descendant who is reputed for having a good knowledge of local history and customs. He explained to me that the reason why Rakamisy and Rainibao became very close was that in the 1880s the Merina Queen requested Betsileo soldiers for her military campaigns, and Rainibao was asked to send one of his children. Since Rainibao was unhappy with the idea of sending his only son to war, Rakamisy proposed to replace him. He went on the expedition and came back alive. According to my free descent informant, it was because of this episode that Rakamisy and Rainibao became very close friends, and this explains why Rainibao and Rakamisy shared the administration of the land on the eastern side of Beparasy:

> Is it the reason why they [i.e., the Berosaiña] say they are *andevohova*, because there is something that Rainibao gave them?

Yes, he really gave them part of the power he had because he [Rakamisy] replaced his child [i.e., Rainibao's child].

Is it only on this that Rakamisy helped him [Rainibao], or did he also work for him?

No, it's only that. He replaced his son for the military, for the government (*fanjakana*). He [Rainibao] had only one son. At that moment each one had to give his eldest son for the government.

Was it at the times of the *vazaha*?

Yes, it was during colonisation [he means the period of conflicts with France that led to colonisation, rather than the colonial period itself].

Did everything go well for Rakamisy there?

Yes, he finished his service and he came back. And then Rainibao gave him power.

That's why Rakamisy's brothers came too?

Yes. For example, you come alone here. You settle down. Then your crops and your settling down are going well. Then people hear your story: 'Ha, I got a good land, I'm very well here.' And the others follow.

Where did Rakamisy's brothers come from?

They all came from the north. Rapitsarandro was their mother but she did not have a husband. Thus they did not have a father. And this woman was someone very rich, she had a lot.

Is it because of what Rakamisy received that she was rich or was she rich before?

She was already rich. She had left, things were over, and there was no slavery anymore. But these people are former slaves. That is, there were *dahalo* [cattle rustlers, i.e. here raiders] who attacked, and when they attacked they took the zebus and they also took the people who were not fast enough [to flee]. And the descendants of the people that the raiders took away [i.e., enslaved people], they came back afterwards [i.e., after abolition].

They were rich then?

They were rich because they helped the ruler (*nanakare satry nilampy ny mpanjaka*). They were the slaves of a ruler, and when colonisation [i.e., the colonial conquest] was over the French announced that there were no slaves anymore, and so they left.

This account is interesting for a number of reasons, but especially for what it says about the relative wealth of the Berosaiña before their arrival in Beparasy and the mention of Rakamisy and his siblings' mother. It seems indeed right that the slaves of rulers and nobles could be richer than the *olomposty* who, for the most part, were poor peasants. Slaves could work in addition to the labour they owed to their owners, and accumulate wealth since they were sometimes allowed to keep as much as two thirds of their earnings (Campbell 1998: 268). Moreover, the fact that slaves lived in proximity to the ruling class and revolved around centres of power presumably gave to some of them more opportunities for personal enrichment than *olon-tsotra* (ordinary people) could have.

There are, however, enough discrepancies between Randriatsoa's account and the stories told by free descendants to provoke suspicions about the versions of both sides. My impression is that while free descendants acknowledge the importance of Rakamisy as a founding figure of Beparasy, they tend to downplay it by stressing that he had come after the other *andevohova*, that he was *andevohova* only for his kinsmen (as explained by Rakoto Jeannot above) and that he had obtained his land and power because he had offered Rainibao a kind of sacrifice, which seems to evoke a relationship between a superior and a subordinate or, perhaps more pertinently here, between an elder and a junior. By contrast, during his interview Randriatsoa stressed that Rakamisy had arrived first (simultaneously with Rainibao and Raikalatsara) and had allocated land to many people (not only to his kinsmen), that the four *andevohova* of Beparasy had equal status and that the Berosaiña today have the same status as the descendants of these other founding figures.

The story of the replacement of Rainibao's son by Rakamisy seems consistent with the historical circumstances. The Merina did recruit southern Betsileo soldiers in 1882, 1888 and 1891 as *fanompoana* (corvée labour, royal service). Ralaikoa (1981: 15) gives the following figures: 3,000 soldiers in 1882 (1,000 from Arindrano), 4,081 in 1888 (1,081 from Arindrano) and 600 (162 from Arindrano) in 1891. Some of these soldiers were sent to Merina garrisons in the west and others participated in campaigns launched by the Merina in the south, notably in Toalañaro (Fort Dauphin) and Toliara. The royal instructions specified that Betsileo 'princes and chiefs' should show an example and send one of their sons (Raveloson 1956: 108). Thus it is plausible that Rainibao was required, as one of the *andevohova* of the polity of Ambatofotsy, to send his unique son and that Rakamisy proposed to replace him. If true, this would have meant disobeying Merina orders and could explain a 'special relation' of complicity between Rainibao and Rakamisy because, according to Raveloson (ibid.), the royal instructions made clear that the free Betsileo affected by the *fanompoana* could not be replaced by someone else.

Conclusion: are the Berosaiña slave descendants?

The picture that has emerged suggests a highly ambivalent local status for the Berosaiña. On the one hand, their ancestral figure, Rakamisy, was one of the four first settlers and an *andevohova* for the region, and therefore the Berosaiña group still enjoys some wealth, prestige and respect from that history. On the other hand, the Berosaiña are considered as people with slave ancestry, and for this reason Beparasy villagers do not want to marry them, as shown by the case of Redison's mother Ramarcelline and Rasamuel. Randriatsoa, the official public voice of the Berosaiña, denied, however, that they were slave descendants. He attributed the insults against them and the ban on marrying them to disputes between former soldiers who fought in the French army during World War I. Ramarcel, on his side, suggested that the jealousy of other families started because their grandfather, Rakamisy, was the first to arrive in Beparasy and was able to secure lands that are among the nicest and largest in the region.

It was not easy to find out whether the Berosaiña were really people with a history of slavery, but these conversations and the piecemeal information I gathered throughout fieldwork led me to think that they were. Their origin in Vinany before their move to Beparasy, evoked by Rakoto Jeannot, was confirmed to me by Randriatsoa and Ramarcel themselves. Vinany, also called Vinanimalaza, was not just any other village in the southern Betsileo region: it was the 'capital', founded by the Betsileo ruler Rarivoarindrano when Radama I tried to unify the Arindrano after his conquests (Raherisoanjato 1984a). Being such a centre of power in the early nineteenth century, it is certain that a large number of slaves lived there. I learned from other sources in Ambalavao that the descendants of these slaves inhabit villages around the former capital. One of them is precisely Mahasoabe, the village mentioned by the Berosaiña as their place of origin.[11]

Notes

1   *Ranomaso* are gifts in cloth, mats or money that attendees bring to the family organising the funeral and to its head, the *tompompaty*. The most valued gifts at funerals are gifts of zebu, which are called *lofo*. The reason why families write down the gifts they receive is that they have to reciprocate them as soon as they have the opportunity. The sharing of *hena ratsy* is of paramount importance to southern Betsileo funerals. About half of the meat of slaughtered cattle is used to feed the guests during their stay in the village, as it is customary to have one or several meals of rice and boiled meat, and the other half is cut into small pieces that are distributed to the guests before they leave.

2 Killing one zebu is the minimum for a funeral in the southern Betsileo highlands. If for some reason a family has no cattle to kill or cannot easily get one from relatives or friends (that they reimburse later), the deceased is buried very quickly and without ceremony. When the family has saved enough money, a kind of delayed funeral called *vokapaty* is organised (Regnier 2012: 215; see also Parker Pearson and Regnier 2018).

3 By 'the duties' done by Ramarcelline 'on the side of her husband', Ramarcel meant that Ramarcelline was more often seen at the ceremonies and gatherings of the Berosaiña, or on the maternal side of her husband, than among her kinsmen in Beparasy.

4 *Lamba arindrano* are coloured pieces of cloth made of raw silk for which the region of Arindrano was famous in the past. Important people wore them on their shoulders at important occasions and they made precious burial shrouds (see an example in Mack 1986: 73).

5 These words had a strong resonance since we had built the house we were in on the land that belonged to one branch of the Berosaiña before Redison bought it off Raboba. During the interview, Randriatsoa kept talking about it as the Berosaiña's land. As I explained in the previous chapter, the Berosaiña thought that Raboba should never have sold this land, although the fact that he sold it to Redison and that Redison was a relative made Raboba's mistake less difficult to accept.

6 The degree in question was, of course, my PhD. I am pleased to report here that Randriatsoa's ancestors managed to make this happen.

7 Redison later confirmed to me that his maternal grandfather, Ramarcelline's father, had also fought with the French in World War I.

8 *Hovavao* is another term used to refer to slave descendants in Madagascar. It refers to the fact that the freed slaves became new (*vao*) commoners (*hova* in the Merina sense). Given the different meaning of *hova* for the Betsileo, the use of the term *hovavao* could be somewhat confusing in the southern Betsileo region. Some of my informants, for example, explained that former slaves were called this because they became rapidly wealthy and behaved as if they were 'new nobles' (*hova vao*).

9 Writing about the Merina kingdom, Graeber (Graeber and Sahlins 2017: 277) states that 'royal service was considered the primary mark of free status within the kingdom: legally, if a slave could demonstrate that he or she had been part of a royal work crew, especially if it was engaged in something intimate like clearing ground for a royal palace, then that was considered grounds for manumission in itself.' One can imagine that Randriatsoa was freed by the southern Betsileo ruler, and then offered a high-status function, for such a reason.

10 A free descendant told me that Rainihosy and Randriatsoakely were actually not Rakamisy's 'true' siblings but more remote kinsmen, perhaps cousins (i.e., siblings in the classificatory sense). My informant did not raise doubts, however, on the fact that Rakamisy's mother (named Rapitsarandro) was his 'true' mother.

11 The following chapters will show that Beparasy villagers have further reasons for ascribing slave status to the Berosaiña.

5   Marriage in Beparasy

Recall that at the beginning of the preceding chapter I put questions to Redison about his mother's marriage with a Berosaiña, most notably: Why was it not possible for Ramarcelline to marry Rasamuel? In this chapter I start answering this question by exploring the issue of marriage. Whereas for the previous chapter I mostly used a wide-angle lens, seeking to reconstruct the local history of the Berosaiña group over more than a century, I now revert to what I have called my 'normal' lens, the ethnographic lens, and provide a descriptive–interpretative account of marriage practices in Beparasy.

An impossible marriage: Andry and his 'slave' girlfriend

In August 2009 I went to a village located outside Beparasy to attend a *vadipaisa*. I had walked westwards for a day through the mountains with a small group of teenagers and with my neighbour, Naina, who had to go to the *vadipaisa* because he had been asked to be the evening DJ for the three-day event. Andry, the boy fostered by Redison in Soatanana, and three Berosaiña young men carried the Catholic community's audio material on their shoulders, as well as Redison's generator. Redison sent Naina because Vohangy had invited him and all the inhabitants of Soatanana to the ceremony. Redison himself could not go since he was busy in Ambalavao, but it was important that representatives of his family attend the event in his name. Naina, Andry and I, as well as Redison's eldest son, were representing his household.

Vohangy, Redison's stepsister, had invited him because her mother, Rasamuel's previous wife, was from this village and had been buried in one of the two family tombs which were going to be opened in order to transfer corpses into the newly built tomb. Even though Vohangy had contributed to the construction of the new tomb, it turned out that her mother's bones could not be moved. The construction of the new tomb had been decided after a bitter dispute within the local descent group, meaning that not everyone wanted their dead to be transported. Such was the opinion of the relatives of the dead who were lying in the same bed as Vohangy's mother; since her remains could not be separated from those of the others, her transfer was deemed impossible.

The building of the new tomb had been decided by Vohangy's cousin, the eldest son of the richest member of the local family. His father had acquired his wealth as a cattle trader at the zebu market of Ambalavao, and at the time of his death he reportedly owned more than 100 zebus. His son paid for the largest part of the expenses involved in the construction of the tomb and the organisation of the *vadipaisa*. Five head of his cattle were slaughtered for the occasion and he also completely refurbished the paternal house, placing new mats in each room and painting the pillars, walls and balconies with bright colours.

The *vadipaisa* was a large gathering of several hundred people that lasted for three days. Upon arrival, guests coming from remote places were allocated to the houses in the village where they would sleep and take their meals. In addition, a large *trano maintso* ('green house', i.e. a temporary shelter made of freshly cut wood with green leaves and sisal) had been built where meals were served to the local guests, who would not spend the night in the village. Because of my special status, we were hosted in a room on the ground floor of the organiser's nicely decorated and centrally located house.

My young companion Andry, the teenager fostered by Redison, and his Berosaiña friends spent most of their time at the *vadipaisa* in search of a girlfriend. Large gatherings of this kind provide opportunities for youth to find an occasional sexual partner who might, someday, if the relation is maintained, become a spouse. After much effort and a few unsuccessful attempts, all the boys had found girls willing to have relationships with them in exchange for a small sum of money.[1] Andry's find was a girl who was from the village where the *vadipaisa* was taking place. As I observed this affair taking off I noted to myself that the relationship between Andry and the girl was very unlikely to lead to marriage. This was because all people living in the village were the descendants of one couple of ancestors who were known in the area as *andevo*. It was therefore a village inhabited by slave descendants only (with the possible exception of some spouses, in cases of mixed marriage), and thus both Vohangy's mother and Andry's girlfriend were of slave descent. Even if Andry and the girl wanted to pursue their relationship, Andry's free descent relatives in Beparasy would never accept his marriage with her.

Customary marriage in Beparasy

To understand the options open to free descent parents who wish to prevent a mixed marriage for their children, it is necessary to have a good idea of what a customary marriage consists of.

The first steps of a customary marriage can start as soon as teenagers become sexually active.[2] Young men and women in Beparasy enjoy relative sexual freedom. When girls reach puberty their parents offer them the option of moving to a separate room in the house, where they will be able to host their *sipa* (boyfriends) for the night. The room is usually not large and often there is no furniture other than mats laid on the ground, but in some families there might be one or two small beds consisting of raphia mattresses placed on wood sticks or roughly assembled planks. The room can be shared by other sexually active female relatives (often sisters) but it is forbidden for male relatives, even for the girls' young brothers, to sleep there. In the most common type of house in Beparasy, which has four rooms (two on the ground floor and two on the first floor), the girls' room is always located on the ground floor, whereas the first floor is occupied by the parents.

The location of the girls' room on the ground floor makes it easily accessible to their lovers, who must come after dusk and leave before dawn so they are not seen by the girls' father, brothers or other male relatives. The furtive nature of these nocturnal visits does not mean parents are unaware that their daughters see lovers at night. On the contrary, the girls are given the option of a separate room precisely to allow them to see their lovers without having to leave the house at night, which is considered a dangerous thing to do. It also prevents the boys from being forced to engage in more formal relationships, which would be the case if the girls had to introduce their lovers to their parents. For these affairs it is always the boy who comes to the girl's place, and never the reverse. Yet sexual encounters are not limited to nocturnal visits or the confined space of the girls' rooms. They also happen during the day, often in the late afternoon, on a discreet river bank or in some nearby undergrowth. Market days offer particularly good opportunities to meet up with lovers, as do all sorts of large gatherings or ceremonies, including funerals.

If a boy is accidentally seen by a male relative of the girl, or if he wants to be able to come to see his girlfriend without hiding himself, he has to give the *tapi-maso* ('closing of the eyes'), which is the first formal relationship of exchange between a potential husband and his potential in-laws. The boy pays a small sum of money, which will be divided between the males of the girl's family, including her brothers. The boy, however, does not give the money directly to the father – this is *fady* (taboo) – but to the girl, who will then pass it on to her mother, who in turn will talk to the father and give him the money. The father will then explain to the male family members who reside locally that the girl is officially 'seeing' someone, and he will give each of them a share of the money. When they receive the *tapi-maso*, if they do not know the boy, parents will ask the girl about his identity, questioning her about his village and his family. At this stage, however, there is no formal relationship between the two families and parents rarely take such unions too seriously, since they are very unstable and frequently break up.

Parents in Beparasy seemed very pragmatic on such matters. For example, I observed unmarried girls having affairs with itinerant workers. Provided they paid the *tapi-maso*, the men were accepted as the girl's *sipa* (boyfriend) in the family, where they lived for a while before moving on to another village. It did not seem to matter much that the men were already married elsewhere, that it was obvious they were not seriously interested in marrying the girls or that they would soon leave the village for *karama* (wage labour) in other places. During their stay, which often lasted for months, they brought resources into the family, most notably money, food, labour force and specialised skills such as carpentry or masonry. Apart from these benefits for the family, a possible explanation for this general tolerance is that it is relatively difficult for girls to get married in Beparasy. Parents therefore seek to maximise the girls' chances to meet potential marriage partners. There is a trade-off, however: many girls get pregnant before being married, making the prospect of finding a spouse even more difficult. This is because these girls' children, despite the fact that they demonstrate their fertility, are often perceived as a burden by junior men looking for a wife.

Once the *tapi-maso* money has been given, the boy can come at any time of the day to see his girlfriend in her village, since they are accepted as a couple by the girl's family. Half-jokingly, people already start using the term *vady* (spouse) alongside *sipa* (boy- or girlfriend). The boy may further show respect to his girlfriend's parents in various ways; for example, by bringing small gifts and taking part in the household's activities, especially in agricultural work. He does not reside permanently in his girlfriend's village, however, because he has to fulfil various duties in his own village. The young couple enjoys a relationship which is already marriage-like, and indeed people refer to the situation of a young girl living by herself and having a lover in her parents' house by saying that the girl *manao kitokantrano*, an expression that comes from *mitokantrano* ('having one's hearth') and can be translated as 'she pretends to have a hearth'.

The next step takes place when the boy informs his girlfriend's parents that members of his family will come to do the *ala-fady* (removal of the taboo). On a previously agreed date, a small party – called the *mpangala-vady* (literally, 'spouse thieves') and consisting of a few men from the boy's local descent group, sometimes accompanied by women – arrives at the girl's parents' house. Sending male representatives is seen as a sign of respect for the other family; women can accompany but are not supposed to intervene in the formal discussions. The party explains to the head of the family that the boy and the girl like each other, and that they would like the girl to come to live with the boy in their village. They then offer a sum of money to the girl's father, who accepts it and gives his blessing. As with the *tapi-maso*, the *ala-fady* money will have to be divided and distributed among the girl's male relatives living locally. In 2008–2010, a gift of 10,000 ariary was considered enough for the *ala-fady*, a sum roughly equivalent to the local value of two or three chickens.

Toaka (local rum) is offered to the guests and a meal is served, usually chicken and rice.[3] If night is about to fall or the journey back takes a long time, the guests are invited to stay for the night. When they return to the boy's village they take the girl with them. She brings only a small amount of luggage: people in her village and family say, euphemistically, that she has gone 'for a walk' (*mitsangatsangana*). At the boy's village, if possible, the young couple will occupy a room in the parents' house, usually a room on the ground floor. If there is no room available at the parents', the couple will temporarily dwell in a relative's house. The girl lives with her partner's patrilineal kin and works with the women for a period that can range from a few weeks to several months. This time is clearly thought of by everyone as being a kind of probation, to see whether she can get along well and work with people. The girl who is in this situation is called *fairindahy*.

After some time the boy's father calls his son and tells him that the girl has been among them for long enough. If there have been serious issues during her stay and the parents are concerned that the girl will not make a good wife, they may tell him that she should be taken back to her village. If, on the contrary, the parents and the family members in the village are satisfied with the girl, the father says that the *tandra vady* ('spouse's gift', often simply called *tandra*) should now be given to her family.[4] Father and son discuss the possibility of paying for the *tandra*. Ideally, it should be the father who offers it, but in poor families it is common for the son to work and save enough to pay for it, although it will always be presented as coming from the father.

The girl is then sent off to her family to announce that the boy's parents will come to do the *fehim-poñena* ('tying of kinship').[5] They choose the date with the help of a *mpanandro* (traditional astrologer) so that it brings good luck to the couple. The *fehim-poñena* is a meeting at the girl's parents' house where the value of the *tandra* will be discussed and part of it will be given, and where the union of the girl with the boy will be blessed by her family. The girl's relatives prepare for the event. Parents buy chickens and rum. Women start weaving mats and collecting items for the girl's trousseau. Male heads of the local descent group's families are invited to attend the meeting. They will bring a *tsiodrano* (blessing) for the boy's parents consisting of *fotsim-bary* (white rice, i.e. hulled rice) and money.

The representatives of the boy's family who attend the *fehim-poñena* meeting consist once again of a few men, sometimes accompanied by women. This time the party is called the *mpanandra-vady* ('spouse givers'). The boy's parents are usually not among the *mpanandra-vady*, and neither is the boy. The boy will wait for his wife in his village. He prepares the room where they will live and is expected to cook something to welcome his wife. When the *mpanandra-vady* arrive at the girl's village they do not enter the house straight away, but instead stay on the threshold. The girl's relatives insist that they should go further into the house to find a better place, but they refuse. One of the male *mpanandra-vady* gives a speech explaining that they come in the name of the *raiamandreny* of the boy's local descent group and that they are there to ask permission for the girl to become the boy's wife.

The eldest of the *mpanandra-vady* puts a small amount of money (usually 100 or 200 ariary) into his hat and places it on the floor, asking for permission to open the door and enter the house, which is a metaphorical way of asking for the opening of the discussion on the value of the *tandra vady*. The money given in the hat is called *vohavaravara* ('the opening of the door'). The girl's relatives respond: 'But you already entered. Please come in, sit in the room.' The *mpanandra-vady* come in a bit further but still stay close to the door, as if they were ready to leave. They then explain that the boy and the girl would like to live together, and the girl's family replies to explain how they value their daughter. The discussion on the value of the *tandra* starts. At this point, I was told, there are two different proceedings, depending on whether the *tandra* is given in cattle or cash. Traditionally the *tandra* should be given in cattle, but nowadays it has become more common for people to only bring money.[6]

If the *mpanandra-vady* have come with a zebu, people go out of the house to examine the animal and to judge whether it is of good value. The benchmark for the discussion of the *tandra* is the value of a *saka-n'aombe* (also called *sakan-dahiny*), i.e. an ox. When I was in Beparasy the price for such an ox at the zebu market of Ambalavao ranged between 400,000 and 500,000 ariary. In most cases the zebu that is brought is deemed enough, but sometimes the girl's relatives will ask for a more valuable or additional zebu. Wealthy families tend to ask for a *tandra* higher than average for their daughters. Some families may also ask for a higher *tandra* because the girl is young, strong and particularly good-looking. The distance between the villages of the boy and the girl can also be used as an argument. The longer the distance, people say, the higher the *tandra*, since the girl will see her family less often. If the ox offered by the *mpanandra-vady* is deemed enough, men will then discuss the value of the *rambon'aombe* ('tail of the ox'), which is a supplementary sum to be given in cash, typically 20,000–60,000 ariary. The amount of *rambon'aombe* is bargained over and, like the *tapi-maso* and the *ala-fady*, it is money that will be divided among the male relatives of the girl. The zebu of the *tandra* itself is usually for the parents, but sometimes it is passed on by the parents to the head of the local descent group as a sign of respect.

If the *tandra* consists of money, the *mpanandra-vady* first propose a low price. The other party responds by detailing the qualities of the girl and asks for a higher price. The bargaining lasts for a while and the discussion progressively arrives at a price that both parties find acceptable, usually close to the market value of a *sakan'aombe*.[7] The final price often has a few 'sixes' in it (for example, 466,000 ariary) as this number is believed to bring good luck. I was told that the reason the *mpanandra-vady* stay close to the door and refuse to enter the room is that they want to show their readiness to step out and leave, either if the *tandra* asked for by the girl's family remains too high or if the family is not ready to let the girl go. This rarely happens nowadays but was apparently more frequent in the past. It is presumably why the boy's parents are not present during the discussions. Were they to be part of the *mpanandra-vady* it would be more difficult to step out and leave without being rude and losing face. This is easier to do if the *mpanandra-vady* party has only limited autonomy in deciding the amount of money that can be paid, the limits being set by the absent father of the boy.

If the *tandra* is in cash it is now common to give it in instalments. This usually means the families agree that the *tandra* will be given 'when possible' but that a substantial part (for example, a quarter) is given immediately. After an agreement on the *tandra* is reached, the *mpanandra-vady* are again invited to enter the room to sit in a better place. This time they accept and sit on a chair or mat on the eastern side of the house – up to this point they have remained on the western side, where the door is located in all southern Betsileo houses. Rum is then passed around. The women of the girl's family, who were busy cooking the meal, are now told to prepare the girl because she will leave the house. During the talks the girl waits in another room of the house, getting dressed and doing her hair with the help of other women. A meal of chicken and rice is served to the guests and the men of the family, while the women and the girl eat with the children in the kitchen. The *vodi-akoho* (chicken's rump), which is normally given to the eldest male present, is given instead to the man who talked in the name of the *mpanandra-vady*, even if he is much younger than the men of the girl's family who are in the room. This is a sign of respect towards the *raiamandreny* (i.e., here all the 'fathers and mothers' in the classificatory sense) of the boy, who have now to be honoured as *havana* (kinsmen).

When the meal is over, the head of the family calls the girl. She appears in her nicest clothes with her hair newly plaited. People bring her luggage, which consists of her personal belongings but also of various household items bought for the occasion or given by relatives: suitcases, mats, baskets, clothes, cooking pots, buckets, spoons, a mattress, a bed and so on. The girl's family makes the inventory, calling out each item and writing down a list on a small notebook or a sheet of paper. This list is for the boy and is given to his representatives. The couple must keep it, because these items belong to the girl and if the two separate she will come back to her village and take these items with her.

The head of the girl's family proceeds to the *tsiodrano* (blessing). Everyone stands up and turns to face the eastern wall of the room, which is the house's side associated with the ancestors. The girl stands between the wall and the group of people. The head of the family, holding a *zinga* (large cup) with water, asks for god's and the ancestors' blessings, and then blesses the girl. He sprinkles her and the audience six times with water from the cup. Everyone congratulates the girl, and her relatives give a small *tsiodrano* (blessing, i.e. here a gift of rice and money) for the boy's parents as well as some money (5,000–6,000 ariary), called *angady* (spade), for the boy so that he can buy a new spade to work efficiently for the new household – in the past a new spade was given in kind. After the *tsiodrano*, the two parties talk about the ancestral *fady* (taboos) on each side and stress that they will have to be respected in the new hearth, especially those that concern food. The *fady* of the girl's family are also written down on the notebook or the paper used for the inventory to be given to the boy.

The *mpanandra-vady* can now set off with the girl and her luggage. When walking in the southern Betsileo countryside, one sometimes meets such a group of people transporting personal items with a girl nicely dressed among them. This is referred to as *mampody vady vao* ('bringing a new spouse home'). In his dictionary, Richardson (1885) translates the expression *mampody vady vao* as 'to marry a wife, but not to make it a time of feasting or rejoicing; to bring home again, or to try to do so, a wife who has been separated from her husband'. Three expressions – *tandra vady*, *fehim-poñena* and *mampody vady vao* – were used almost interchangeably by my informants to refer to the last stages in the process of a customary marriage. These expressions actually stress different aspects: *tandra vady* refers to the negotiation and the offering of the gift; *fehim-poñena* refers to the 'tying together' of the two families; and *mampody vady vao* refers to the 'definitive' return of the girl in the boy's village.

In the past it was customary for a young female relative to accompany the girl; she would live for a while with the couple to help them with the running of their household. This is less common today. On her way to her new village, the girl is not allowed to greet people. When they arrive at the village, the *mpanandra-vady* are welcomed and the new couple is congratulated. A communal meal is organised for relatives and friends, again with chicken and rice. The leader of the party reports the outcome of the meeting to the boy's parents and to the head of the family. The girl presents her parents-in-law with a particular kind of basket with a lid and two plates in it, which is called *vahin-dovia* ('guest's plate') and was traditionally used by the head of family, as well as two *fitoeram-bositra* (small woven poufs on which important guests are often invited to sit when they enter a house). The girl's relatives' *tsiodrano* (the blessings, which consist here of gifts of rice and money) are also passed to the boy's parents, who thank the girl. The head of the family asks *zanahary* (god) and the ancestors to bless the new couple; he then gives his own blessing and the blessings from the rest of the family follow.

After all this has been done, the couple should customarily live for some time in the boy's parents' house, even if a separate house has already been built – ideally, the boy should build the new house in the period between the *ala-fady* and the *fehim-poñena*. After a month or two the couple asks permission of the boy's father to set up their own *tokantrano* (hearth). If the father agrees, this is announced to the boy's whole family, whose members are invited to eat the *sakafo maraina* (morning meal) the day after the couple has moved to their house or to a separate room where they will have their own hearth. This morning meal must be very simple and it usually consists of *vary sosoa* (rice broth), or *kaza* (cassava), or *bageda* (sweet potato), sometimes with *tantely* (honey). All members of the local descent group as well as friends and neighbours are invited to eat a small portion of the meal, after which they congratulate the couple by saying: 'Let your house be hot!' (*'Mafanà trano!'*) – a wish for the stability of the couple (Michel-Andrianarahinjaka 1986: 979). They then depart to leave room for other visitors. With the *sakafo maraina* completed, it becomes clear to people that a new hearth now exists in the village.

Divorce

In spite of the wishes for the couple's stability, customary marriages in Beparasy are unstable and separations happen frequently.[8] A woman will leave the village of her husband's family either because her husband repudiates her or because, for various reasons, she wants to go back to her village. Although I witnessed several cases of separation in Beparasy, I never observed a single case of a woman leaving her husband's village to go to live with another man without first going back to her own village. Both men and women have extramarital affairs, but if a woman wants to abandon her husband and live with another man she should first go back to her village and the new man should ask for her in the customary way.

When a separation is about to happen, or has already happened, husband and wife should talk separately to the man's parents, who will then attempt to find a route to reconciliation. If their son offended his spouse, they will go to see the woman's parents to ask them and their daughter for forgiveness. Conversely, if a fault is on the woman's side her parents will go to see the husband's parents and ask them and their son to accept her back. If the attempt at reconciliation is unsuccessful, the *tandra* is usually not given back if the girl has given birth to at least one child; even so, the girl has the right to take back the items she brought into the household. I was told that when the union has lasted only a very short time after the *fehim-poñena* and no child has been born, the girl's family feels ashamed and, out of fear of being accused of dishonesty, sends representatives to the boy's village to return the zebu or the money received as *tandra*. In such instances it is also possible that the boy's family will not take the *tandra* back, out of honour and pride. In any case, it is considered very shameful if the boy's relatives go to the girl's village to reclaim the *tandra* after a separation, even if the couple has remained childless.

Separations also occur when women go back to their parental village to give birth and to spend their *mifana*, the postpartum period that normally lasts a few months. I was told that traditionally it is not considered an offence for a man to sleep with another woman while his wife is away for the postpartum period. But when the *mifana* is over, a man should go to his wife's village to take her back with the newly born child. Yet it is not uncommon for the husband to fail to return, either because he has found another partner in the meantime or for a range of other reasons. The woman has therefore no other option than to stay in her village with her kinsmen, since it is clear to everyone that her husband does not want her anymore. Such a sad story happened twice to Redison's cousin from his maternal village. Each time she had been married according to the *fomba* (customs) and had lived in her husband's village until she fell pregnant. She then went back to her village to give birth and to spend the *mifana*. Time went by but neither husband ever came to take her and the baby back. The girl's parents were poor and thus they accepted a very low *tandra* in both cases, which arguably made it easier for the men to decide to abandon her. During our stay in Beparasy, the girl and her parents were struggling to raise the two small children, receiving no support from the children's fathers, and the girl was worried that the fathers would claim the children when they were older. We heard that she had had various affairs with married men, but was never asked to marry again during our stay.

If a separating couple has children and the *tandra* has been given, the man's family can keep them. Very young children go back with their mother to her village, but when they are older the father can take them back to his village. If the *tandra* had been agreed upon but only the first instalment paid, the father will keep rights over the child providing he gives the remainder of the *tandra*. The rights over children here mean essentially the right to keep them in the local descent's group village, where they will contribute to economic activities from an early age (herding cattle, fetching water or firewood, pounding rice, etc.). The rights that are acquired after the payment of the *tandra* also involve the right, for the father's group, to bury the children in their ancestral tomb, although it does not have to be so because, as we shall see in a subsequent chapter, the burial place is always negotiated by families. However, the delayed payment of the *tandra* precludes the negotiation since, in such cases, the father's group is not in a good position to claim the corpse of a dead child.

The process of marriage

As my description makes clear, marriage in Beparasy is highly processual, a characteristic already noted by Kottak (1980: 200–210). The
marriage process is punctuated by events and exchanges where local
descent groups progressively strengthen their relationships as *havana*
(kinsmen) and where a couple receives blessings from elders of both
sides. Bloch analysed this kind of marriage as a 'double filiation' and
stressed that it is not a transfer of a woman towards the man's descent
group (Bloch 1971: 194; Bloch 1978; see also Dubois 1938: 897). For
this reason, following Bloch, I avoid the terms 'bridewealth' or 'bride
price' to translate *tandra vady* because, even though it is sometimes
presented as such, the *tandra* does not represent a compensation for
the loss of a woman, since married women retain all their rights and
affiliations with the groups of their parents, and if married locally they
continue to work for their family by participating in labour-demanding
activities such as weeding, planting and harvesting. If anything, the
tandra represents a compensation for the loss of the couple's descendants, since, as I have just explained, in cases of divorce the father's
family has the right to claim the couple's children if they have paid the
tandra in full.

It is remarkable that during the marriage process the parents of the
couple are not expected to meet each other. Indeed, marriage can take
place without the parents knowing each other, until they meet at a
particular occasion; for example, when the girl's parents pay a visit to
their daughter, or when the girl's or the boy's parents are invited to a
ceremony in their counterparts' village. In the past, such a situation
was not uncommon but probably rare in Beparasy, because many
marriages were initiated and partly arranged by parents, who in consequence knew personally the family of the potential candidates they
selected for their children.

Because of the processual nature of southern Betsileo marriage, it is
not easy to say whether a couple is married or not. The word *manambady*, usually translated as 'to marry', is a verb that literally means
'to have a spouse'. In practice it is used in Beparasy to distinguish
between people who share a household with a partner and those who
do not. Accordingly, Raboba and Ravao, for example, are said to be
vady (spouses) because they live together, even though, as we shall see
in the next chapter, they have not been through the formal exchanges
of customary marriage.

To enquire whether a couple has been through this process, one
would have to ask: '*Efa nanao ny fomba nareo?*' ('Have you already

performed the customs?') or '*Efa vita ny fomba?*' ('Are the customs over?'), or something along these lines. But, depending on the context, it might be a rude questions to ask. The absence of a clear linguistic distinction between people living together and people who have been through the customs must be understood as a consequence of the gradual process of traditional marriage. There is no sudden, clear-cut change of status after any one particular stage, and none of the meetings where the *tandra* is discussed or given should be seen as a discrete wedding ceremony. There is no speech act of the kind 'you are now husband and wife'.[9] For the southern Betsileo, one is said to 'have a spouse' (*manambady*) as soon as one lives permanently with a partner and has a *tokantrano* (hearth in a house). But to establish an alliance between families (in the sense of the *fehim-poñena*), with all its implications in terms of rights and duties, one has to go through the *fombandrazana* (ancestral customs).

Another point to note is that customary marriage procedures in Beparasy have undergone significant changes over the last decades. One of the most important of these changes concerns the choice of the spouse. I was told that before the 1960s or 1970s most marriage discussions were initiated and arranged by parents, who selected potential partners for their children, even though the youngsters also had their say in the final choice. Nowadays, although there remain cases where parents play a major role in selecting their children's partners, the marriage process is most often initiated by the children themselves, who express their wish to their parents. In the above account I described what my informants referred to as traditional practices, although in various ways these 'ancestral customs' might now differ significantly from what they were only a few decades ago. My account also slightly differs from those of Dubois and Rainihifina (Dubois 1938: 395–410; Rainihifina 1975: 28–38). This is not too surprising, since Dubois' and Rainihifina's inquiries were conducted more than half a century ago. Moreover, their work attempted to describe in a unified way the customs of different places in the Betsileo region. Even if they are not very different, these customs in my experience show significant local variation (as explained in Chapter 1), so speaking of 'Betsileo marriage' in general can be somewhat misleading.

The entire process of customary marriage among the southern Betsileo can be viewed as a gradual process by which the information that one has found a partner to live with is diffused among one's network of kin; the relationship between local descent groups is built up through the exchange of gifts; and the couple receives the blessing of the senior members of their respective local descent groups. It is thus necessary to analyse southern Betsileo traditional marriage as an alliance between descent groups rather than as an agreement between two individuals, two sets of parents or two extended families. The parents' authority in the process is always subordinated to that of the senior relatives of their local descent groups who, although not normally involved in directly choosing the spouse or in deciding the amount of the *tandra* that should be offered or accepted, will nonetheless have their say if they disapprove of the marriage. Their say is, of course, backed up by the fact that they can refuse to bless the couple.

Civil and Christian marriages

Against the background of traditional marriage, the respective places of civil and Christian unions in Beparasy can be seen as further steps in the overall process of marriage, even if they are much less important and even unnecessary steps in local society. Many people did not seem interested in them and married according to custom only. They viewed civil marriage in particular as something superfluous, partly because traditional marriages are recognised by the Malagasy state, which calls them since the French colonial era *mariages coutumiers* (customary marriages). Members of the various religious communities of Beparasy were encouraged to marry in church, but often this occurred fairly late in life and long after a spouse had been taken according to the customs. In any case, before being allowed to marry in church, by law they needed to marry at the *mairie* (i.e., to contract a civil marriage). In Beparasy I sometimes met old couples who had married in church only

Figure 5.1 An elderly couple from Beparasy

very recently, even though they had been married according to custom in their twenties and had been Christians for most of their adult lives.

It seems that religious marriages in Beparasy are often carried out in order to gain prestige. Local big men told me how many zebus they had given for their wives, adding proudly that they also married at the *mairie* and in church, as if these two steps added further value to their marriages because they had meant more expenses. People refer to both kinds of wedding ceremony with the word *mariazy* (from the French *mariage*), a word that they do not use for traditional marriage. Since these two ceremonies usually involve a feast with relatives, most people cannot afford a *mariazy* without making substantial savings. The Catholic father in charge of the area of Beparasy was very active in promoting church marriages, and when I visited him he boasted that since his arrival in Beparasy the region had reached one of the highest rates of marriage in all of the Catholic districts around Ambalavo. However important these religious marriages may be for Christians, even for them the primacy of traditional marriage cannot be underestimated. In Beparasy I did not hear of cases where people married at the *mairie* and in church without having first married traditionally.

The only exception I knew of was the marriage between Ramarcelline and Rasamuel, which I will discuss in the next chapter. They were married at the *mairie* and the church, but never went through the customs because of the refusal of Ramarcelline's kinsmen. The difference between these forms of marriage and a customary marriage is clear: two individuals can contract a civil and a religious marriage without needing the blessing of their parents or of the senior members of their descent group. This is not possible in the case of a customary marriage, because, as I have explained, it is above all an alliance between local descent groups. It is the parents and the group's senior members who decide whether or not they will give their blessing to a couple and, by doing so, engage in kinship relations with the other group.

Blood bond as wedding

Although free descendants in Beparasy avoided marriages with the Berosaiña, they could nonetheless make kinship links with them through the *vakirà* (blood bond) ritual. People explicitly compared this ritual to civil or religious weddings, stressing the sort of reciprocal vows of fidelity that are uttered by the two spouses in these circumstances. By contrast, such formal vows or promises are absent from the process of customary marriage. A free descent woman explained to me the kind of relationship that is engendered by the *vakirà* and its

importance in making durable relations with the Berosaiña. This discussion followed a conversation with her father, where they had both
told us it was 'really forbidden' (*tena tsa azo atao mihitsy*) for free
descendants to marry slave descendants (here called *hovavao*):

> But is it possible to do a *vakirà* with the *hovavao*?
>
> Yes, it's really possible. It's that way that we can have *relations*
> [she used the French word] with them. We can receive them.
>
> Then they are like family?
>
> Yes, they are. Ha! This thing is really a strong link, for example
> one does not lose sight of each other. 'Doing' *vakirà* is like 'doing'
> a wedding (*ohatrany manao mariazy ny manao vakirà*).
>
> What has to be done to do a *vakirà*?
>
> If, for example, *maman'i Camille* and I we want to become
> *mpivakira* we go to the *kaky* (old man, i.e. here a healer/diviner)
> and we have really the blood 'broken' (*vaky*), we really throw with
> a razor blade here [she indicates a place on her upper chest] and
> we let the blood flow. Then we add ginger to it and you eat my
> blood and I eat your blood. After that we talk about the things we
> must do and those we cannot do, then we agree like in a wedding
> (*mariazy*): for better or for worse, whatever happens. Then you
> cannot get rid of it. 'Doing' a *vakirà* is really like 'doing' a
> wedding.

A close friend of Redison and Raely, and like them an active member
of the Catholic community, the woman also referred to the practice of
doing a *vakirà* on the Bible (in church) if one does not want to do the
'more serious' traditional custom. Although this is an option in
Beparasy, at least for Catholics, I was told that most *vakirà* are still
contracted in the traditional manner, by drinking each other's blood.

To understand the situation of the Berosaiña within the community
of Beparasy it is very important to take into account the role of the
vakirà ritual, used as it is by people of free descent to make alliances
with slave descendants, despite the avoidance of customary marriages.
As the free descent woman stressed, in the absence of possibilities of
marriage with the Berosaiña it is essentially through *vakirà* that free
descendants can have very strong kinship relations with them. Indeed,
many free descent people had *vakirà* with the Berosaiña, and so did
their forebears in previous generations. Randriatsoa, for example, had
a *vakirà* with five free descendants of Beparasy. When I interviewed
him, I asked questions about his *vakirà* and he explained that these
relations were even more important than 'true' family relations. There

is little doubt that *vakirà* relations greatly facilitated the integration of the Berosaiña into the community of Beparasy even though, as we shall see in the next chapter, these relations were also proposed to the Berosaiña with ulterior motives.

Notes

1 It seems to be customary among the southern Betsileo that during funerary events women ask for a gift of money when they have affairs with men. In a more ordinary context they also expect gifts from their lovers but it does not have to be money and the gifts often consist of food, clothing and so on. This practice must be understood in the light of the marriage process, which as we shall see involves various forms of exchange between different stakeholders.

2 My description of customary marriage in this chapter is based on people's accounts rather than on direct observation, although I did observe some marriage-related events. My account thus provides some kind of 'ideal type' of the marriage process in Beparasy.

3 Meat is highly valued but not easily available in Beparasy, where the ordinary diet is vegetarian, sometimes supplemented by small quantities of fish, crayfish, sweet-water crabs, insects or larvae. Beef and pork are consumed only at special occasions, such as funerals (beef) or national independence day (pork). It is therefore common practice to kill a chicken to honour special guests or the ancestors in domestic rituals.

4 In the past, southern Betsileo commoners gave a *tandra hova* ('ruler's gift') each time they killed an ox or harvested rice, to show their allegiance to the polity's ruler. The *tandra vady* must be understood in this context, since with this gift the family of the boy shows its willingness to strengthen the new kinship link with the girl's family.

5 *Fehy* means 'the act of tying' and Michel-Andrianarahinjaka translates *foñena* as the 'ensemble of relations born from the fact of cohabitation and sociability; kinship and its obligations' (Michel-Andrianarahinjaka 1986: 978, my translation). Thus it seems that *fehim-poñena* can be glossed by 'alliance'.

6 The reason for this change has to do with the general impoverishment of Beparasy peasants. Zebus have become too expensive and unaffordable for many families. By proposing a *tandra* in cash, people not only have the opportunity to pay in instalments but also to negotiate the value of the *tandra* to levels much lower than that of the traditional zebu (see next endnote). However, it is still more prestigious to offer cattle.

7 Sometimes the *tandra* can also be significantly less than a zebu. I heard that a family of Beparasy received a *tandra* as low as 50,000 ariary and two chickens. The girl in question was particularly difficult to marry because she already had several children. Unmarried girls and their children can be an economic burden for poor families, who feel obliged to let them go with a 'symbolic' *tandra*.

8 Similar observations about the instability of customary marriages have been made in other Malagasy societies (e.g., Sharp 1993: 107; Astuti 1995: 65–70).

9 Among the Merina, the giving of the *vodiondry* (i.e., a rough equivalent of the southern Betsileo *tandra*) is often marked by a small feast, and this step is often said to be the ceremony that renders customary marriage effective. Westernised urban Merina tend now to consider this event as an equivalent of Western betrothal, before contracting a civil and religious marriage. The need to find a discrete moment of change of status in Malagasy marriage came from the influence of Western ideas about marriage and from state organisation (Kottak 1980: 223).

6 Unilateral unions and their consequences

Because of the processual character of customary marriage in Beparasy, described at some length in the preceding chapter, it is often difficult to judge whether marital unions have been blessed by both sides. My first goal in this chapter is to explain that getting this kind of information is crucial when discussing 'mixed unions' between free and slave descendants, because it is essential to discriminate between those mixed marriages that may have been accepted by the descent groups involved and those that have not. My second aim is to provide empirical evidence suggesting that no 'bilateral mixed marriage' has ever taken place in Beparasy. My third goal is to discuss the case of the 'unilateral marriage' of Ramarcelline (the mother of my host, Redison) with the Berosaiña Rasamuel, together with two other cases of unilateral marriage. I end the chapter by explaining how free descendants can refuse to engage in a marriage process with the Berosaiña, even when the circumstances seem favourable to such unions.

Unilateral and bilateral marriages

For the sake of clarity I shall call a union that has been blessed by elders on both sides a 'bilateral marriage', whereas I shall call a marriage that has been blessed by elders on only one side a 'unilateral marriage'. My use of 'unilateral' and 'bilateral' to describe southern Betsileo marriages differs much from the usual meaning of these terms in kinship theory (cf. 'unilateral cross-cousin marriage'). I use 'unilateral marriage' to highlight the fact that a marriage can occur without the consent of one side, just as we speak of 'unilateral divorce' when one spouse decides to terminate the marriage without the consent of the other. Unless distinctions such as these are used, talking about 'mixed marriages' of free descendants with slave descendants can be very confusing since nothing indicates whether the local descent groups have given their agreement to the union and, thereby, to the relation of alliance between the two groups.[1]

The cases of the two 'mixed couples' I have already mentioned (in Chapter 1 and Chapter 3) will illustrate the difficulties. First, everyone in Beparasy considered Raboba and Ravao as married (*manambady*). Nobody ever told me that the two were not 'appropriately' married, even though some people clearly disapproved of Ravao's decision to take Raboba as *vady* (spouse). Many of the people I asked were not even able to tell me with certainty whether or not Raboba and Ravao had gone through the customs; although they said they had probably not. The truth is that they had not and thus Ravao's kinsmen did not behave towards Raboba and the Berosaiña group as their relatives. This 'non-behaviour' is not obvious though, since Ravao's kinsmen live together with a Berosaiña branch in the village of Mahasoa and inter-act with them on a daily basis. But it becomes clear in situations where a particular gathering takes place among Ravao's kinsmen: Raboba is never invited to attend. The opposite, however, is not true: I could see that Ravao was always invited to the Berosaiña's gatherings and, for example, she attended the funeral of Randriatsoa's sister's son I men-tioned in Chapter 4. I would therefore say that Raboba and Ravao were unilaterally married because Raboba's family treated Ravao as a relative (i.e., as an affine) whereas Ravao's family did not treat Raboba in the same way. The same can be said about Ramarcelline and Rasa-muel: they were unilaterally married, because the Berosaiña behaved towards Ramarcelline as a relative, whereas her kinsmen did not do the same for Rasamuel. As a general point, it is important to note that, as far as I could see, slave descendants always accepted their members' *vady* (spouse) as an affinal relative, even if the couple had not been through the customs because the free descent side had not accepted the union.

A mixed couple can thus be viewed as 'appropriately' married by some and not by others, since such a couple will receive blessings from the senior members on the slave descent side but not from those on the free descent side. Whereas for the slave descent group the couple is considered to be 'in the process' of customary marriage, it is not really considered as such from the point of view of the free descent family, and they do not think they are bound by the customary duties towards relatives. In the case of mixed couples, free and slave descent families may have (and do in fact have) opposite views on how they should act towards each other. The fact that no (or little) exchange 'according to customs' has taken place does not prevent the slave descent elders from giving their blessings to the couple, or even from continuing to try to engage in formal kin relations with the free descent family through invitations, the sending of gifts and so on. Members of the free descent group, on the contrary, systematically refuse these attempts at 'normalising' the situation. In other words, even though there is no *fehim-poñena* ('tying of kinship', i.e. no binding alliance between the two groups), the slave descent group recognises the marriage of the couple and tries to act in consequence in spite of the reluctance of the other side, whereas the free descent group does not. An important point needs to be made here: it would be a mistake, in my opinion, to say that mixed couples are not 'appropriately' or 'really' married, since that would mean privileging the free descendants' perspective at the expense of that of the slave descendants, for no good reason.

Assessing the reality of marriage avoidance

One of the problems I encountered when I tried to investigate the avoidance of marriage with slave descendants in Beparasy was the difficulty in assessing its reality. Was it really the case that free descendants refrained from marrying the Berosaiña? Did they really avoid slave descendants in general? Or was the stated avoidance only wishful thinking? I had listened many times to free descendants saying that people in Beparasy do not marry the Berosaiña because of their slave ancestry and that 'mixed' marriages with slave descendants were *vitsi-vitsy* (rare). At the same time I knew of the mixed unilateral marriages of Ramarcelline and Rasamuel as well as that of Ravao and Raboba. I therefore wondered whether breaches of the rule might get dissimulated because of the embarrassment they caused for free descent families. I also wondered: had there been any bilateral marriages in Beparasy? Was it possible that a free descent group had, in the past, contracted an alliance through marriage with the Berosaiña but that people were hiding such an alliance – at least to me?

From the numerous conversations I had on this topic it became evident that, in general, free descent families among the southern Betsileo probably never engage in bilateral marriages with slave descendants if they are fully aware of their slave ancestry. If a free descent family suspects that the potential partner of their child might be of slave descent, it is very unlikely that the meetings and exchanges between the two families will reach the *fehim-poñena* and the *tandra vady* stages of the marriage process. Sometimes, however, the families have already been through the previous stages of the process, such as the *tapi-maso* and even the *ala-fady*, before learning that their child's potential partner is of slave descent. This can occur because in the initial stages of the process a free descent family may still have to carry out an intensive investigation of the 'origins' of the potential spouse or because, if they have started the investigation, they have not been careful enough – an issue which I will come back to in the next chapter. However, during the late stages of the process the members of the local descent group become progressively more involved, increasing the likelihood that a senior member of the group will raise suspicions and oppose such an alliance.

The limited number of mixed bilateral marriages I was told about during my fieldwork appeared to be unions where the free descent family was not aware of the slave origins of the other side until a very advanced stage in the process.[2] In such instances, the marriages went ahead because it became too late to back away – for example, because the *tandra* had already been given or the couple already had children. I never heard of a single case where a free local descent group had accepted, in full awareness from the start, a slave descent spouse for one of their members.[3] Somewhat naïvely, I had assumed that from time to time impoverished families of free descent would probably accept the marriage of one of their daughters to a wealthy slave descendant who owned good lands and many zebus, and was ready to give a high *tandra*. This, I was repeatedly told in Beparasy, never happens, because it would be *tena diso* (deeply wrong) and too shameful. Several times I heard that people would rather stay poor than allow their children to marry slave descendants.

After I became good friends with Ramarcel at the *vadipaisa* ceremony mentioned at the beginning of the previous chapter I eventually had the opportunity to enquire about the Berosaiña's genealogies and marriages. Ramarcel kindly agreed to help me map out genealogies and to give me the names of the villages where his kinsmen had found their spouses. I thus have a list of villages located in regions around Beparasy and Ambalavao, as well as much more remote places in Betsileo country. When I compare these data with similar genealogical and marriage data I had obtained from free descendants, it is clear that the Berosaiña do not marry close by, whereas many free descendants marry very locally. The majority (i.e., about sixty-five per cent in the sample of marriage data I collected) of free descendants have married within Beparasy, although it is now becoming increasingly difficult to find a suitable spouse due to the *fady* (taboo) on marrying close kin, a point to which I will return later in this chapter.

Table 6.1 shows the number of marriages I recorded in the genealogies of the three branches of the Berosaiña (over five generations), the number of marriages for which I obtained the village of origin of the

Table 6.1 Spouses of the Berosaiña

	Number of marriages recorded on my genealogical diagrams	Number of marriages for which I have data on the village of origin of the spouse	Number of spouses from Beparasy	Number of spouses from outside Beparasy
Branch of Rakamisy and his descendants	49	37	2	35
Branch of Rainihosy and his descendants	81	51	2	49
Branch of Randriatsoakely and his descendants	11	9	1	8
Total	141	97	5	92

spouse, and a breakdown of these figures between the number of spouses found in the five *fokontany* of Beparasy and the number of spouses found outside Beparasy.[4]

Among the five *vady* (spouses) of the Berosaiña who are from Beparasy, one was confirmed to have come from a household dwelling in a small hamlet in the *fokontany* of Beparasy-II. This household had come to Beparasy recently from Ambalamasina, a village located halfway between Beparasy and the Ambatofotsy hill, where the former rulers of the polity had their royal residence (see Chapter 1). It is notorious in the region that a relatively large number of slave descendants live in Ambalamasina, since in pre-abolition times there were *hova* (nobles) and a number of their slaves remained on this land after abolition. There is a clear pattern of marriage alliances between the Berosaiña and the families of (alleged) slave descent in Ambalamasina, since several Berosaiña from the branches of Rakamisy and Rainihosy appear to have found a spouse there. That the marriage in question was not a 'mixed marriage' was also confirmed by free descendants, who regarded the household from the small hamlet in Beparasy-II as *olo tsy madio* (unclean people, i.e. slave descendants).

Another spouse of the Berosaiña recorded in my data is from a village in Beparasy-I. I had already heard that there was one house inhabited by a slave descent family in this village, but I was never able to learn their story and whether they had any connection other than through this marriage with the Berosaiña. My understanding of Ramarcel's explanations is that the spouse came from that slave descent household, thus this does not seem to be a 'mixed marriage' either. Of the three remaining spouses of the Berosaiña who are from Beparasy, two are the free descent women I have already mentioned: Raboba's wife Ravao and Redison's mother Ramarcelline. I will introduce the third case of 'mixed marriage' later in this chapter.

When drawing the genealogies and writing down the spouses' villages of origin I refrained from asking Ramarcel whether the *fomba* (customs) had been carried out for each marriage because I was aware that this was a very sensitive issue. The loose meaning of the words *vady* and *manambady* appeared to be convenient for Ramarcel in this case since he did not have to explain the unilaterality of the possible mixed marriages that were in this list; i.e., the fact that some of these marriages had not been accepted and blessed by the free descent families. But if the spouses found by the Berosaiña in Beparasy were slave descendants (apart from the three cases of mixed marriages), what about the spouses found outside Beparasy? My free descent informants tended to assume that 'the Berosaiña marry other Berosaiña', as I was once told. That is, free descendants firmly believe that the Berosaiña, on the whole, marry other slave descendants.

Trying to find out whether this was really the case was no easy task, but one method I used went as follows. I picked up a few names of villages where the Berosaiña had found spouses, according to the genealogies provided by Ramarcel, and asked a friend of mine who was an active politician in Ambalavao to do his best to gather some information about whether these villages were inhabited by slave descendants or not. This was an easy thing to do, he boasted, since he was well-connected in the region because of his political activities and his kinship network. To check whether his information was correct, I had given him, in my list of villages, the name of the village where I attended the *vadipaisa* mentioned at the beginning of the preceding chapter, since I had already found out from other sources that it was a slave descent village. My friend came back to me a few weeks later with the information that the *vaidpaisa* village was entirely inhabited by slave descendants, whereas the other villages I had enquired about were 'mixed'. He had obtained the information about the *vadipaisa* village from his wife's cousin, who had relatives in a village nearby, and he said that it had been further confirmed by some of his acquaintances in Ambalavao. I did similar triangulations on various occasions and with different people. I found that they were usually consistent with the data on marriage obtained from Ramarcel: the villages where the Berosaiña found their spouses were, most of the time, villages with slave descendants. In sum, my regular triangulations, though admittedly patchy and of limited value, were consistent with the free descendants' view that the Berosaiña's spouses are, for the most part, people who are reputed to be of slave descent.

There are certainly many exceptions to this general trend and I would suspect that some of the male Berosaiña of Beparasy have managed to bring free descent women from outside who agreed to marry them unilaterally. For example, a free descent friend told me he had heard that Randriatsoa's wife was of free descent. Randriatsoa had already been married four times before he found this new wife a few years ago. As he once explained to me during one of my visits to his house in Mahasoa, Randriatsoa had separated from his former wives because they had not given him children, which he finally achieved with his fifth wife. A free descent friend of mine, whose own wife came from the same region, had heard stories about Randriatsoa's wife when visiting his in-laws. The woman was of a free descent family and had decided, despite the opposition of her family, to follow Randriatsoa and set up a hearth with him in Mahasoa. This was yet another case of unilateral marriage, but, given the distance between Beparasy and the woman's region of origin (about twenty-five kilometres through the mountains), it was not possible for me to investigate.

In spite of the limited number of cases that I could observe, two general points can be made about gender asymmetry in mixed marriages. First, because post-marital residence is viri-patrilocal it is much easier for a free descent girl to marry a slave descent man unilaterally (i.e., she leaves her village and goes to live in her partner's village) than for a free descent boy to marry a slave descent girl unilaterally, because in that case the couple would have to reside neolocally. They could of course live in the girl's village, but it is considered very shameful for a man to live with his in-laws and so it happens rarely. Second, for the free descent girl who marries unilaterally the slave descent family will not have to bring a *tandra* (since the free descent family refuses it), whereas if a free descent man marries a slave descent girl unilaterally he will have to find means for the *tandra* by himself, without the support of his kinsmen. For these reasons it seems easier and more likely for a free descent girl to marry a slave descent man than the opposite. The three cases of mixed unions I observed in Beparasy seemed to confirm this pattern, but of course more data is needed to show that this is the case across the board.

Learning who not to marry

It seems that free descent children in Beparasy learn at an early age that they are *olo madio* (clean people) and that the Berosaiña are not. A primary school teacher told me that very young children already knew that their Berosaiña contemporaries were *olo tsy madio* and that they should not marry them. Yet children seem not to be told why this is the case until they are much older (I shall return to this issue in Chapter 8), perhaps because parents are afraid that young children will tell their Berosaiña friends, who may in turn tell their families, or perhaps because they think that young children are not yet mature enough to learn about difficult issues (see Astuti 2011). But when learning who they cannot marry, children have to identify many more people than just the Berosaiña. Redison told me how, when he lived in Beparasy as a very young boy, he was told that they should not *mitady ampela* (look for girls) in particular places. This is because, with the exception of the Berosaiña, the handful of families who arrived in Beparasy at the end of the nineteenth century have intermarried during several generations and, as a consequence, there are many houses or entire hamlets where children should not look for a spouse because they are too closely related.

I was told that, ideally, people should not marry if they have common ancestors in their genealogy. People are aware, however, that such a rule is difficult to observe in practice and that, in the end, 'Tsiataha marry Tsiataha' (i.e., people marry a relative) as a local saying goes. The degree of closeness that was acceptable varied across my informants, but all agreed that second cousins should not marry, as this would mean breaching a serious *fady* (taboo). Third cousins were also regarded by many of my informants as too closely related. But I was told that families could make this marriage acceptable by the ritual killing of an ox on both sides in order to 'cut' the kinship links existing between the two individuals, thus allowing them to marry. My informants stressed that different families often have different views on the distance necessary for an acceptable marriage. Some of my friends in Beparasy had married a third cousin and were always a bit embarrassed when someone mentioned this fact in jest. I did not hear of *lova tsy mifindra* marriages, i.e. marriages between close cousins to keep the land within the group (Bloch 1971: 175).

I had the impression that most parents turned a blind eye to their children's affairs, including those with prohibited partners such as their second cousins. Similarly, free descent parents also seemed to turn a blind eye to affairs that their teenagers or adult relatives had with the

Berosaiña. This applies not only to single people, since in Beparasy everyone was aware that married free descendants, both men and women, sometimes had extramarital affairs with the Berosaiña. This again suggests that what matters most is parental or descent group control over the process of marriage, and the offspring produced as the result of alliance, rather than over sexuality per se. Indeed, the allocation of an individual room to teenage girls, mentioned in the preceding chapter, shows that parental vigilance directed towards their children's sexuality is voluntarily limited. The only exception pertains to relations between siblings: it is strictly *fady* (taboo) for teenage boys to sleep in the same room as their sisters.

Parents of marriageable children also have to be careful when they explain to their offspring why they cannot marry a Berosaiña, out of fear they will repeat the explanation to their boy- or girlfriend. This is what happened to the grandfather of the politician I have mentioned above. When he learned that one of his daughters was engaged in a long-term affair with a slave descendant and wanted to marry him, the grandfather explained to her in direct terms why she could not go on with such a relationship: 'This boy is an *andevo*.' The girl told her boyfriend, who in turn told his parents and soon enough the boy's family asked for public reparation for the insult. The politician's grandfather had to pay the customary fine of one zebu, which was publicly slaughtered to wash out the insult with its blood. The meat was distributed to the two families involved in the dispute and to the *fokonolo* (village council). As I have already explained, the possibility of being fined in this way was commonly mentioned to me to explain people's unwillingness to talk about slavery and slave descendants.

In the preceding chapter I described the process of customary marriage, which people in Beparasy have to go through in order to produce an alliance – the *fehim-poñena* ('tying of kinship') – between two local descent groups. I have stressed that this process can hardly take place without the consent of one's parents and family elders. However, given the relative sexual freedom that youth (and adults) enjoy in Beparasy, one might expect that, from time to time, some long-lasting affairs take place between free and slave descendants and that these can potentially disrupt the ban on mixed marriages that free descendants seek to maintain. I came across a few such cases in contemporary Beparasy, but I was told about similar cases that had occurred in other regions or in the past. The three cases I will now discuss were the only instances of mixed unilateral marriages that I could observe more or less directly during my fieldwork. Although limited in number and unevenly documented, a close analysis of these cases offers some insights into the

consequences faced by those who choose to ignore the free descendants' ban on mixed marriages and engage in socially disapproved
relations. As I have already emphasised, these issues are extremely
sensitive. I was able to talk almost openly about the prohibited character of the marriage with only one of the free descendants involved in
these stories. The closest I came to a conversation about the decision to
go against the family's will was during an interview with Ramarcelline,
Redison's mother, whose case I will now discuss.

Ramarcelline and Rasamuel

Ramarcelline currently lives in Ambalavao but she is from a village
that was founded in Beparasy by her patrilineal grandfather about a
century ago. As a young woman, Ramarcelline was bilaterally married
to a free descent man from a village in the vicinity of Beparasy and
gave birth to a son. The marriage did not go well and soon after the
birth she came back to her village with her baby. A few years later she
married another free descent man from another village outside
Beparasy. She moved to her husband's village and later gave birth to
her second child, Redison. Once again the marriage did not last long
and Ramarcelline returned to her village in Beparasy, where she raised
her two sons, until her eldest son's father took him back to his village.
Ramarcelline remained single with her young boy Redison, until she
met Rasamuel, a Berosaiña from the village of Mahasoa. They got
along well with one another and Rasamuel wanted to marry Ramarcelline. His request was met with a strong refusal on the part of
Ramarcelline's parents and elders. Facing a stubborn opposition from
Ramarcelline's descent group, Rasamuel and Ramarcelline decided to
leave Beparasy to seek fortune elsewhere.

They worked as petty traders for more than twenty-five years, first in
the south of Madagascar, in Ambovombe and Betroka, and then in
Ambalavao. During this time Ramarcelline had few contacts with her
patrilineal kinsmen in Beparasy. A devout Catholic, she married
Rasamuel at the church in Ambovombe, having previously contracted
a civil marriage. In their old days, the couple decided to go back to
Beparasy. They settled in Rasamuel's paternal house among the Berosaiña of Mahasoa and lived there until the death of Rasamuel. When
they returned to Beparasy, Ramarcelline's family had to a certain
extent buried the hatchet and accepted the status quo. It seems that the
unilateral marriage between Ramarcelline and Rasamuel was by now
considered more tolerable by Ramarcelline's kinsmen mainly because,
by the time they returned, Rasamuel and Ramarcelline were elders and

thus deserved respect from the young generation of Ramarcelline's kinsmen – many of the group's elders who had opposed the marriage, including Ramarcelline's parents, having passed away. Moreover, the couple did not have children together. As explained in Chapter 3, Rasamuel, like Ramarcelline, had children from a previous marriage and together they had raised some of their respective offspring.

One day, before going to Ambalavao, I went to see Redison to ask his permission to interview his mother. I also enquired whether he thought I could ask her questions about the difficulties she faced when she chose to marry Rasamuel. Redison gave me his permission and once again, as with Ramarcel, my wife and I set up an afternoon meeting in the empty dining room of a Chinese-run hotel in Ambalavao to make sure that Ramarcelline could talk freely about difficult issues. While she had been very talkative during the first part of the interview and had told us stories about her childhood in Beparasy and her love of the place, when we broached the subject of her marriage it became obvious it was very difficult for her to answer our questions. Feeling a bit uncomfortable ourselves, we did not prolong her uneasiness and returned to more benign questions after just a few minutes. I quote this short moment extensively because, despite their brevity, Ramarcelline's responses are extremely interesting:

It's possible, *maman'i Redison*, that we're now going to ask you some weird questions, but it is for a study that we're going to ask them. Is it a problem for you?

No, go on.

We have already talked to Redison and asked him some questions. He told us that the reason why his mother's family didn't like her husband was because he did not have the same ancestry. That is, you didn't have the same ancestry as he and they weren't happy that you married him.

Yes, maybe it was so.

What did they mean by 'not the same ancestry'? Apologies *maman'i Redison* but this is for a study.

Because they didn't know his 'roots' (*tsy nahalala ny fototrany*). Because they [Rasamuel's family] were strangers (*vahiny*) when they arrived and they didn't know his descent group (*firazana*).

Whose descent group?

The descent group of my husband.

Were they strangers (*vahiny*) when they arrived in Beparasy?

They were in the east [of Ambalavao] and they came up there. It's his grandmother who came there in the past.

Your husband's grandmother

Yes. She lived here, to the east [of Ambalavao], in Mahasoabe, and she went there [to Beparasy] to marry. In the past, there were *mpandia tany*.

Mpandia tany?

That is, people who divide land (*mpizara tany*). Their grand-mother was someone who divides land.

Before that they were only in Mahasoabe or were they in other places too?

No, they were only there. And they [Ramarcelline's family] didn't know his origin [Rasamuel's origin]. And they made out as if he had not the same ancestry. But much later we did the history (*natao ny tantara*) and he wasn't [implied: of slave descent].

But what did they mean when they said that he was not of the same ancestry?

In the past, there was something which was not very different from the helpers (*mpanampy*) today. [They said] there were helpers like that.

What they meant was, like, in the days of the kings, there were nobles, slaves and the rest ...?

Yes, like that. But we did the history after we arrived in Betroka and everything was clear (*mazava*).

Where were they from? Apologies for asking these questions, it's for a study.

According to what they said of the history, they came from the east and went to the west.

From where in the east?

From the east of the Tanala, maybe. I don't know. I don't know the place where they were. They went to the west and arrived in Betroka. And in Betroka there is a place where they are, where their relatives are. We arrived there, we did the history and we saw their origin.

Didn't he [Rasamuel] cry and say 'So these people are like that,' because these were strong words from your family? Didn't it make him sad?

It didn't make him sad since he knew his origins. When we arrived in Betroka, where his family were, we did the history and it was clear, the history was the same [the same history as that told by Rasamuel to Ramarcelline]. It was as if we [i.e., Ramarcelline, Anjasoa and Denis] are relatives (*mpihava*) but we don't know the place of origin (*toera fihavy*) [of each other]. Then I come to you and you don't know my ancestry (*firazanako*) and then you suspect (*mihahihay*): 'Is she not a slave (*andevo*)?' Because you don't know my origin (*niandohako*). That's why this story started, but when we went to the place where he has his roots (*am-pototrany*) we did the history and he wasn't … he was clear (*mazava*) … clean (*madio*).

Is that the grandmother of your husband who arrived first in Beparasy?

Yes, his grandmother. The mother of his grandmother.

And do you know the name of this grandmother?

Rapitsarandro gave birth to Ravolamana. Ravolamana gave birth to my husband's mother.

When she arrived there [in Beparasy], did she come alone or did she come with someone else?

She came there and got married. She married the lord who measures land (*nanambady ny andriana mpandia tany*).

Was it his grandmother who came from Betroka?

His grandmother came from Betroka when her ruler friend (*ny mpanjaka namany*) brought her here [to Vinany, now called Mahasoabe, close to Ambalavao]. She was brought to Ambalavao [i.e., Vinany] because the ruler there had a kinship relation (*nisy fihavana*) with the ruler here. The ruler in Betroka and the one here had established a relation like family (*nifampihavana*) and he brought her here. And when she arrived here she married another ruler, a ruler who divides land.

And do you know the name of her husband? The name of the husband of your husband's grandmother?

No, this I don't know, I don't remember.

Ramarcelline attributes the reason for her family's opposition to her marriage with Rasamuel to the alleged slave origins of her husband's great grandmother. The great grandmother she refers to, Rapitsarandro, was the mother of Rakamisy who, as explained in Chapter 4, is remembered as one of the founders in Beparasy. My understanding of the story is that the elders in Ramarcelline's family in Ambalabe opposed her marriage with Rasamuel, not by questioning the status of Rakamisy – who had been a slave before being freed and becoming one of the *andevohova* in Beparasy – but by questioning the status of his mother, Rapitsarandro, who, according to my free descent informants (see Chapter 4), had been a slave in Vinany (now called Mahasoabe) until she joined Rakamisy with Rainihosy and Randriatsoakely after the abolition.

Some details of the story told by Ramarcelline appear to be incorrect. First, according to my other sources, both from the Berosaiña and the free descent side, Rasamuel's great grandmother Rapitsarandro was not married when she arrived in Beparasy and never married there. Randriatsoa had explained to me that Rakamisy had no father in Beparasy and that his mother had lived with him in Mahasoa. Moreover, Ramarcelline gives a genealogy for Rasamuel that is not correct: she indicates descent from Rapitsarandro through women, whereas it is in fact through his father and then his grandfather, Rakamisy, that Rasamuel is related to Rapitsarandro (see Figure 3.1). This is interesting, nonetheless, since her insistence on women (and their status) indicates perhaps that, since Rakamisy was regarded as a 'clean' commoner when he arrived, people in Beparasy might have developed suspicions about the unclear origins of some females in this branch, i.e. Rakamisy's mother and his descendants' wives.

Finally, Ramarcelline seems also to have somewhat mixed up the stories about the 'ruler who divides land', i.e. the *andevohova*. There is no doubt that Rakamisy was the *andevohova* – it was not Rapitsarandro's husband, as implied in Ramarcelline's story. The fact that Ramarcelline did not remember the name of this husband and that nobody told me about this man is also evidence that she is mistaken, since, had this man existed, he would have been the apical ancestor of the Berosaiña in Beparasy and would have been remembered as such. These discrepancies aside, her version of the story is interesting because, in spite of Ramarcelline's explanations, it does suggest that Rapitsarandro may have been a slave who was originally kidnapped in an eastern region by a Bara ruler – Betroka is in the Bara area – in the nineteenth century, and that at some point she was offered to the ruler of Vinany because he had an alliance with the Bara ruler.[5]

It was rather moving to hear Ramarcelline explaining that Rasamuel had taken her to a *mpitantara* (historian) among his great grandmother's relatives when they left Beparasy and arrived in Betroka. He had done so in order to convince her that his version of the story was true and that his great grandmother was not a slave – it is indeed possible that Rasamuel was able to trace the origins of his great grandmother to a Bara descent group in Betroka – and that she got a particular status and function (she 'divided the land') when she arrived in Ambalavao. While Ramarcelline certainly did try to make the story she told us sound unproblematic, I believe she spoke the truth when she said that at that time she became convinced that her family had been wrong and that there was no history of slavery in her husband's family. But if this is true, it would also mean that before that moment she too had wondered whether Rasamuel could be of slave descent. And yet she had decided to flee with him, against the will of her kinsmen.

Ramarcelline clearly did not want to speak ill of her own family during the interview. She is a sweet, very polite elderly woman and since Rasamuel's death these stories had probably lost much of the importance they once had. She insisted several times during our conversation that everything became clear for everyone, including for her relatives, implying that in the end they had even accepted her choice to marry Rasamuel and were not upset with her anymore. Yet this nice version does not correspond to what I was told by Beparasy villagers or by Redison himself. Although it does seem that some of Ramarcelline's relatives never completely cut relations with her, in spite of disapproving her unilateral marriage, none of her kinsmen ever recognised Rasamuel as her husband. This means that Rasamuel never accompanied Ramarcelline when she visited her relatives and that her family never adopted the kind of behaviour towards Rasamuel and his descent group in Mahasoa that is customary when descent groups are tied together through a marriage. In other words, because Ramarcelline and Rasamuel never married bilaterally, Ramarcelline's kinsmen never acknowledged a marital alliance with the Berosaiña of Mahasoa and never felt bound by the duties that such an alliance entails. This was particularly obvious at Rasamuel's funerals, held in Mahasoa, which nobody from Ramarcelline's village attended, even though they had all been invited. None of them offered the kind of support – i.e., help with organising the funerals and gifts of money, cloth or zebu – that they should have provided in these circumstances had they truly accepted Ramarcelline's marriage. Rasamuel, for his part, had tried to establish such relationships. At Ramarcelline's father's death, for example, he had sent a *lofo* (i.e., a gift of a zebu) for the funerals, as is customary for men when their father-in-law dies, but the elders in Ramarcelline's family refused the gift and sent it back to Mahasoa. This was a very strong sign that they had no intention to normalise the situation.

During the interview, Ramarcelline also explained that her family did not try to directly take her out of her marriage, but again the truth seems to be a bit different since her relatives threatened her with exclusion from her paternal tomb if she persisted in her decision. Redison mentioned these threats to me as the reason why Ramarcelline's preference was to be buried with her mother in a tomb that her maternal descent group has recently built in Beparasy, since apparently this side of her family had not been so harsh with her after her marriage (even though they disliked it) and, on the whole, this group had continue to keep good relations with her. Redison added that he had personally contributed to the tomb's construction and to the *vadipaisa* that had followed, stressing that he would prefer to be buried in the tomb of his maternal grandmother rather than in that of his maternal grandfather, because of the intolerant attitude that her mother's father's kinsmen had shown towards his stepfather Rasamuel. He said that in the near future he wanted to build a tomb (for his mother as well as for himself and his children) on a plot of land that he would like to buy again from Raboba, just below Soatanana. If this project materialises, the tomb would then be situated, somewhat ironically, on the Berosaiña's land.

Raboba and Ravao

The second case of mixed unilateral marriage I could observe is that of my neighbours in Soatanana, Raboba and Ravao. It is interesting to compare it with the case of Rasamuel and Ramarcelline. Before marrying Ravao unilaterally, Raboba was bilaterally married to a slave descent woman. I know this fact with certainty since one of this woman's forebears, Raboba told me, was from the slave descent village where I attended the *vadipaisa* mentioned in the previous chapter. I subsequently learned from Ramarcel that Raboba had, moreover, family relations in this village on his mother's side. So Raboba had relations to this village through both descent and marriage, and consequently he attended the ceremony, taking his teenage son with him.

Ravao, for her part, had married several times in the region of Ivohibe and had two children with two different free descent husbands. When they decided to live together, Ravao and Raboba were already in their mid-forties. Unlike Ramarcelline, Ravao was neither born nor raised in Beparasy but in the south, outside Betsileo country, in a village close to Ivohibe. She came to Beparasy because she followed her mother, who was from Mahasoa. Ravao's mother had left Beparasy when she was married to a Betsileo migrant living in Bara country. When her husband died, Ravao's mother came back to her paternal village, Mahasoa, to cultivate a small plot of her family's land. She was later joined by Ravao after she separated from her last husband, at which point she did not want to go back to her paternal village because she was not on good terms with her brothers and therefore had few prospects there. Shortly after Ravao came to live with her mother in Mahasoa she started a relationship with Raboba. The relationship was not accepted by Ravao's maternal descent group, even though the family lived in the same village as the Berosaiña – in Mahasoa, the village founded by Rakamisy – and had good relationships with them. Ravao, who has a strong and often rebellious character, apparently did not care about the ban on marrying the Berosaiña and went to live with Raboba in the 'big village'.

The fact that Ravao had spent more than thirty years outside Beparasy and outside Betsileo country certainly made it easier for her to ignore the free descendants' ban on marriage with the Berosaiña and her own maternal family's dislike of her relationship with Raboba. In my experience, people like Ravao who have lived outside their Betsileo homeland in an ethnically diverse community of migrants do not care so much about the issue of slave descent.[6] In any case, Raboba never tried to ask Ravao's family in Mahasoa for permission to do *ny fomba* ('the customs', i.e. to engage in the formal exchanges of the marriage process), in all likelihood because he knew all too well that they would never allow it. Since Raboba and Ravao were my closest neighbours, I could see that Ravao had very few interactions with her maternal relatives, and that she seldom participated in ceremonies, gatherings or agricultural work in her mother's village. Someone once described her relations with her maternal kinsmen as *tsa mifandevy maty* ('they don't bury each other's dead'), meaning they do not help to organise or attend each other's funerals – probably the gravest level reached by any family dispute.

Ravao does not participate in family gatherings on Raboba's side either. She was not present, for example, at the aforementioned *vadipaisa* ceremony. Ravao's behaviour in this matter contrasts with Ramarcelline's, who was present at the *vadipaisa* even though her only connection to the local descent group was through her stepdaughter Vohangy – recall that the village is home to Vohangy's maternal family since it is the village of Rasamuel's first wife. Unlike Ravao, Ramarcelline maintains very good relationships with the Berosaiña and, even after Rasamuel's death, continues to attend family gatherings among them whenever she can.

A further difference is that, unlike Rasamuel and Ramarcelline, Raboba and Ravao have not moved out of Beparasy in the hope of finding a better place to live and have not contracted a civil or a religious marriage. Nonetheless, a feature common to both couples is that, like Ramarcelline and Rasamuel, Raboba and Ravao did not have any children together. Again, this certainly makes their marriage more acceptable to Ravao's free descent family, for reasons that will be clear in the next chapter. The price they pay for their relationship is that, as I have illustrated in Chapter 3, they live more or less on their own, having little contact with each other's families and therefore little support from them. But it seems also true that they were able to carry on with their relationship precisely because both of them were already living much on their own before they met, so they had little to lose in this matter.

Yet Ravao does not refuse to have contact with Raboba's Berosaiña kinsmen. She was present, for example, at the funerals of Randriatsoa's sister's child described in Chapter 4. She also goes once a year to *manetsa* (planting of rice seedlings) among Raboba's kinsmen in a village not far from Ambalavao where rice can be harvested twice a year (unlike in Beparasy, where it can only be harvested once because of the cold climate). Thus, for a few weeks each year, Raboba and Ravao leave their house in Soatanana and stay at Raboba's relatives, presumably with people of alleged slave descent, where they are paid for their work.

Fara and Mamy

How do people in Beparasy refuse to engage in the marriage process with the Berosaiña if, on the other hand, they can be their neighbours, friends or their allies for various reasons? It is in fact less easy than it may seem. It is out of the question that people would refuse to engage in the process of customary marriage with the Berosaiña by saying (or even implying) that it is because they do not have the same ancestry. First, this would be interpreted as implying that they have slave ancestry and, as I was endlessly reminded, it is forbidden by law and custom to say that someone is of slave descent. Second, this would spark the kind of dispute that would threaten the social cohesion of the small community. Free descendants are well aware that any word in this sense would be considered as highly insulting by the Berosaiña, and that they would seek compensation at the *fokonolo* (village council). The third case that I would like to discuss shows how a marriage offer can be declined even when the circumstances make it difficult to refuse.

This case concerns a much younger couple. Mamy is the son of Randrianja Albert, the head of the Berosaiña branch I introduced in Chapter 3. Fara is the daughter of a free descent teacher at the primary school. Mamy and Fara are both in their twenties and studied together at a junior high school in Ambalavao, where they had a relationship. Fara fell pregnant while in Ambalavao and had to leave school and come back to her village to give birth to her daughter. When Mamy finished school he too went back to his paternal village in Beparasy to work on his father's estate. As soon as Mamy had returned, Fara abandoned her village without authorisation, leaving her daughter with her parents. She established a *tokantrano* ('hearth in the house') with Mamy in a ground-floor room of Randrianja Albert's spacious house.

As explained in Chapter 3, Mamy's father, Randrianja Albert, is the wealthiest Berosaiña and is a rather powerful man precisely because of his wealth. But in Beparasy he is also well-known for his strong character and outspoken demeanour. A few months after Fara had arrived at his house, Randrianja Albert felt confident enough to make contact with Fara's young father – he was in his forties – to propose a marriage between Fara and his son Mamy. I was told that in response to this demand Fara's father had gone to Randrianja Albert's house to discuss the issue personally with him. Before going to see Randrianja Albert, however, he had sought the advice of Redison, whom he had asked for help to solve the problem he had with his daughter. Redison repeated the teacher's words to me: 'Can you help me Redison? I don't know what to do. I cannot let this situation go on because it is very shameful for me and my family. You know why. You have good relations with the Berosaiña, can you come with me and explain that it cannot carry on like this?' Redison, however, categorically refused to be involved in the affair. He told me, with his characteristically impatient attitude towards what he once called 'Betsileo hypocrisy': 'I don't know why they do not want to let their daughter marry Mamy. If they have problems with that, well, too bad, they will sort out this situation themselves.'

Fara's father went alone to Randrianja Albert's and tried to convince him that it was not appropriate for their children to go through the *fomba* because Randrianja Albert's father, Randriatsoakely, had a *vakirà* (blood bond) with one of Fara's forebears. Thus, the teacher said, his family was too closely related to Randrianja Albert's to accept the alliance. Such a marriage, he insisted, would be shameful for both parties. The teacher later reported to Redison and other free descendants that Randrianja Albert became very upset when he heard these arguments. He said he knew the true reason why Fara's family did not want to let her marry his son. Fara's father denied there was any other hidden reason. He stuck to the argument that his family's refusal was only motivated by fear of breaching the *fady* (taboo) of marrying close kin. Randrianja Albert did not believe him for a second. He nonetheless called Fara and, in a rage, told her to go back to her village with her father.

Refusing marriage with the Berosaiña

The story of Fara and Mamy provides a striking answer to the question I asked above: how do free descent families refuse marriage with slave descendants? There are, of course, many excuses that could be invoked to refuse a marriage, but in some situations it can become very difficult. Since, according to custom, it is always the boy's family who approaches the girl's, parents of free descent girls are the most likely to face the problem. I was told that parents in this case would say that their daughter was too young to marry or that they still needed her at home. They would ask for a high *tandra*, hoping that the cost would deter the suitor, or they would say they were waiting for the opinion of a family elder who lived far away, thereby delaying the decision-making process ad infinitum in the hope that the suitor's family would take the hint and give up. In the case of Fara and Mamy, however, the situation was not so easy to handle for four reasons: because Randrianja Albert was a powerful man in Beparasy; because Fara was extremely determined to marry Mamy; because there was already a child; and because Mamy was clearly the father of this child.

In this case the free descent family's strategy involved manipulating the *vakirà* practice to avoid marrying the Berosaiña. We can see here that the 'fictive kinship' created by the ritual of *vakirà* is not only used to integrate some Berosaiña in one's network of kin, as I explained in the preceding chapter, but also to exclude them from the wider kinship network that relates all the descent groups of Beparasy through bilateral marriages. I once asked an elder why the first inhabitants of Beparasy had done *vakirà* with the Berosaiña, and I received the following answer: the first reason was that the first settlers were strangers to each other and so they had to 'make' kinship ties, even with the Berosaiña, to strengthen mutual support in difficult material conditions; the second reason was that by so doing they would be able to refuse the marriage of their children with the Berosaiña's children, on the pretext that they were already *fianakavy raiky* ('one family') and that it would be wrong to marry one's close kinsmen. In the case of Fara and Mamy, we see that this old strategy is still very much in use in Beparasy. My guess is that it has been the most commonly used official reason for refusing to marry the Berosaiña since the end of the nineteenth century. What are now left to explore are the hidden reasons: how do free descendants in Beparasy explain their reluctance to marry the Berosaiña? And how can they be sure that their marriage partners do not have slaves among their ancestors? I tackle these two questions in the next chapter.

Notes

1 The discussion of mixed marriages by Evers (2002: 54–71) suffers from this ambiguity, since it is never clearly explained whether the marriages with migrants of alleged slave descent were blessed by the elders from the free descent side.

2 None of these stories happened in Beparasy and therefore I will not mention them here, because I was not able to investigate them. These stories concerned people's relatives who lived far away in Betsileo country and thus they were more easily reported to me than the stories that concerned persons from Beparasy.

3 Evers (2002: 61–62) reports a case where a free descent family has actively promoted the marriage of one of its members with a girl of alleged slave descent because the family was desperate as the man could not find a spouse in the village. It remains unclear, however, whether the girl was really of slave descent and why this man had to find a spouse necessarily in his village, since most southern Betsileo marry outside their village.

4 Ramarcel was unable to provide any kind of information about the marriages of Randriatsoakely's children because the sons had moved to the region of Ivohibe a long time ago (see Chapter 3) and the daughters had married away from Beparasy, meaning that he hardly knew them. For this branch of the Berosaiña I only found information about the marriages of Randrianja Albert's children and grandchildren.

5 Slaves, like cattle, were commonly exchanged as gifts by rulers and nobles, for example at the occasion of marriages (Michel-Andrianarahinjaka 1986: 631).

6 This was also true, for example, of Redison's wife Raely and his brother Naina, who were born and had lived among Betsileo settlers in the region of Betroka. Naina told me that before coming to Beparasy as a young man he had never heard that one was not allowed to marry slave descendants.

7 Mixing ancestries and keeping a memory of origins

Are there differences here between the descendants of slaves and the others, like those that existed in the past?

Yes, such differences still exist.

How does one see these differences? How do they matter in daily life?

One can have relations with slave descendants but one should never marry them. Because history goes on, goes on, goes on … Up to this date people know who is of slave descent. Because grandparents tell children: 'These people, there, they are slave descendants … watch out!' And these people also know that they are descendants of slaves, so they do not seek spouses among the others.

They marry other slave descendants?

Yes, that's it.

(Conversation with an elderly woman in Beparasy)

Asking questions about slave descent and the Berosaiña as slave descendants was quite challenging in Beparasy. During interviews, many free descendants avoided answering my questions directly and some merely refused to talk about these topics, thereby maintaining a meaningful silence. It has been suggested that the widespread 'silence about slavery' in Madagascar is purposely maintained among the Betsileo by both free and slave descendants because it creates a livable 'fiction of equality' (Somda 2009; Freeman 2013). In Beparasy I found such a fiction. Free descendants carefully avoided saying or implying that someone is of slave descent because they could be fined a zebu by the *fokonolo* (village council) for doing so.

The Berosaiña, on their end, had no interest in bringing up the issue of their slave reputation in public discussions, unless they felt they had been insulted and wanted to obtain reparation – but this seems to have occurred only rarely. Moreover, in daily life, the relations between the free descendants and the Berosaiña appeared to be rather egalitarian:

they were never considered inferior partners when they tilled the fields with their free descent friends or helped them to organise a funeral. Yet, as I showed in the previous chapters, there is one issue that regularly disrupted the fiction of equality and brought social inequality back to full light: marriage.

The goal of this chapter is to provide answers to the following questions: Why do free descendants consider slave descendants as unmarriageable 'unclean' partners? And how do they ascribe someone's clean or unclean status? To answer these questions I use my wide-angle (i.e., historical) and normal (i.e., ethnographic) lenses.

Marrying equals

The Berosaiña's wealth and *tompontany* status were apparently never sufficient for them to be judged 'marriageable' by free descent families. In the previous chapter I explained that for the ninety-seven Berosaiña marriages I recorded across five generations, none of them was a bilateral marriage with a free descent family of Beparasy. Although incomplete, these data seem to indicate that the Berosaiña never had marital alliances with local free descent groups during the four or five generations that followed the arrival of Rakamisy and his 'brothers' in Beparasy. Indeed, my free descent informants denied there had ever been any marriages between a free descent family of Beparasy and the Berosaiña. This absence of local marriages for the Berosaiña sharply contrasts with free descent families. The free descendants' repeated local alliances have resulted in their view that all people in Beparasy are kinsmen sharing common ancestors – all people, that is, except the Berosaiña.

This situation is not the result of the Berosaiña's preferences and choices. Despite what free descendants sometimes seem to think (see the quote of the elderly woman at the beginning of this chapter), the Berosaiña are not avoiding marriage with the free descendants of Beparasy, and unlike the free descendants they do not tell their children that there is a *karazan'olo* (kind of people) that they should not marry.[1] As I could observe with the case of Andry at the *vadipaisa* (see Chapter 5), relations between free and slave descent teenagers are frequent, but free descent parents turn a blind eye to them as long as they do not last. If, however, the relationship becomes serious and the teenagers say they would like to proceed with the marriage process, the free descent parents then have recourse to various strategies, including the threat of heavy sanctions, to deter their child from continuing the relationship and to prevent the first formal stages of customary marriage from being undertaken.

When I asked free descendants why they did not want to marry the Berosaiña, they told me that one should only marry 'people of the same ancestry' (*olo mitovy raza*), or people more rarely said 'people of the same rank' (*olo mitovy saranga*) – the 'same ancestry' means marrying people from the same status group (i.e., *hova, olompotsy* or *andevo*), whereas the term *saranga* ('rank') refers more explicitly to the ranking system that existed for nobles and commoners during the pre-colonial era (Dubois 1938: 578–579). In both cases the idea is that people should marry equals or, in anthropological terms, that they should marry isogamously. A free descent elder and his daughter explained to me the reasons for this rule of isogamy in striking terms:

DAUGHTER: Commoners (*vohitse*) and slave descendants (*hovavao*) cannot marry each other. We cannot marry nobles either, since if we marry nobles we become their slaves and we lose our honour (*zo*). We become their slaves because we prepare their meals and it is very difficult for us Malagasy.

ELDER: The nobles, too, they lose their grade.

DAUGHTER: The nobles are 'destroyed' too.

ELDER: The nobles do not rule anymore if they marry people who are not nobles.

DAUGHTER: If they marry ordinary people (*olon-tsotra*) [i.e., commoners].

ELDER: Nobles marry nobles. But if nobles marry people who are not nobles, 'what makes them noble' (*ny maha-hova*) falls and their honour (*zo*) is lost.

DAUGHTER: Commoners marry commoners. And if ordinary people marry slaves, then they become slaves too.

ELDER: If nobles marry slave descendants they do not fall because they [the slave descendants] are still their slaves (*andevo*).

DAUGHTER: Slave descendants can marry nobles. Because they are still their slaves (*andevo*) and therefore it's not a problem. Because they will still be under their command, they will go to work; they [the nobles] will give them food.

DENIS: Does it occur that nobles marry slave descendants?

DAUGHTER: It happens, because they are still really their slaves and they are still made to work, they go back to what they were in the past.

ELDER: It's like going back to their former work.

DAUGHTER: They marry them and at the same time they make them work. But with ordinary people it doesn't work at all.

ELDER: Ordinary people cannot do that.

DAUGHTER: If ordinary people marry nobles, they become their slaves. If ordinary people marry slave descendants they go into a very bad situation (*lasa ratsy be*). People won't let them enter the ancestral tomb when they die if they marry them.

In this discussion the elder and his daughter think about marriages across status groups and talk about what happens to the honour (*zo*) of nobles and commoners in cases of intermarriage and in instances of their marriage with slave descendants. If they marry commoners, nobles lose their honour (*zo*) but also their ability to rule (*manjaka*), their grade (*girady*) and 'what-makes-them-hova' (*ny maha-hova*). They are destroyed (*potiky*). If they marry nobles, commoners are said to lose their honour too and to become the slaves of the nobles, being obliged to cook for them. It is not too difficult to imagine that the latter refers to real-life situations where, for example, two such families jointly organise a funeral for the descendants they have in common. The commoner family may feel obliged or could even be asked to do the low-status tasks, whereas the noble family will take the leadership of the funerals. Commoners seem to dislike marriage with nobles precisely because they fear that the alliance will not be egalitarian and they end up in an inferior position to the other family. It is of great interest that this line of reasoning is not applied by the elder and his daughter to a marriage with slave descendants: it is not that in such a marriage commoners will be the superior and will have inferior relatives that they will dominate. On the contrary, commoners who marry slave descendants are said to become 'slaves' in this case too.

The conversation above suggests that commoners think that any kind of marriage outside their status group will result in them becoming 'slaves'. Slavery, for contemporary southern Betsileo – or, to be more precise, for southern Betsileo commoners – seems to be a major idiom to talk about marriages and the ensuing relations between families.[2] But if these two kinds of out-marriage for commoners have the same consequence (commoners become slaves), one could expect that they lead both to similar patterns of avoidance of marriage. Nowadays, however, bilateral marriages between descendants of nobles and commoners do occur, even though both noble and commoner descent groups disapprove of them. If a couple insists, in spite of their respective families' attempts to discourage them, the partners will be allowed to go through with a customary marriage.[3]

By contrast, such tolerance was totally absent in Beparasy when a marriage with the Berosaiña was at stake. The strict pattern of avoidance I observed in Beparasy was striking given the aforementioned fiction of equality, which could have been extended to marriage and affinal relations, at least by the free descendants who were on very good terms with the Berosaiña. A strong preference for isogamy thus does not seem sufficient to explain why free descendants did not, and still do not, marry the Berosaiña. A further reason given by my free descent informants sounded much more serious, although I did not understand all of its implications when I first heard it: 'If we marry slaves then we become slaves too' ('*Lasa andevo koa anay raha manambady andevo*'). My first understanding of this statement was that their group's honour (*zo*) and local reputation would be damaged by such a marriage, as explained by the elder and his daughter above. This interpretation is correct (and I shall come back to it later), but the phrase also has two less obvious meanings, which follow from the way Beparasy villagers think about the mixing (*mifangaro*) of ancestries (*raza*).

Mixing ancestries through procreation

The first case of 'ancestries mixing' I was told about involved procreation, which is crucial because it concerns the production of *taranaka* (descendants), so valued in Madagascar (Keller 2008). I asked free descendants: What would happen if *olompotsy* (commoners) and *andevo* (slaves) had children together? What would be the *raza* (ancestry) of the children?

Beparasy villagers could only describe the procreation process in vague terms, but their views seemed very similar to that of their immediate southern neighbours, the Bara, as reported by Richard Huntington (1973: 79). In short, the mother contributes the raw material – *ra* (blood) – and the father provides the building principle – his semen, which *manamboatra* ('arranges') the foetus out of the mother's blood. Since, on the other hand, my interlocutors had sometimes told me that the Berosaiña were *tsy madio* (unclean) because they had dirty blood (*ra maloto*), I expected them to say that children inherit their status from their mother, and so a child's status depends on which parent is of slave descent. Their response was, again, different from what I expected.

The children born from unions between commoners and slaves are called *lambo-tapaka* ('split wild boar'). Pastor Rainihifina writes in his book on Betsileo customs (Rainihifina 1975: 29–30, my translation) that one of the reasons why the spouses must 'have the same ancestry' (*mitovy razana ny mpivady*) is:

To make sure that the descendants will not have a mixed blood and that their name will not be weakened, since people give the names of 'split wild boar' [*lambo-tapaka*] or 'split noble' [*hova-tapaka*] to children born from people who do not have the same ancestry. Children born from people who have a nice ancestral land [*soa tanindrazana*] are called 'children with roots' [*zana-potots'olo*].

The term *lambo-tapaka* evokes some kind of hybrid status because of its implicit reference to two halves – the children being, I was told, half *lambo* (wild boar, i.e. *andevo*) and half *omby* (zebu, i.e. *olompotsy*). My informants stressed that the children would be *lambo-tapaka* irrespective of whether the mother or the father was of slave descent. This is consistent with the Betsileo kinship system, which is bilateral in spite of a strong patrilineal bias (Kottak 1980: 172). Bilaterality, however, does not mean that *lambo-tapaka* children could – like the descendants of former slaves among the Sakalava, according to Michael Lambek – 'assert social identity derived from non-slave ancestors' and 'be absorbed into the social order' (Lambek 2004: 109). To the contrary, my informants explained that *lambo-tapaka* children were of slave status. They unambiguously considered them as unclean persons. Thus, unlike what the term suggests, *lambo-tapaka* is not a hybrid status at all, since the children are not mixed as far as their social status is concerned. Beparasy free descendants apply here a rule of hypodescent: the children of an *andevo–olompotsy* couple are ascribed the social status of the parent of the inferior ancestry (*raza*). The term 'hypodescent' was coined by Marvin Harris and Conrad Kottak (1963) to discuss racial categorisation in Brazil and has been used to analyse other cases, the best-known example being the one-drop rule in the United States. It also applies to the way in which Beparasy free descendants think about children born from unions with slave descendants. The phrase 'if we marry them, we will become slaves too' thus means that all the descendants born from such marriages will be ascribed slave status, despite having one commoner parent and many other commoners among their ancestors.

The rule of hypodescent, however, does not apply systematically in the southern Betsileo context. In the case of descendants of nobles who have children with slave descendants or commoner descendants, the ascription of status follows other rules, as I was told by a local historian of noble descent in Ambalavao:

Why do people refuse to marry slave descendants?

(Laughing). Listen, here is what happened in the past. For commoners, it was forbidden to marry with a slave, but for a noble it wasn't, because the children that the noble had with slaves were not considered slaves but nobles. A noble man could take the children and raise them as his children.

Did it not pose any problem?

No, there was no problem. For us [i.e., the nobles], even today it is not a problem to marry slaves.

But why is it a problem for commoners then?

(Laughing) I don't know why but it's really humiliating for commoners because of the customs, because their children will be children of slaves. If a commoner marries a slave, the children will be slaves. But for the nobles, it's not the case, it's the contrary.

Was a marriage of a noble with a commoner possible in the past?

Yes, it was possible. A noble man can marry whoever he wants, and the child will be noble. But a noble woman cannot marry a commoner.

Why is this case not possible?

Because [in this case] it's the father who transmits the status.

The rules of status ascription proposed by the historian are sum-marised in Table 7.1. What he said does not exactly correspond to what commoners told me in Beparasy. Table 7.2 shows that the com-moners' views are simpler: people in Beparasy explained that when nobles marry commoners their children are *always* commoners, irre-spective of the father's status. In other words, they apply a strict prin-ciple of hypodescent to the mixed marriages between nobles and commoners, and between commoners and slaves, but not to the mixed marriages between nobles and slaves. This is an important point because, as we shall see in the next chapter, commoners often hold the view that most southern Betsileo nobles have lost their ritual power, precisely by marrying commoners.

Table 7.1 Status of mixed children according to a noble in Ambalavao

	Noble mother	*Commoner mother*	*Slave mother*
Noble father	NOBLE	NOBLE	NOBLE
Commoner father	COMMONER (*Hova-tapaka*)	COMMONER	SLAVE (*Lambo-tapaka*)
Slave father	NOBLE	SLAVE (*Lambo-tapaka*)	SLAVE

Table 7.2 Status of mixed children according to commoners in Beparasy

Mixed marriage	Satus of the child
Noble – commoner	COMMONER (*Hova-tapaka*)
Commoner – slave	SLAVE (*Lambo-tapaka*)
Noble – slave	NOBLE

Mixing ancestries in the tomb

The second case of 'ancestries mixing' mentioned to me was the mixing that would occur in the free descendants' ancestral tombs if they had to bury *lambo-tapaka* children. In an attempt to explain why the corpse of an 'unclean' slave descendant should never be placed inside a free descent tomb, one of my friends quoted the proverb '*Fandoto iray tandroka mahaloto rano iray sinibe*' ('The dirtiness of a horn [used to pour water] makes the water of a jar [used to store water] dirty') to mean that such a corpse would *mahaloto* (dirty) the entire tomb. Others, following the same logic, told me that if such a person were to be placed in the tomb the ancestors would become *maloto* (dirty) as well and therefore 'the ancestors [would] become slaves too' (*lasa andevo koa ny raza*). This is particularly significant because in southern Betsileo tombs the dead are placed close to one another on beds or, if the beds are already full, piled upon one another, so that when corpses decompose the bones are mixed up. In this process, individual corpses progressively lose their identity and become a single entity of the ancestors. The phrase 'if we marry them, we will become slaves too' thus implicitly refers to this kind of mixing: not only would the descendants of the couple be unclean, but their free descent ancestors in the tomb could become unclean too. In Beparasy, people strongly felt that placing a *lambo-tapaka* child in the tomb would have serious negative consequences. They stressed that the ancestors would become angry and would retaliate by bringing misfortune to their descendants. In other words, free descendants feared the 'ancestral violence' (Graeber 1995) that could be unleashed on them.[4]

'If we were to marry the Berosaiña,' an elderly woman once asked me in response to my questioning, 'where would we bury the children, then?' The sense of this question follows from what I have just explained about the placing of an unclean child in the tomb. In the eventuality of a marriage with the Berosaiña, there would be no obligation, for the free descent side, to bury the *lambo-tapaka* children in their tombs: they could simply leave the corpses to the Berosaiña, who would bury them in their own tombs. But this idea is very difficult to accept for free descendants, not only because it goes against the local practice of sharing the dead between descent groups (Parker Pearson and Regnier 2018: 52; see also Beaujard 1983: 446–456 for the neighbouring Tanala) but also because relinquishing the children means that 'the descendants are lost' (*very ny taranaka*) – that none of the descendants of the couple will ever be buried in a free descent tomb, and therefore the contact with their free ancestors will be lost forever. The future generations of the couple will never receive the blessings of their free descent ancestors. For free descendants, this would be too high a price to pay.[5]

'Superficial' versus 'deep' uncleanliness

But would it not be possible, I wondered, that *olompotsy* families somehow 'cleanse' *lambo-tapaka* children in order to bury them in their 'clean' tombs with their 'clean' ancestors? This option seemed plausible to me because I had learned that the southern Betsileo make frequent use of *fandiova* (ritual cleansing) to remove various kinds of pollutions, insults and wrongdoings. As I have already mentioned, people who have prolonged and intimate contact with a slave descendant will need to be cleansed because they have become *maloto* (dirty). Is it the same kind of uncleanliness that *andevo* and *lambo-tapaka* children are thought to have?

Despite the fact that people use the words *maloto* and *tsy madio* for both cases, the two types of uncleanliness seem crucially different. My *olompotsy* informants explained that those who have become 'dirty' because of sexual contacts or a prolonged relation with a slave descendant always have the possibility of being cleansed by a ritual if they want to come back to their village and have a chance to be buried in an ancestral tomb. This is because, I was told, their uncleanliness comes from becoming *ota* ('guilty of wrongdoing').[6] Thus, although it does look as if there was some contamination going on, not all the southern Betsileo think that the dirtiness they will get if they have sex or 'set up a hearth' with a slave descendant will come from a supposedly 'contagious' dirtiness of their partner.[7] Rather, they would consider that they become *maloto* because they become *ota* as a consequence of their misbehaviour.

I was told in very general terms that one becomes *ota* when one does something wrong with respect to ancestral customs. Since there are many things that ancestral customs forbid, there are many occasions when one can behave badly and become *ota*. Breaching an ancestral *fady* (taboo) is a particularly frequent way of becoming *ota* and the person is then said to be *ota fady*. Being *ota* can have harmful consequences because ancestors are upset and they may bring bad luck to the guilty person and his/her close relatives. The only way to remedy this situation is to ask the ancestors for forgiveness and to remove the 'dirtiness' that resulted from the wrongdoing.[8] This is usually done by the elder heading the local descent group and, in cases where the consequences of the breach have been particularly serious and have affected people's health, by an *ombiasa* (a traditional healer and diviner – see Legrip-Randriambelo and Regnier 2014). Southern Betsileo rituals of purification (*fandiova*) always require *hazomanga*, a wood to which powerful virtues are attributed.[9] *Hazomanga* is finely grated and mixed with water, silver and plants – all ingredients that are considered to be purifying and to be endowed with curing or protective power. Besides the mix of water, *hazomanga*, silver and plants, the other powerful means to cleanse is the blood of cattle slaughtered for the occasion.

Usually only individuals become *ota* – and thus 'dirty' – because of their misbehaviour. But I was also told that entire families could become guilty and 'unclean' as a consequence of a collective wrongdoing. In such cases the group is said to be *hazo fotsy*. Cases of families being considered *hazo fotsy* seem to be rare nowadays, but people in Beparasy recalled one that occurred in the 1960s–1970s. This is the story I was told. One day someone in Beparasy discovered human faeces in a water spring that nearby villagers used for cooking and drinking. Having heard about this, the *raiamandreny* of Beparasy decided to forbid the use of this water for cooking or drinking. A family living in a *vala* (hamlet) close to the spring did not observe the prohibition and kept on fetching water as usual. Their behaviour was exposed and discussed at a meeting of the *fokonolo* (village council). The *raiamandreny* ruled that the family should be considered *hazo fotsy* from that moment on. The ruling implied that the people of Beparasy could not have close contact with them until they performed the necessary ritual to be cleansed from their guilt. According to my informants, the family was truly ostracised. They could not even visit their relatives or be visited by them. To get out of this situation, the family had to kill a zebu and share the meat with the *fokonolo*.

All the people who had been considered *hazo fotsy* drunk a bit of purifying water mixed with silver, *hazomanga* and plants. A *raiamandreny* pronounced an ancestral invocation and put a drop of the zebu's blood on their foreheads. They were cleansed, and Beparasy villagers were allowed to resume normal relationships with them.

Given the power of rituals to cleanse individuals and entire families, I wondered why it was not possible to cleanse slave descendants and addressed the question to my friend Rakoto Jeannot, the old man I introduced in Chapter 4. He had some authority in Beparasy as a ritual specialist because he had been an *ombiasa* (traditional healer and diviner) during half of his adult life until he converted to Catholicism. He first laughed when he heard me asking whether it was possible to ritually remove the uncleanliness of the Berosaiña and of slave descendants in general. Then he paused, thought about it again for a moment and eventually moved his head in a sign of resignation – no, it was not possible.

It thus seems that an important distinction must be made between a 'superficial' uncleanliness that one can individually or collectively contract by becoming *ota* or *hazo fotsy*, and the 'deep' uncleanliness that the descendants of slaves are thought to have and to transmit to their children. The first kind of uncleanliness was perceived in Beparasy as contingent: it was unequivocally believed that cleansing rituals could remove it. The second kind of uncleanliness, from the point of view of Rakoto Jeannot, seemed impossible to cleanse. I will come back to this important issue in the next chapter.

A social memory of origins

My account would be incomplete without examining how free descendants can obtain reliable knowledge about the social status of their marriage partners. All of the villagers in Beparasy know the slave status of the Berosaiña, but what and how do they know of the ancestry of a person who is not from Beparasy? If free descendants had no way of knowing this, their self-confident assertion that they never marry slave descendants would be nothing more than wishful thinking. When free descent parents first explained to me that they would never marry their children to someone with slave ancestry, I doubted that it was possible, in practice, to obtain reliable information on such a sensitive issue. Recall, moreover, that given bilaterality and hypodescent, for people to have slave status it suffices, in theory, that only one of their ancestors living in 1896 was a former slave who had not been ritually cleansed. Given that today's young Betsileo had a large number of forebears living in 1896, how could one check all of these possibilities? Moreover, during the twentieth century both free and slave descendants moved continuously within and outside the Betsileo area in search of land or paid labour, and the Betsileo population increased from about 408,000 in 1900 (Kottak 1980: 54) to more than two million today. I therefore assumed it would be much more difficult today than in the early twentieth century to ascertain whether someone had slave status or not. My informants, however, told me that it was still fairly easy. 'But how come it is so easy?' I asked, sceptical. 'It's easy,' I was told, because 'we Betsileo all know each other' (*anay Betsileo mifankafankatse aby*).

The reason the Betsileo feel they all know each other, in spite of their mobility and population growth, is in large part due to their keeping of a certain kind of social memory. Social memory in Madagascar has been studied most notably by Jennifer Cole in reference to colonialism (Cole 1998, 2001) and by a number of other authors (e.g., Feeley-Harnik 1991; Graeber 1997; Larson 1999; Walsh 2001; Osterhoudt 2016). What interests me here is how knowledge about status differences, and especially about the cleanliness or uncleanliness of families, is passed on and maintained through generations. In Madagascar, the most common way to approach the social memory of inequality is through its inscription in geography (e.g., Thomas 2006; Evers 2002; Freeman 2013; Somda 2014). Anyone familiar with a particular place can usually 'read' social hierarchy in the landscape or in village organisation. Among the Betsileo, for example, slave descendants who live close to where their former masters lived usually reside in poor dwellings to the west of free descent villages, in the least favourable location according to the Malagasy astrological system (Hébert 1965; Kottak 1980: 137–138; Freeman 2013: 600). As I have already stressed, in Beparasy such analysis is of limited relevance because the Berosaiña do not live peripherally or in locations considered to be inferior. Yet, even if it cannot be deciphered in the landscape, a geography of inequality permeates the cultural practices that produce and reproduce the vast amount of memorial knowledge about status differences that I call the Betsileo 'memory of origins'. Two practices in particular play a crucial role in facilitating the retrieval, learning and remembering of people's 'origins' (*fiavy*, or *fototse*, which can be translated as 'roots' – see Thomas 2006: 32–33): premarital inquiries and genealogical speeches.

The Betsileo undertake extensive investigations of potential marriage partners (Rainihifina 1975: 29; Kottak 1980: 205). Although such premarital inquiries seem common throughout Madagascar, in Beparasy they are taken particularly seriously. When children inform their families that they would like to marry, parents or other senior group members set off, often on foot and sometimes journeying more than 100 kilometres, to visit relatives living close to the native village of the potential future spouse. This information-gathering inquiry can last for weeks. Family members are predominantly concerned with one question: 'What is the ancestry' (*Inona no raza*) of these people? My informants stressed that, when undertaking such an inquiry, it is important to question relatives, even very distant ones, since they will be serious and committed contributors in the process of gathering information, as they, too, are concerned with excluding unclean people from their family. Relatives living close to the village of the family under investigation are most likely to know whether the family is of slave descent, just like everyone in Beparasy knows the slave status of the Berosaiña. If they don't, they may know someone who has a relationship with this family and has attended their funerals. At these funerals this person may have listened to a kind of speech called *tetiharana*.

Tetiharana speeches constitute the other cultural practice that is crucial to the social memory of origins. All Malagasy peoples highly value oratorical performance, and *kabary* (speeches) are pronounced on many occasions, especially (albeit not only) in the highlands (Ochs 1974a; Haring 1992; Jackson 2013). In Beparasy, *tetiharana* are speeches made at the end of funerals to resituate the deceased in descent groups. A *tetiharana* starts with a male ancestor of the deceased, usually a founding ancestor, and alludes only briefly to previous forebears. The name of this first ancestor is mentioned, in addition to his village of origin and his descent group name. Then his wife is named, as well as her descent group and her native village. The name of the village they founded, or their original place of settlement, is recalled, followed by the names of their children. The speech continues to name the descendants of the couple's children over the generations, providing similar information until reaching the deceased. Once the *tetiharana* of the patrilineal founding ancestor has been completed, another *tetiharana* that includes the deceased's mother should follow. Two *tetiharana* are typically given – one on the paternal side and one on the maternal side – but occasionally other *tetiharana* are added; for example, on the sides of the deceased's father's mother or mother's mother. The *tetiharana* recall not only the names of the descendants of two ancestral couples but also their geographical dispersion, mentioning migration, hiving off and residence. Importantly, they also provide information about the marriages of the apical ancestors' descendants, since they name their spouses, their descent group and their native villages.

The *tetiharana* is therefore much more than a genealogical recounting of the dead person's local descent groups: it also offers a mapping of the marital alliances that these two local descent groups have contracted with other groups. Since a *tetiharana* should recall the names of all the descendants of the couple it starts with (i.e., all the members of a cognatic descent group or stock) and their spouses, only a small

Figure 7.1 People gathering in a village for a funeral

number of generations (usually four or five above the deceased) are considered, for reasons of time and complexity. To prepare for their speeches, the *mpikabary* (orators) who are in charge of the *tetiharana* often consult the family history manuscripts that are kept and regularly updated by the heads of descent groups. In addition to the manuscripts and genealogical knowledge kept within families, both *tetiharana* speeches and premarital investigations thus preserve a 'distributed memory' (Salomon 1993) of origins that is stretched over the people who live and regularly attend funerals in a particular region.

Vigilance about origins and its consequences

While attending funerals in Beparasy I was sometimes told that *tetiharana* speeches provide the best opportunities to learn about someone's slave ancestry, or at least to develop suspicions about the origins of some families. It is remarkable that vigilance about origins is not only present when free descendants conduct lengthy investigations about marriage partners or listen to *tetiharana* at funerals. It also pervades everyday forms of communication. One of my informants told me how, when he introduces himself to people who live outside Beparasy and announces the name of his village, he is frequently asked to specify the exact area of the village. In such cases his interlocutors clearly know that in his village in Beparasy there is a Berosaiña family, and they are subtly inquiring about whether he is one of them. My friend, on the other hand, knows very well why his interlocutors are asking these questions and takes care to convince them that he belongs to one of the free descent families and thus has no kinship links with the Berosaiña, in spite of living in the same village. However, he does not answer the question directly if he suspects that his interlocutors are slave descendants themselves, so as not to offend them. In conversations of this kind, people show a high level of vigilance when investigating people's origins in order to find out about each other's social status and update their knowledge of the distribution of slave descent families in the Betsileo countryside.

Slave descendants are well aware that free descendants are extremely vigilant about origins, and this explains their frequent elusiveness about family history. Elinor Ochs notes that in Betafo, central Vakinankaratra (highland Madagascar), slave descent households do not usually possess family history manuscripts – unlike nobles and commoners – and 'prefer not to refer to their familial histories' (Ochs 1974a: 219). Although she does not explain why, it is easy to guess that this is because slave descent households are aware that publicly recalling their family history would provide food for thought to free descendants, who would find confirmation of the slave status they have already ascribed to them. For slave descendants, public disclosure of family history would contradict their hope of someday shedding their slave status. It is tempting to see, in their reluctance to talk about family history, a spontaneous strategy of resistance to being categorised as 'slaves' (*andevo*). This strategy, however, is doomed to remain unsuccessful because by not disclosing their familial history, or by omitting certain details, a family can quickly become suspicious.

When Beparasy free descendants conduct premarital investigations they might fail, in spite of their efforts, to obtain reliable information on someone's ancestry. The person's origins will be then judged as unclear (*tsy mazava*). The origins may be considered unclear when, for various reasons, the parents are unable to ascertain clean origins or when serious doubts are raised about a family's cleanliness. In that case, as with families clearly identified as unclean, parents typically refuse the marriage for fear of discovering the slave ancestry of their affines at a later stage. Thus, in practice, a family who is considered to have unclear origins faces almost the same difficulties as a family with a publicly recognized slave ancestry and unclean origins. This makes it even more important for free descent families to take every precaution to preserve their clean reputation – this is the third meaning of the phrase 'if we marry them, we will become slaves too' mentioned earlier. For slave descendants, the fact that free descendants prefer to avoid people with unclear origins makes it almost impossible to escape slave status by hiding or remaining elusive about one's family history. Of course, it is possible for free descendants to make mistakes and wrongly judge a family's origins to be clean. Such mistakes, however, can only be short term, since in the long run the widely distributed social memory of origins inexorably catches people up. Indeed, in Beparasy I heard a number of stories about bilateral marriages that free descendants had started 'by mistake' with slave descent people from outside Beparasy because they had not been vigilant enough in their premarital investigations. They had discovered only at a later stage of the marriage process that the other side had an unclean or unclear reputation. In such cases, free descent families would step back, stop the formal exchanges of the marriage process, and cut all relations with the couple and the now unwelcome affines.

Because of their role in the settlement of Beparasy, their relative wealth and their rooting in a *tanindrazana* (ancestral land), the Berosaiña are more fortunate than the slave descendants mentioned by Ochs. As we have seen, like free descendants they have family history manuscripts. Randriatsoa, their main *mpikabary* (orator), who is regarded by all Beparasy villagers as an excellent one, also acts as the *andevohova* representative of the Berosaiña group and frequently speaks in public. In his long and elaborated speeches he never misses an occasion to refer to the arrival of Rakamisy on the land of Beparasy, and to stress that all the descendants of the four men are relatives (*havana*) since their ancestors once lived together in the same village (i.e., in the fortified hilltop village). Thanks to the role of Rakamisy, the Berosaiña have a locally prestigious family history to tell and they can speak proudly about it in public. This is a double-edged sword, however, especially when it comes to *tetiharana* speeches. When they mention the names of the places where several generations of Berosaiña have married, the free descendants who attend the funeral can recognise the names of villages exclusively inhabited by slave descendants, or those notorious for having some slave descent families living there. This is because, as I have explained, most Berosaiña have married other slave descendants in the regions neighbouring Beparasy. By not shying away from mentioning these marriages – in spite of the fact that this indicates their alliances with other slave descent families – the Berosaiña thus provide precious information to free descendants about the marriage networks of slave descendants in the region, which adds up to their knowledge of places where their children should not marry. The village I mentioned at the beginning of Chapter 5 – the one where the *vadipaisa* was held and where Andry found a girlfriend – is one of these villages outside Beparasy where the Berosaiña have found a number of spouses over several generations.

Conclusion: the paradox of 'marrying equals'

In this chapter I have explained that Beparasy villagers, because they are descendants of *olompotsy* (commoners), are very cautious of not marrying 'people who do not have the same ancestry' (*olo tsy mitovy raza*). They say that if they marry descendants of nobles or descendants of slaves they will become 'slaves' in both cases. They do not like marrying nobles because they feel that in such cases they will not have equal relationships with them due to the 'superiority' of noble descent; this, they fear, can potentially lead to conflicts and disputes between families, which they prefer to avoid. On the other hand, they do not want to marry slave descendants like the Berosaiña because, if they make alliances through marriage with them, their descent group will risk becoming progressively identified as a slave descent group too by other free descendants. Were they to be considered so, it would become increasingly difficult for them to marry people other than slave descendants.

Moreover, the offspring of the mixed couple will be ascribed the status of 'slave' by the application of a rule of hypodescent. The offspring of this couple will therefore be considered *tsy madio* (unclean) as well as *very* (lost) for the group of commoner descent, with none of the mixed couple's descendants being allowed to be buried in the free descent ancestral tombs. This too goes against another egalitarian principle, namely that families should share the dead children of a couple to receive at least some of them in their ancestral tombs. Accepting a bilateral marriage with the Berosaiña – or another slave descent family – would therefore be very costly for the descent groups of Beparasy, especially because they think that the uncleanliness of the children from such a marriage will be impossible to cleanse. The gathering of information about one's origins and alliances is thus a crucial issue when a marriage is at stake. Investigations are made possible by the social memory of origins and alliances, which is kept alive by the practice of giving *tetiharana* speeches at funerals and conducting extensive investigations before marriage.

I have suggested that descendants of commoners in Beparasy do not like marrying people who do not belong to the same status group because they are very sensitive to the idea of equality between allied families or, to put it differently, because they have egalitarian views on marriage: they do not like to marry people who are *ambony* (superior, i.e. nobles) or *ambany* (inferior, i.e. slaves). This may sound like something of a paradox. The apparent paradox lies in the fact that, by refusing marriage with other status groups, and especially the slave descendants, Beparasy commoners perpetuate the existence of the hierarchy and the inequalities that they seek to avoid. In spite of their dislike of marriages with descendants of nobles, bilateral marriages between descendants of commoners and descendants of nobles do occur and they do not pose intractable problems, unlike those with slave descendants. Families of commoner descent can cope with these unequal marriages even though they are not their preferred choice. A marriage with a slave descendant remains, on the contrary, unacceptable. What we still need to understand, however, is why slave descendants are considered as irredeemably *maloto* (dirty) and *tsy madio* (unclean) by Beparasy commoners. I dedicate the next chapter to this crucial question.

Notes

1 Recall that in Chapter 4 Randriatsoa said: 'We marry whoever we want.' Yet towards the end of the interview we came back to the issue of marriage prohibitions and he explained that they (the Berosaiña) avoid marrying people who have the reputation, after death, of waking up as *kinoly* – a kind of 'living dead' (see Astuti 2011). I suspect, however, that this response was provoked by my repeated questions and that Randriatsoa felt somewhat forced to answer that the Berosaiña too can be 'choosy' when it comes to marriage.

2 The idiom of slavery to mean unequal exchanges or relationships or historical situations seems to be widespread in Madagascar. Rafidinarivo (2000) underlines its constant use in economic transactions. Graeber (2007: 49) stresses that slavery is an idiom used to talk about all kinds of power relations. See also Sharp (2002: Chapters 4–6), Cole (2010: 57, 142), Jackson (2013: Chapter 6) and Sodikoff (2012: 66–67).

3 Cases of mixed marriages between nobles and commoners seem to have been rare in Beparasy and I could not find many in the genealogies I collected. As I have already explained, *hova* (noble) families never resided in Beparasy but in Ambatofotsy and Ambalamasina. I met a few Beparasy villagers who had some of these *hova* among their forebears. The grandfather of one of my friends, for example, had married a *hova* woman from Ambalamasina. It was in no way a shameful marriage and my friend was rather proud of telling me about the noble origins of his grandmother, even though, in accordance with the rules of status ascription I will explain later in this chapter, he was not considered by Beparasy villagers as a *hova* but as an *olompotsy*.

4 I did not hear of precedents in Beparasy, but people explained they could become sick or experience various sorts of problems because of ancestral wrath. Interestingly, the mixing of different ancestries is the main reason

why the communal ordeal described by David Graeber (2007) in western Imerina was considered so disastrous. In this case, the earth of noble and slave descent tombs had been mixed in the ritual.

5 As will be illustrated in the next chapter, another possible option open to the free descent side would be to claim the corpses of the mixed couple's children and bury them in the ground, close to but outside the ancestral tomb. But this compromise is considered unsatisfactory by free descendants.

6 The word *ota* was chosen by Christian missionaries to translate 'sin' in the Bible. According to Richardson (1885), the word, both a noun and an adjective, means: 'Guilt, sin; guilty, sinful, mistaken, in error.' The verb *manota* means 'to err, to make a mistake, not to go in the right direction' (Ruud 1960: 265) or 'to commit sin, to transgress, to violate' (Richardson 1885). *Ota* and *manota* have, therefore, a high moral meaning since they mean transgressing the rules of society.

7 Some scholars have argued that a belief in contagion is the main reason why commoner descendants think they will become 'unclean' when they have affairs with (or marry) slave descendants (e.g., Evers 2002: 53, 70).

8 The association of ideas of cleanliness and uncleanliness with those of morality and immorality is common to many societies. For a classic account on these issues, see Douglas (1966). Dubois (1938: 860–873) explains that, for the Betsileo, moral wrongdoing is a sort of disorder which leads to 'a kind of poisoning' (ibid.: 861) and will have to be cleansed.

9 The *hazomanga* was once the sacrificial post that was found in every Betsileo *vala* (hamlet), but Christian missionaries succeeded in eradicating its presence because of 'idolatry'. Today, *hazomanga* consists of a small piece of wood that family elders keep for all ritual occasions where its powerful powers are needed.

8 Essentialism: evidence, development and transmission

> Why is it that one can do many things together with a slave descendant but cannot be buried in the same tomb?
>
> Because, for example, you are an *olompotsy* and I am an *andevo*. I work hard, I clean the dirt (*ny maloto*) everywhere …
>
> But this was in the past. Their descendants don't do that anymore.
>
> Yes, but it's the spirit (*c'est l'esprit*), they are the descendants of the persons who took the dirt.
>
> Are they still considered dirty (*maloto*)?
>
> Yes, they are dirty.
>
> Even though they don't do dirty things?
>
> Yes, that's it.
>
> (Conversation with an elderly woman in Beparasy)

As previous chapters have made clear, in spite of the actively maintained fiction of equality there is an important social divide in Beparasy: a divide between *olo madio* (clean people) and *olo tsy madio* (unclean people). At least since the pioneering work of Durkheim and Mauss (1903), anthropologists have been interested in categorisation and classification. While classification refers to the way categories are related to each other, categorisation is the process of sorting 'things' into groups (categories) based on similar characteristics. Both are evidence of what Roy Ellen (2006: 1) aptly calls the 'categorical impulse', namely the human mind's impulsive capacity to create and manipulate categories that are 'asserting absolutely'. The way Beparasy commoners thought of slave descendants aroused my interest in categorisation, and particularly in one aspect of it: the fact that some categories can be essentialised.

This chapter deals with social essentialism and the essentialisation of slave descendants by free descendants. To explore these issues I add a long-focus lens (i.e., a 'cognitive' lens) to the wide-angle and normal lenses I have used so far. By doing so I seek to bridge my ethnographic and historical analysis, on the one hand, and research on essentialism in cognitive science, on the other. What follows can therefore be viewed as the most experimental chapter of the book. It is experimental in the sense that I experiment in the practice of ethnographic writing by weaving together ethnography, history and cognition. It is also experimental in a more literal sense because I describe and analyse a field experiment I carried out in Beparasy.

Social essentialism

I was frequently told by the *olompotsy* (commoners) in Beparasy that nowadays '*mitovy aby*' ('everyone is like everyone else'). This statement was meant to stress the equality of economic conditions between the *olompotsy* and the *andevo* who live among them, i.e. the Berosaiña. Yet the *olompotsy* were also quick to clarify that it is strictly forbidden for them to marry the *andevo*. The issue of marriage, my informants often added, is their only problem with the *andevo*. As we have seen, a number of sociological and historical reasons account for the *olompotsy*'s reluctance to marry the Berosaiña and slave descendants more generally, but one of the most striking aspects of the problem is that the *olompotsy* call them *olo tsy madio* (unclean people), or *olo maloto* (dirty people). A number of euphemisms are also used to refer to slave descendants, mainly because the *olompotsy* are afraid to be fined an ox for using insulting words, but in secretive conversations *olo tsy madio* and *olo maloto* are by far the most commonly employed terms.

Whereas a minority of my *olompotsy* informants explained they would be polluted (and could become sick) if they shared a plate or a glass with an *andevo*, most of them considered that it is only through intimate and regular contacts that this can happen. People often illustrated the issue of pollution by referring to the case of mixed unions, i.e. *olompotsy–andevo* couples setting up a *tokantrano* ('hearth in a house') together in spite of the prohibition. As I have explained, in such cases *olompotsy* families repudiate their members who have breached the prohibition and exclude them from the ancestral tomb, and this exclusion is arguably the most serious social sanction for the southern Betsileo. But another important aspect of the problem is that, in the eyes of their *olompotsy* relatives, the excluded members have become unclean through sexual contact with their *andevo* partner. Consequently, if they want to be buried in the ancestral tomb – for example, if their union breaks up and they go back to their family asking for forgiveness – they will have to be cleansed through a costly ritual involving the killing of an ox.

This issue of pollution becomes even more sensitive if the mixed couple produces children. In that case, the couple's children are also considered to be unclean by the *olompotsy* side, but, unlike their *olompotsy* parent, the children cannot be cleansed through a ritual because their *olompotsy* relatives view them as irredeemably unclean – recall the distinction between superficial and deep uncleanliness discussed in the preceding chapter. From the *olompotsy*'s point of view, therefore, the couple's unclean children can only be buried in *andevo* tombs or, alternatively, in a separate tomb that the *olompotsy* build for them. The *olompotsy* thus seem to think that *andevo* parents inevitably transmit their uncleanliness to their children.

When I asked my *olompotsy* informants why the Berosaiña were unclean, they explained that slaves in the past had to deal with *zavatra maloto* (dirty things) all the time. When asked what kind of dirt, they almost unanimously stressed the daily handling of *tay* (excrements) and other soiling tasks such as cleaning the cattle pen. Some explained that the blood of slave descendants had become unclean through their frequent contact with dirt (see also Evers 2002: 70). *Olompotsy* in Beparasy thus seemed to consider that *andevo* have something that cannot be observed directly, but which makes them intrinsically unclean and permanently bestows on them the identity of unclean people.[1] Their uncleanliness – conceptualised either vaguely or somewhat more precisely in terms of unclean blood – seems to be conceived by the *olompotsy* as if it were lodged 'deep inside' them. Moreover, as I have already explained, the *olompotsy* hold that the uncleanliness transmitted by the *andevo* parent to the children of mixed unions is impossible to cleanse. All this seems to bear a clear signature of psychological essentialism.

The term 'essentialism' is employed somewhat differently across different disciplines and thus it is useful to explain what I mean by it. In sociology, anthropology and other social sciences, essentialist views are often opposed to constructionist approaches (see Sayer 1997). Social scientists having 'essentialist positions', for example on race or gender, are those who consider some traits to be fixed and invariable, as opposed to being culturally, socially or historically constructed. This is not the way I use 'essentialism' here. I am using this term in the specific sense of 'psychological essentialism' as it has been discussed in cognitive, developmental and social psychology in the last three decades. Psychological essentialism is a claim about how people think, not a theoretical position in social science or philosophical debates.

The term 'psychological essentialism' was coined by Medin and Ortony (1989). It refers to people's tendency to believe that an entity or a category has an underlying essence that determines its identity (Haslam and Abou-Abdallah 2015). Developmental psychologists have documented young children's essentialist thinking about biological and social categories (see Gelman 2003, 2004; Gelman and Legare 2011), and a growing body of experimental studies has provided evidence of essentialism's pervasiveness as a cognitive bias across cultures (e.g., Mahalingam 1998; Astuti, Solomon and Carey 2004; Rhodes and Gelman 2009; Birnbaum et al. 2010). In anthropology, psychological essentialism has been notably discussed in relation to ethnobiology (Atran 1998), racism (Hirschfeld 1996; Hale 2015), ethnicity (Gil-White 2001), language (McIntosh 2005, 2009) and shamanism (Stépanoff 2014, 2015).

Social psychologists' interest in the essentialisation of social categories dates back to the work of Gordon Allport (1954). In a seminal article, Rothbart and Taylor (1992: 12) suggested that 'whereas social categories are in reality more like human artifacts than natural kinds, they are often perceived as more like natural kinds than human artifacts' and, like natural kinds, they are often assumed to have an underlying essence. This line of research linking essentialism and natural kind-ness has been widely followed in social psychology to investigate a variety of domains (including gender, religion, sexual orientation, personality and political groups – see the studies in Yzerbyt, Judd and Corneille 2004). Studies have shown that psychological essentialism is associated with social stereotypes (e.g., Bastian and Haslam 2006) and prejudice (e.g., Haslam, Rothschild and Ernst 2002). Others (e.g., Yzerbyt, Corneille and Estrada 2001) have examined the relations between essentialism and entitativity (i.e., the perception of a strong degree of similarity and organisation among the members of a group). More recently, some scholars have argued that 'psychological essentialism about social categories' (Prentice and Miller 2007) – now often referred to as 'social essentialism' – should be strictly differentiated from natural kind-ness and entitativity, and restricted to the attribution of an underlying essence to social groups (Demoulin, Leyens and Yzerbyt 2006). For these authors, what matters is whether groups are perceived as 'forced social categories' (i.e., categories whose membership is imposed on people) or 'chosen social categories'(i.e., categories whose membership is dependent on group members' personal choice). According to them, both categories can be equally essentialised, but forced social categories are essentialised because they are perceived as highly 'natural' groups, whereas chosen social categories are essentialised because they are perceived as highly entitative.

Slave descendants in the southern Betsileo region are clearly perceived as a forced social category by the *olompotsy*, who are very well aware that this inferior status is not the slave descendants' choice and that this identity is imposed on them. Moreover, the slave descendants' forced endogamy – a consequence of the fact the *olompotsy* strictly refuse to marry them – strengthens the perception that they are a *karaza olo hafa* (different kind of people) and a 'natural' category.

A field experiment

In order to explore the issue of whether *olompotsy* essentialise slave descendants, I conducted a field experiment during a follow-up stay in Beparasy from September to October 2012 and in April 2013. I told people three stories about an adoption, a cleansing ritual and a blood transfusion that focused on either an unclean or a clean fictional character (see Appendix). These stories were followed by the following question: 'In your opinion, has this person become clean [or unclean] or has s/he remained unclean [clean]?' The tasks were designed in such a way that the stories sounded familiar, and the question seemed relevant and easily understandable. The question was followed by an open conversation during which I asked people to explain their answer.[2] Each of the tasks found their rationale in issues that arose from my long-term participant observation fieldwork in Beparasy.

The idea of using an adoption task came to mind while I was in the field, after I had heard about a kind of 'natural experiment' bearing much resemblance to adoption stories used in cognitive psychology. It concerned two villagers who had arrived in Beparasy as babies in the 1960s. As I was told it, a man from the eastern coast had proposed the babies for adoption because they were twins. Twins are thought to bring bad luck among some populations of the east coast of Madagascar and are therefore often abandoned by their parents. A childless couple of Beparasy decided to take these two babies to raise them as their children. In 2008–2010 the twins were about fifty years old. A member of the local descent group of the twins' adoptive father told me that there had been on-going discussions within his family about whether the twins could be buried in the ancestral tomb. When I first heard the story I thought that these difficulties had to do with the reputation of bad luck attached to twins, but I was told that the Betsileo do not believe that twins bring bad luck. The problem was of a different nature: at stake was the fact that nobody knew the origins (*fiavy*) of the twins and what their *raza* (ancestry) might be. The fear, I was told, was that they might be unclean persons, i.e. slave descendants. The matter was not yet settled at the time of my last visit – indeed, it will be definitely settled only at the time of the twins' deaths – but in the family the prevailing opinion was that the twins, as well as their children, should be buried outside of the ancestral tomb as a precaution.

Adoption and fosterage are very frequent practices in Madagascar, reflecting the 'fluidity' and 'optativity' often attributed to Malagasy kinship in general (Southall 1986; Kottak 1986). A person's affiliation with a particular kin group and social identity is not fixed at birth but changes throughout life; it is only fixed at the time of death, when this person is placed in an ancestral tomb (Bloch 1993). Adoption and switched-at-birth tasks have already been used in Madagascar to explore issues of biological inheritance among Zafimaniry (Bloch, Solomon and Carey 2001) and Vezo adults and children (Astuti, Solomon and Carey 2004). My aim was to use an adoption scenario to explore essentialism since I thought that if *olompotsy* had an essentialist view they would hold, contrary to ideas of fluid social identity, that a baby of slave descent adopted and raised by a free descent family would not become a clean person in adulthood. On the basis of the real-life story about the twins, I expected that a number of *olompotsy* would provide such a negative answer, although the fact that there was an on-going discussion within the twins' adoptive family indicated some degree of disagreement. The adoption task's main goal was thus to get an idea of the proportion of respondents who would hold an essentialist view.

The cleansing ritual task had a similar goal. As I have explained above, the children of mixed *olompotsy–andevo* couples are considered by the *olompotsy* side to be irredeemably unclean; for this reason they cannot be buried in their tombs. Moreover, my *olompotsy* informants insisted on the impossibility of cleansing these children. I found this particularly striking because the southern Betsileo make frequent use of rituals to remove various kinds of pollution, and because southern Betsileo rituals for cleansing slaves after manumission are attested in oral histories. I was thus interested in knowing whether contemporary southern Betsileo would think that, under some specific conditions, a ritual could be powerful enough to cleanse a slave descendant. I made up a story where a young man of slave descent is in love with a free descent girl. Since they cannot marry, the young man decides to ask a ritual specialist to perform a cleansing ritual so that he becomes a clean person.

I have already mentioned the alleged uncleanliness of the slave descendants' blood. The idea of using a blood transfusion story came to mind because I knew that when *olompotsy* create fictive kinship links with slave descendants through a *vakirà* ritual they do not drink their blood – as it normally should be for this ritual – but replace it with rum, out of fear of being polluted. Among the southern Betsileo, as in many other cultural contexts (see Carsten 2011), *ra* (blood) is an important symbol. During ceremonies the blood of slaughtered cattle is ritually used to bless, cleanse and protect people as well as material things such as houses. The goal of the blood transfusion task was therefore different from the previous ones since it examined the possibility, for a clean person, to become 'deeply' unclean after receiving blood from an unclean person. In other words, the issue I wanted to explore with this task was one of extremely serious pollution through blood mixing.[3]

Each task had two slightly different versions: the second version (which I call task #2) was identical to the first version (task #1) except for one sentence added at the end of the story, which mentioned that local people had reached a consensus with regards to the question under consideration (see the additional sentences in the Appendix). This consensus consisted of the view opposite to the one articulated by the majority of respondents in task #1. The goal was therefore to see whether respondents to task #2 would be sensitive to the consensus and significantly change their answers in comparison with the results of task #1.

All the interviews took place in people's houses. We tried to avoid bias in the selection of respondents by choosing randomly a direction everyday (e.g., south) and by walking in this direction from one hamlet to another in search of potential participants. The age of respondents varied from about twenty to about seventy and for each task we kept a balance across gender. All the participants were *olompotsy*. The results of the adoption task are given in Figure 8.1. All the results are presented in rounded percentages for comparative purposes. For this task we had twenty-four respondents for the first version (Adoption #1) and eighteen for the second version with the consensus (Adoption #2).

The responses to the first version of the task show that a large proportion (seventy-five per cent) of the participants judged that an unclean baby raised by a clean couple does not become a clean adult person. In other words, a significant majority thought that the baby could not become clean through adoption by clean parents and long-term affiliation with a free descent group in a free descent village. In the discussion, many stressed that 'nothing could be done' for the unclean child. I take this as evidence that most *olompotsy* essentialise *andevo*. Some of the respondents who judged that the baby had

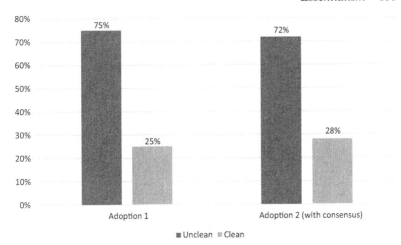

Figure 8.1 Results of the adoption task

become a clean adult justified their choice by explaining that the child 'follows the ancestral history (*tantarandraza*) of his/her [adoptive] parents'. I understand this as meaning that these *olompotsy* overrode the essentialist construal of 'slaves' that prevails among their peers and gave more weight to their 'fluid' conceptions of kinship and identity. Others justified their answer by referring to Christian beliefs and stressing that there were no such differences between people.

Interestingly, the results show that the mention of a consensus on the view that the adopted baby had become a clean adult person had no significant effect on the pattern of the responses (χ^2 (1) = .04 and p = .84, so we cannot reject the null hypothesis because the p-value is greater than .05). This apparently suggests that essentialist thinking might be impervious to what other people in the village would think. Moreover, the similarity with the results obtained with the first version of the task seems to indicate that *olompotsy* consistently essentialise the *andevo*.

The cleansing ritual task provided very similar responses and thus also showed that a large proportion of *olompotsy* essentialise slave descendants (see Figure 8.2). We had eighteen respondents for Cleansing ritual #1 and twenty-four for Cleansing ritual #2.

A large majority of respondents held that the most powerful cleansing ritual one can think of in the southern Betsileo context (and which was used in the past for cleansing slaves) could not cleanse present-day slave descendants. Interestingly, during the discussions people stressed that such a cleansing could not be performed successfully today

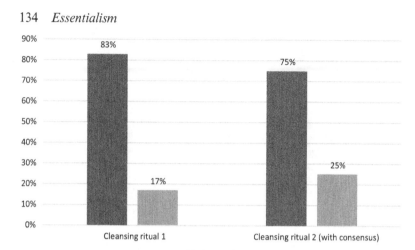

Figure 8.2 Results of the cleansing ritual task

because, they explained, the *hova* have lost the power they had in the past. The two reasons they gave for this loss was French colonisation, which put the *hova*'s role as rulers to an end, and the *hova*'s inter-marriages with *olompotsy*, which resulted in corrupting *ny maha-hova* ('what makes them *hova*') – recall the discussion with a free descent elder and his daughter in the previous chapter. These comments were made even though I had anticipated the second reason and mentioned in the script that the ritual specialist was a *hova tena hova* (*hova mbola tsy nanambady vohitse*), i.e. a 'noble really noble (nobles who have not yet married commoners)'.[4] Moreover, as in the previous task, the mention of a consensus did not seem to have any significant effect (for this task, χ^2 (1) = .04 and p = .51, so here again the p-value is greater than .05 and we cannot reject the null hypothesis).

The results for the first version of the blood transfusion task do not show a clear preference for one response over the other, and their interpretation is thus less straightforward (see Figure 8.3). We had twenty-four respondents for Blood transfusion #1 and eighteen for Blood transfusion #2.

The running of the two versions of the task and the discussions that followed provided interesting insights nonetheless. First, it should be noted that, unlike the other tasks, the blood transfusion story seemed unfamiliar to the participants. They clearly knew about the medical act of transfusing blood, but, because the region is far away from the closest hospital and most people in Beparasy have never been hospitalised, the question sounded less familiar than those about adoption,

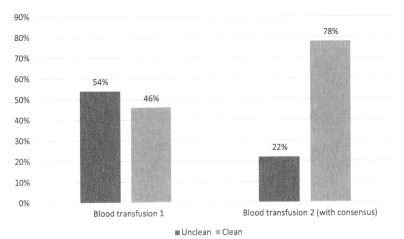

Figure 8.3 Results of the blood transfusion task

marriage or cleansing ritual. Whereas people understood the other stories as a real possibility and could answer the question quickly, during this task they expressed surprise at the question and took some time before giving their judgement. Moreover, during the discussions it became clear that their responses depended on their interpretation of the task's question. Most of them answered that Rakoto, the character who received blood, had become unclean if they interpreted the question to be about the kind of 'superficial' pollution that I have already mentioned in the case of mixed couples and which can be cleansed through a ritual. The other half answered that Rakoto had not become unclean if they interpreted the question to be about Rakoto's transformation into a slave descendant and 'deeply unclean' person. Therefore, once the answers are put in the context of the discussions that followed the task, it becomes apparent that only a handful of respondents thought that Rakoto had become as unclean as an *andevo*. Most of them judged instead that Rakoto was only superficially polluted after receiving the unclean blood. They explained that he could be cleansed by a ritual and buried in an ancestral tomb.

Unlike the previous tasks, the mention of a consensus on the view that Rakoto is still clean after the transfusion seemed to have a significant effect (χ^2 (1) = 4.36 and p = .04, so the p-value is less than .05 and we can reject the null hypothesis). As I have just explained, the words 'become unclean' in the task's question could mean either 'become superficially polluted' or 'become deeply polluted' (i.e., become an *andevo*). I would therefore argue that the difference of results between the two versions of the task means that the respondents were somewhat perplexed about how to interpret my question and therefore most of them followed the consensus mentioned in the second version, while in the first version indecision was predominant. Overall, the results of the tasks suggest that, for most respondents, receiving unclean blood from a slave descendant does not cause a deep and irreparable pollution. I interpret this as meaning that, in spite of what *olompotsy* sometimes told me, they do not perceive the alleged unclean blood of slave descendants as the causal factor for their uncleanliness. I would rather argue that the *olompotsy* tend to conceptualise the 'inner essence' of slave descendants in terms of blood because it is a bodily substance that is particularly 'good to think', to use the famous phrase of Lévi-Strauss (1963: 89). As Medin and Ortony (1989: 184–185) argued, psychological essentialism is a placeholder notion: one can believe that a category has an essence without knowing exactly what the essence is.

Essentialism in historical perspective

The data obtained with the field experiments confirmed what I had inferred from my ethnographic observations, namely that present-day *olompotsy* essentialise slave descendants. One of the main points that emerged is the extent to which people hold that the slave descendants' unclean status is irredeemable. The conversations with respondents also confirmed my intuition that the essentialist construal of *andevo* needs to be understood in a historical perspective. In this section I would like to argue that before abolition slaves must have been differently conceptualised to how their descendants are today, and suggest that after abolition a subtle but important conceptual change occurred in the way southern Betsileo *olompotsy* think of the *andevo*.

As far as we know, slavery is probably a very ancient institution in Madagascar (Regnier and Somda 2019). It increased in scale, however, with the arrival of Europeans and their need for slave labour in the Indian Ocean (Allen 2014), as well as with the rise of the Merina empire in Madagascar (Campbell 2005). From the end of the eighteenth century and during most of the nineteenth century, enslavement became so widespread in the Malagasy highlands that commoners and nobles alike were continuously at risk of being enslaved (Larson 2000). In consequence, everyone was at risk of someday becoming a slave. Virtually every individual – noble or commoner, rich or poor, man or woman, adult or child – could be captured and sold, being the victim of a local war, of a raid operated by the bands of *mpangalatr'olo* ('men's thieves') that plagued the highlands until the end of the nineteenth century, or of ill-intentioned neighbours who wanted to make some money. As Pier Larson writes, 'By 1820, perhaps as many as 70 per cent of highland Malagasy households experienced the loss of a member to the export slave trade' (Larson 1999: 341).

At the same time, in the pre-abolition era, slaves could be freed through a legal process and could rid themselves of the unclean status associated with enslavement through ritual cleansing. As I have already mentioned – and illustrated with the case of Rakamisy – slaves could work in addition to their duties, save money and buy themselves back from their masters (Rakoto 1997; Campbell 1998). The ubiquity, frequency and the very possibility of these changes of status make it very likely that free people regarded slave status as a contingent rather than a fixed status. People must have conceived enslavement as a shameful yet reversible condition, the uncleanliness of which could be removed if one could do the necessary ritual. In other words, the uncleanliness of slaves was probably not viewed as immutable and irredeemable. Furthermore, in pre-abolition times the category of *andevo* was not necessarily perceived as a 'forced social category'. Oral histories attest that frequently poor *olompotsy* proposed their own enslavement to the *hova* because their slaves had better living conditions than the poorest segments of the free peasantry. It is therefore likely that the category *andevo* was, in pre-abolition times, not perceived as a natural kind, as it is today. The category of slaves was probably not perceived as highly entitative either: given the precariousness of their condition and the diversity of their trajectories, *andevo* were probably viewed more as a collection of individuals than as a coherent group, in spite of the practice of giving them an *anarampoko* (group name) that I explain in Chapter 3.

I found historical evidence supporting my argument in a document that was only recently discovered in the archives of a Norwegian missionary (see Razafindralambo 2008) and translated and published by Gueunier, Noiret and Raharinjanahary (2005). The published material consists of three texts. In the first, a southern Betsileo man named Isambo of noble origin explains how he was kidnapped as a child in Betsileo country, brought to Antananarivo to be sold on the slave market and then finally bought by Lutheran missionaries, who freed him. Isambo became a primary school teacher in Fianarantsoa. In the second text, Isambo tells the story of how, after many difficulties, he managed to contact his relatives in the southern Betsileo region of Ikalamavony, ten years after having been kidnapped. The third part of the document is a manuscript entitled 'The customs to accomplish to "wash the tongue," or to give the blessing to a child who has been rejected but will become a child again' (literal translation of: *Ny fomba fanao raha manoza lela na hanao tsiodrano zaza nariana ka haverina ho zanaka indray*). According to the editors, although the manuscript is not signed it is very likely to have been written by Isambo, as indicated by the resemblance of the handwriting with Isambo's autobiographical accounts mentioned earlier and by the use of Betsileo dialect in parts of the description (Gueunier, Noiret and Raharinjanahary 2005: 72–73).

Isambo wrote his account shortly before the abolition of slavery. The ritual of *manoza lela* ('washing the tongue') – a variant of the *mikaodela* ('scratching of the tongue') that was described to me in Beparasy – is presented as a ritual that could be performed with two different aims: to reintegrate people who had been freed from slavery, or to reintegrate children who had been previously repudiated by their parents. Thus, in both cases, the cleansing ritual serves the purpose of reintegrating an individual into a local descent group and, consequently, into a wider local community of kinsmen.

Isambo's account provides evidence that slaves were indeed considered as dirty and extremely diminished persons, because of the inferior tasks they had to perform for their owners, because they had to forgo their own ancestral taboos and because they had to serve other people that should have been their equals or their inferiors. Yet Isambo's detailed description of the ritual also shows beyond doubt that it was always possible to ritually remove the deep uncleanliness associated with enslavement. Indeed, it seems to indicate that, at that time, people thought these cleansing rituals were all-powerful. As the speech reported by Isambo states, 'there is nothing dirty that [sacred] water cannot remove' (*tsy misy maloto tsy ho afaky ny rano*). In the description, when the ritual performer put sacred water on the head of the person that needed to be cleansed he says:

> Although you served others who were people like you, although you did what your ancestors did not, although you were subject every day to the imprecations of your master, we cleanse you with this water. However you were soiled, may the misfortune not follow you, may the fault not follow you. We pray for you with this water [...] so that you become 'nicely accomplished' [*vita soa*], so that you become 'well accomplished' [*vita tsara*].
>
> (Gueunier, Noiret and Raharinjanahary 2005: 167–168, my translation)

At the end of his account, Isambo comments:

> It is when all this has been accomplished that his/her family can count him/her again as one of its members, and that it is allowed to bury him/her in the ancestral tomb. Because as long as this ceremony of 'washing the tongue' has not been performed he/she is not allowed to be buried in the ancestral tomb and he/she cannot marry someone of the same 'kind' [*karazana*] in the local community.
>
> (Ibid.: 168–169, my translation)

Isambo's description of the ritual of *manoza lela* shows that free southern Betsileo did not think of slaves as people who could not fully regain their free and clean status once they had lost it. To my knowledge, there is no historical evidence that a strong stigma or taint comparable to that of today's slave descendants was attached to having been a slave during part of one's life or to having ancestors who had been enslaved. As indicated by Isambo, former slaves were considered as suitable marriage partners by the 'clean' local community as soon as they had performed the cleansing ritual and had been reintegrated into their descent group. I would therefore assume that, provided they went through the appropriate ritual, any kind of formerly enslaved persons were completely redeemed, did not suffer from any prejudice and discrimination because of their personal history and did not 'transmit' any uncleanliness to their children. If so, this means that the crucial features of the essentialism observed today were absent.

Historical development of essentialism

If I am right, the essentialist construal became entrenched only after the abolition of slavery. An important shift seems to have taken place – but why? I suggest that the explanation for such a shift is to be found in the context of the colonial abolition of slavery. To understand why the abolition might have significantly modified the way southern Betsileo people think about slaves, former slaves and their descendants, it is necessary to go back to its circumstances and most immediate consequences.

On 30 September 1895, a French expeditionary force entered Antananarivo. The military takeover was soon followed by the annexation of Madagascar, on 6 August 1896. On 27 September 1896, only one year after the French troops had reached Antananarivo, slavery was abolished and hundreds of thousands of slaves – perhaps as many as

500,000 (Deschamps 1972: 221) – were set free in a total population of about three million Malagasy (Campbell 2005: 136). 'In a fit of pique,' the resident governor, Hippolyte Laroche, had decreed the abolition just before leaving his office to Joseph Gallieni (Randrianja and Ellis 2009: 157).

The question of whether the French administration should immediately emancipate the slaves or adopt a more careful approach, abolishing slavery step by step, had been discussed in the French parliament in June 1896. The context was particularly difficult, since the French occupiers faced an anticolonial rebellion. Opponents of an immediate abolition feared an increase in social disorder that could damage French interests in Madagascar (Jacob 1997: 262). In spite of these concerns, the parliament unanimously voted in favour of an immediate abolition. Up to this point, resident governor Laroche had worked on a plan to abolish slavery progressively over the course of ten years, but when the minister of the colonies asked him to examine how to execute the will of the parliament, he replied: 'I am ready to abolish slavery whenever you want.' A few days later, he added: 'The best would be to rush the decision. We should not fear troubling what is already troubled. Abolition will pass unnoticed (or less noticed) during the insurrection' (quoted in Jacob 1997: 265, my translation). Laroche then convened a committee in Antananarivo to work on a draft of the decree. In this committee, anxious voices were again heard about the unpredictable consequences of an immediate abolition. Yet, once again, the vote decided on immediate abolition. On 26 September, Laroche received a message from the Ministère des Colonies requesting that he follow the decision of the committee and that he abolish slavery immediately. He signed the decree on the same day and published it in the *Journal Officiel de Madagascar* the day after. On 28 September, Laroche handed over his powers to Gallieni.

To the satisfaction of many – including Gallieni, who opposed the immediate abolition – the emancipation of slaves in 1896 did not lead to social disorder prejudicial to French interests in Madagascar. But what was the effect of the abolition on Malagasy society? Did it provoke a social change of great magnitude? Three years later, Jean Carol, a French official, wrote that it 'hasn't changed anything to the customs of the Malagasy so far' (Carol 1898: 30, my translation). Scholars have tended to endorse this view, stressing in particular that traditional hierarchy and the rules governing relations between status groups, including those related to marriages, continued to be observed as if nothing had happened (e.g., Rantoandro 1997: 283). Unlike these authors, I argue that, for the southern Betsileo at least, the abolition caused an important change in the way people conceived of slaves and their descendants.

Many of the freed slaves left their masters within hours of hearing the news of their liberation (Cousins 1896). Those who had been recently enslaved went back to their region. We can assume that most were welcomed by their kinsmen and ritually cleansed by their elders in the way described by Isambo. They could resume the life of a free man or woman, and most probably did not suffer from stigmatisation because of their former enslavement. They were able to find a 'clean' spouse and to have offspring who found their place in the ancestral tombs. However, a large number of slaves whose forebears had been born into slavery for several generations had been severed from the links with their descent groups, and after their liberation were unable to go back to a region where they could be reintegrated into a kin group. In the aftermath of the abolition there must have been a large number of former slaves moving around who could not identify with a *tanindrazana* (ancestral land) other than that of their former masters. But if they did not want to stay on their former masters' estates on a share-cropping arrangement they had no place to establish themselves.

Some, like the Berosaiña in Beparasy, found free land to cultivate in remote places. In 1896, land suitable for cultivation must still have been relatively easy to find in the Betsileo region, for two main reasons. First, the region of the Malagasy highlands is one of the most productive in sub-Saharan Africa and can sustain relatively high population densities (Campbell 2005: 135). Second, the population of Madagascar seems to have remained constant during most of the nineteenth century, remaining at between two and three million people while the population of Imerina and Antananarivo, the capital, grew (ibid.: 137). As missionary James Sibree (1870: 223) observed in 1870:

> The country is so sparsely populated that the land is, comparatively [compared to Europe], of little value, so that almost everyone possesses some piece of ground which he can cultivate; even the slaves have their rice-patch. [...] Except in the near vicinity of Malagasy towns, a good deal of the land appears open to anyone living in the neighborhood to cultivate and enclose at pleasure, so that no one need want at least the bare necessaries of life.

It thus seems that, as long as they moved away from towns and the most densely populated areas, the freed slaves who settled in the southern highlands after 1896 must have easily found new lands to clear and cultivate. If this is right, the former slaves' most immediate problem after emancipation was not access to land.

Their main problem was ritual uncleanliness. As the description of the cleansing ritual mentioned above clearly shows, the nineteenth-century Betsileo viewed enslavement as a highly polluting condition. Slaves were viewed as 'insipid' (*matsatso*) and strongly diminished persons, since they had to obey their masters' orders to perform the most dirty and inferior tasks, and they could not follow the customs of their *fombandrazana* (ancestral customs), including their ancestral *fady* (taboos) (Regnier 2014b). Betsileo rulers and nobles, on the other hand, were considered *masina* ('sacred') and revered 'almost like gods' (Dubois 1938: 567; Regnier 2014b).[5] Having the highest ritual efficacy, they had the power to cleanse the slaves they freed. Although they were less powerful than rulers and nobles, the heads of commoner descent groups had enough ritual power to cleanse their kinsmen who had been freed and needed to be reintegrated in the group. The French colonial government, by contrast, did not have the legitimate ritual power to properly free the slaves, and so the abolition decree of 1896 did not meet the minimal conditions to be considered by the southern Betsileo as a proper cleansing. Given that the southern Betsileo commoners had, as we have seen, a strict rule of status isogamy – one should only marry people of equal status – after abolition the *olompotsy* families became extremely vigilant and put much effort into avoiding any marriage with people they regarded as freed but not properly cleansed. These efforts included checking more carefully than ever the *raza* (ancestry) and *fiavy* (origins) of their marriage partners, and imposing strong social sanctions against the group members who breached the prohibition.

By contrast, Eva Keller reports that slave descendants in Masoala, north-east Madagascar, were able to shed their status as slaves through access to land and intermarriage (Keller 2005: 31–36; 2008: 659–660). Since they found access to new land in Masoala, they could recreate a kin group rooted in the land and could turn this new land into their *tanindrazana* (ancestral land) over the course of successive generations. Now that slave descendants are no longer people without a *tanindrazana*, Keller writes, 'they are no longer people who are deprived of caring for their ancestors and of receiving the latter's blessing in return' (Keller 2008: 660). Although she does not explain the historical circumstances that led to intermarriage between free and slave descendants, it is presumably the slave descendants' re-creation of an ancestral land that opened up marriage opportunities. As we have seen, the Berosaiña too have achieved the reconstruction of a kin group and their rooting into a new land that is now their ancestral land. Yet this has not resulted in the shedding of their slave status – far from it. It should be clear by now that it is because free descendants essentialise them as unclean people and strictly refuse to marry them that the slave status of the Berosaiña has had no chance of being shed.

I have already described the situation into which the Berosaiña were 'locked' in Beparasy after the arrival of Rakamisy's uncleansed mother and 'siblings'. Because free descendants avoided marrying them, they had no other choice than to marry other former slaves who had been 'improperly' freed in 1896. In so doing, they have 'fed back' the commoners' views, further preventing intermarriage. The Berosaiña, therefore, are stuck in a 'vicious circle': as *olompotsy* (from Beparasy or elsewhere in the region) still strictly avoid marrying them, they have no other choice than continuing to marry people who have an unclean reputation and, by so doing, continue to reinforce the *olompotsy*'s prejudice against them. Such a circular process of marriage avoidance and prejudice reinforcement must have been going on since the aftermath of the abolition in the southern Betsileo highlands. It must have played a key role in driving and fuelling the essentialisation of slave descendants as a 'natural' kind; i.e., their construal as a *karaza olo hafa* (different kind of people) who will stay 'unclean' and 'slave' forever because their uncleanliness and inferior status will be always transmitted to their children, whatever they do.

Ontogenic development of essentialism

Given the difficulty of observing the process of learning about such a sensitive issue, I am not able to provide a precise account on how, in practice, children and adolescents in Beparasy come to essentialise the *andevo* in general, and the Berosaiña in particular, as 'unclean people'. Yet in spite of this lack of detailed knowledge, a few important points can be made.

Scholars working on psychological essentialism have insisted on the fact that little input is necessary to trigger essentialism because, it is argued, essentialism is an early bias of the human mind (Gelman 2003). This is particularly true of 'natural kinds' and of social categories, which are readily essentialised with very little cultural prodding. Thus it would seem that all that children need to learn is which categories are to be essentialised in their particular cultural context, rather than having to learn from scratch how to adopt an essentialist stance (see Hirschfeld 1996).

Figure 8.4 Beparasy women and children at a rice harvest

Following this model, one would expect that children of commoner descent in Beparasy will easily home in on the category of 'slaves' and deploy their 'essentialising mind' to it. This is arguably because they are often around when adults converse. The best opportunity for children to listen to adults' conversations is at the evening meal, when the night has already fallen and members of the household (as well as their eventual guests) are confined in the small space of the *lakozia* (kitchen) around the fire. Presumably, at these moments, adults sometimes talk about 'slaves' and children listen in. Yet I find it unlikely that the category 'slaves' is made available to children as simply as such an interpretation suggests. One of the problems is that, as I have already mentioned, adults are very careful when they talk about slave descendants and use many euphemisms to replace the word *andevo*. These euphemisms are unlikely to be transparent to a child, which means that their essentialist bias could not be triggered until they understand what the adults really mean. Moreover, as I have already mentioned, it seems that children know very early on that the Berosaiña are 'unclean people' (*olo tsy madio*), even though teenagers and young adults are often not able to explain why this is so and do not understand what the terms *andevo* or *hovavao* really mean.

This was confirmed to me by a primary school teacher who was a good friend and a particularly reliable informant. The existence of slavery in Madagascar before colonisation should be explained by teachers – it features in the curriculum – but history is taught only in the final years of primary school, and slavery is only mentioned in passing (when it is mentioned at all). When I asked my friend whether primary school teachers used this opportunity to discuss this sensitive topic with their pupils, he replied that they did not, because it would be too complicated to do so. But he confirmed that at that time most pupils of commoner descent knew that the Berosaiña were considered *olo tsy madio* (unclean people). I did not question primary school children about slave descendants but I did put some questions to a few teenagers. They all knew about the uncleanliness of the Berosaiña and they were also aware that, as clean people, they should not marry them, but they did not seem to have a precise idea of why this was so.

This suggests that children and young teenagers have not yet made *andevo* – that is, 'slaves' in general – the target of their psychological essentialism. By contrast, they probably start very early to essentialise the Berosaiña, probably because they sometimes hear the label *olo tsy madio* that is most commonly attached to them. This label presumably triggers essentialism in young children since it leads them to look for a hidden, non-obvious property. However, even though they essentialise the Berosaiña, children lack the knowledge of why they are 'unclean' and why people cannot marry them. It is only much later that they will build up this knowledge.

The following example of an interaction between a mother and her son provides some support for my claim that children first essentialise the Berosaiña long before learning why they are 'unclean people' and why people do not marry them. It took place when my wife and I were interviewing the mother. Her son, in his late teens, had listened to the discussion from the start and had remained silent throughout the interview. Yet when questions about slave descent and marriage were asked, he jumped into the conversation, showing an obvious interest in the topic:

DENIS: According to the ancestral customs, what kind of people is it not possible to marry?

MOTHER: (Hesitating) People who do not have the same ancestry.

SON: [People with] other ancestry (*raza*).

MOTHER: In the past, there were people fleeing (*olo lefa*). And people took them. They made them slaves. That's how a custom like this arrived, and now all people look for the *raza*. And then [they ask]: 'How is the ancestry (*raza*)?' And then [people reply]: 'They do not have the same ancestry (*raza*) as we have.' That's how it started in the past. (Whispering) We do not say it aloud but we talk about it and it's like a secret. It's like that. And only people like them can marry them.

SON: Only people who have the same ancestry can marry each other.

DENIS: What does it mean exactly that they do not have the same ancestry (*raza*)?

MOTHER: That's how I said, they were people fleeing. And people sold them. And they made them slaves. That's how it became so. And then it continued, continued and people inherited all this.

SON: (To his mother) As slaves, what did they do?

MOTHER: I don't know what they did but they were slaves. If people are not like them they cannot marry them and have children [with them]. They can only marry each other. Even if it's on the side of the mother or on the side of the grandmother [that they have a slave ancestry] but the father is clean, we do not give [our child] at all, unless the child insists, insists.

DENIS: And why are some people 'clean'?

MOTHER: Clean people are people to whom nobody did that [i.e., people who were not enslaved].

SON: (To his mother) Are you not going to say that the name of the 'clean' is so-and-so and the name of the 'unclean' is so-and-so [implied: in Beparasy]?

MOTHER: I don't know what to say for the clean but the unclean are called *hovavao*.

SON: [They are called] Berosaiña!

DENIS: When someone wants to marry, how do people know that the person is *hovavao*?

SON: When one goes to get a spouse it is necessary to examine people in detail.

MOTHER: One needs to investigate.

SON: 'What kind of ancestry (*raza*) do you have?'

MOTHER: 'These people, how are they? Are they clean people?'

SON: (To his mother) What is the exact wording?

MOTHER: 'Are these people clean?' That's the question. 'How are the origins of these people?' In this case it is really necessary to go where they have their roots (*tafototriny*). One must look into the father's side and into the mother's side if a child is going to have a spouse. 'How is it for the father? How is it for the mother?' And the people who live close to them must tell us: 'No, this cannot be done since it's a *lambo-tapaka*.' They have to tell us. Because you cannot enter into something like this and give your child for marriage without thinking about it. People who live close by must investigate, maybe they know and then [they say]: 'These people are clean' and then we can receive/ take them. Or [they say]: 'These are people with whom it can't be done because they are like this [implied: they are unclean].'

SON: It's necessary to ask people who are their neighbours.

During this interview the teenager was obviously eager to answer our questions on the avoidance of marriage with slave descendants but he also seemed very curious about what his mother had to say on the issue of slavery and on the way parents investigate the status of their children's potential partners. He had some reason to be particularly interested in the discussion: some time after the interview we were told by one of his sisters that he had recently brought a girlfriend to his paternal village for the trial period of a customary marriage. The *tapi-maso* and the *ala-fady* had already been given to the girl's parents (cf. Chapter 5). The girl was *tamana* (well) in the young man's village but his relatives' investigations about her origins led to the conclusion that she was from a slave descent family of the region of Ambalamasina. As soon as her slave ancestry was confirmed, the boy's parents told him that the girl should be sent back to her village. The teenager then followed his parents' instruction and sent his girlfriend home. We were not told about the 'official' reason given to her for sending her back home, but since this stage in the marriage process is clearly conceived as a trial period there was no need for elaborate explanations.

The above discussion was particularly interesting because the son had probably known for a long time that one must marry 'people with the same ancestry' and that the Berosaiña are 'unclean people', but he did not seem to know much about the reason why this was so. He seemed to have only a vague idea of slavery. It looked as if he was still in the middle of the process of learning why he could not marry his girlfriend. At the same time, however, he knew already why such a marriage would cause problems: he knew that his children could not have been buried in his family's ancestral tomb. This was clear in the following passage of the same conversation, after the mother had just told us that the children of a mixed couple were called *lambo-tapaka*:

DENIS: What makes them *lambo-tapaka*?

MOTHER: Because one half is clean and the other half is *hovavao*. That's how they become so.

DENIS: Are there bad things that befall to their life if people marry them?

MOTHER: Yes, there are. If children are stubborn [and want to marry a *lambo- tapaka*] then there they are [i.e., people let them go]. But if their children die, the parents from here will not take them [to bury them in their ancestral tomb], they will let them be outside [the tomb] because they do not want to mix with them at all.

DENIS: They cannot be with their parents?

SON: They cannot be put into the ancestral tomb. People will break the earth (*hamakia tany*).

MOTHER: They really cannot be put into the tomb but [have to stay] outside of it. There is no asking [for the corpse] from their side [i. e., from the free descent side].

DENIS: Break the earth? What does it mean?

SON: It means that there is no tomb [i.e., that they are buried in the earth].

MOTHER: If they [the free descent family] do not want to break the earth, they [the children] will be placed in the tomb where they are [i.e., in the slave descent tomb] because they [the free descent family] do not take them, not even on the side of the mother [of the free descent parent] or on another side. They do not take them in their tomb. They [i.e., the children] are buried at the place where they are [implied: in the slave descendants' tomb].

On the basis of this and similar evidence gathered in interviews, I would argue that children of commoner descent learn from an early age that the Berosaiña are 'unclean people' and that they cannot marry them. Maybe they are told that the reason is that they are 'clean people' themselves, that the Berosaiña 'do not have the same ancestry' and that 'clean people' should only marry 'clean people' and 'people who have the same ancestry'. Beyond that, however, I doubt they learn about the reasons why the Berosaiña are 'unclean' and what 'having the same ancestry' really means before they reach adulthood. Nonetheless, the fact that the Berosaiña are commonly referred to as 'unclean people' invites children to assume the existence of hidden, non-obvious properties in a group of people who, superficially, are just like them, so that they conceive of them as essentially different and unmarriageable because of their hidden essence.

I would therefore schematically (and tentatively) describe the learning process as follows: first, young children learn about the 'uncleanliness' of a few persons in their neighbourhood (e.g., Raboba or Ramarcel) because they have heard the label *tsy madio* commonly used to refer to them. At this point, because of their 'essentialising mind', children already 'look beyond the obvious' and attribute a hidden essence to these individuals – an inner 'uncleanliness'. Then they learn that it is not only these individuals who are 'unclean' but their entire group of kinsmen, like, for example, the Berosaiña in Beparasy. Thus they now essentialise the descent group, attributing an 'unclean' essence to all its members by inductive inferences (i.e., by learning that someone is a Berosaiña they will infer that he/she is an 'unclean' person, even if they have never heard such a statement about this person). Later on, when children reach puberty and start having *sipa* (boy- or girlfriends), they will catch more from adults' conversations about 'unclean people' and they will, like the teenager in the above conversation, be increasingly receptive to what is said about marrying them. When they reach marriage age they may even be taught about the issue by their parents or by elder members of their family, and have explained some of the reasons why they should be careful to not find a spouse in villages or parts of villages inhabited by slave descendants. As they grow up they will take an active part in various gatherings, ceremonies and rituals, where issues of 'slaves' and people's 'origins' will be further evoked or discussed, albeit secretively, adding more cultural content to the way they think about 'slaves'. The point that I want to stress in this developmental story is that children, because of the essentialist bias of the human mind which makes them 'natural essentialisers', most probably essentialise their slave descent neighbours, the descent group to which these neighbours belong and the category 'slaves' long before they are explicitly taught why they should do so.

Language and the transmission of essentialism

Developmental psychologists have explored the role of language in the promotion of essentialist thinking and the transmission of social essentialism from parents to children (see Rhodes and Mandalaywala 2017). Their work shows that 'apparently innocuous and everyday uses of language may play a role in engendering essentialist thinking', therefore 'nourishing the child's tendency to see a social world populated by deep divisions and stable hierarchies' (Haslam 2017: 14–15). Recent studies have highlighted, in particular, the role of generic statements (i.e., generalising statements such as 'girls like pink' and 'boys like cars') and provided experimental evidence that the essentialist thinking of adults may be transmitted to children via such statements.

One such study showed that both four-year-olds and adults tended to develop essentialist beliefs about a novel category ('Zarpies') that had been described using generic rather than specific (i.e., non-generic) language (Rhodes, Leslie and Tworek 2012). In the same study – but with another experiment – the researchers induced adults to hold essentialist beliefs about a novel social category (called 'Zarpies' again). This led these adults to use more than twice as many generics when talking about Zarpies while showing a picture book about this novel category to their children. These experiments, and others in the same vein, suggest that adults' essentialist thinking is reflected in their language use, which in turn promotes essentialist thinking in the young children who are spending much time with them. Thus generic statements are increasingly considered central to the development of social essentialism in children and, by extension, to the construction of folk sociological knowledge in adults. Such a view is well summarised by the catchphrase of philosopher Sarah-Jane Leslie (2014): 'generics carve up the social world.'

In Beparasy, however, the early transmission of essentialist thinking does not seem to be easily explained by the frequent use of generic statements in a child's environment. *Olompotsy* children are unlikely to hear many explicit generic statements about slave descendants since, as I have explained, there is a widespread 'silence' about slavery and, when they want to talk about the Berosaiña as slave descendants, adults most often resort to various euphemisms and implicit statements. They may also lower their voice, whisper and seek to avoid being heard by anyone other than their interlocutors. Furthermore, even in the unlikely circumstances when adults would express a few generic statements about *olo tsy madio*, for example, it seems unlikely that young children would easily pick up this expression (and the associated generalising statements) from the conversation, since without a concrete idea of the persons to whom this expression refers it would remain too abstract to catch children's attention.[6] The adults' careful linguistic behaviour and the abstractness of expressions such as 'unclean people' or 'slaves' (in the absence of a context in which children can map them on to particular persons) thus make it implausible that the development of essentialised views about 'unclean people' is triggered and promoted by listening to carers' generic statements. I would rather argue that the transmission of essentialism from *olompotsy* adults to children is – at least in its early stage – more guided by deictic language than by generic language.

Deictic statements are expressions with words such as 'this', 'that', 'here' and 'there', whose meanings depend strictly on the occasions of their use (see Hanks 2005). In Beparasy, deictic language seems to play an important role in the transmission of social essentialism, for the simple reason that people walk a lot and these frequent journeys on foot provide opportunities for increasing and updating one's social knowledge. Recall that there are no cars or motorcycles in Beparasy, and that the region's human settlements are relatively scattered: about 5,000 people live in more than 100 *vala* (villages). Many households have, moreover, built their house at a distance from these villages, mainly because they want to live closer to their rice fields. As a result, the landscape of Beparasy is criss-crossed with myriad narrow paths, which form a large network linking together villages, hamlets, single houses, primary schools, churches, rice fields, threshing floors, bridges, ancestral tombs, cultivated lands and so on.

When walking on these paths it is very common to meet small groups of people who are, for some reason, heading to a particular place, and who may have to walk for hours before they reach their final destination. During my stay in Beparasy I often walked through the countryside with such a small group. It struck me on these occasions that people, while walking, were frequently commenting on the people and places they encountered. For example, one of our co-walkers would explain: 'relatives of mine live in this house here', or 'the new tomb over there is our neighbour's family tomb, they built it two years ago', or 'these rice fields there, to the east of the river, they belong to such-and-such family'. The others would then ask questions on these comments or add further information. By so doing, they check and update their knowledge about Beparasy's society and history.

Children take part in these journeys on foot from an early age. Until they are old enough to walk they are carried on adults' backs, tied in a *lambahoany* (i.e., a piece of thin, printed cloth). So they too are exposed to the frequent sharing of social knowledge that takes place among groups of walkers. This sharing is, for the reasons I have explained in the previous chapter, particularly important when it concerns slave descendants. On a few occasions I witnessed that my walking companions made comments about the Berosaiña, or about other slave descendants if we were outside Beparasy. They expressed statements such as *'misy olo tsy madio eto'* ('there are unclean people here'), *'ny olo anatin'io trano io tsy madio'* ('the people in this house are unclean'), or *'olo tsy madio ny tompon'ny omby ambany aty'* ('these zebus down there below belong to unclean people'). Like the other comments mentioned above, these statements about slave descendants were deictic, not generic.

Sentences like these are more likely to catch young children's attention and trigger their essentialist thinking than generic statements, for at least three reasons. First, these statements attribute properties that children can directly map on to concrete persons, animals or places. Just like adults, children will value this kind of information to increase their (at first very limited) social knowledge. In other words, they might learn very early on that *olo tsy madio* live, for example, in a house next to their mother's village – and this even though they have no clue at all about what *olo tsy madio* means. Second, these properties (i.e., uncleanliness or dirtiness) will easily appear as non-obvious to them because they will notice that the people in question are not particularly unclean or dirty when compared with others. Thus they will infer that these properties must be, somehow, 'hidden' inside the person. This idea – i.e., that there is something 'mysterious' that makes people unclean or dirty – seems particularly catchy for a child's mind because cleanliness and uncleanliness are very familiar properties; children are taught from a very early age what *madio* and *maloto* mean. Third, since children will continue to walk frequently on Beparasy's paths, they will cross the same villages again and again. Thus they will have endless opportunities to expand and strengthen their social knowledge, and in particular the knowledge that concerns the individuals who belong to the 'mysterious' category of unclean people. As they grow up they will increasingly walk in the company of peers, for example when they go to school, and these groups of children will also share and update their social knowledge about Beparasy villagers.

I believe this is the main route to the early development of social essentialism in Beparasy. Children's essentialism, I would argue, is triggered mainly by deictic statements and develops during their long walks in the inhabited landscape of Beparasy. On these occasions they learn, by listening to adults and other children, that some Beparasy villagers are very different from the others because they are unclean.

Notes

1 In other regions of Madagascar, such as in Imerina, slave ancestry is often suspected or ascribed on the basis of phenotype (Razafindralambo 2014; Regnier and Somda 2019). This is not the case among the southern Betsileo.

2 These conversations were remarkably open in comparison with more ordinary contexts where a 'silence' on slavery is usually observed. Retrospectively, running the three tasks proved a very effective way to circumvent the southern Betsileo reticence to talk about slavery and slave descent.

3 I am grateful to Jonathan Parry for bringing to my attention the issues of blood and uncleanliness in medical contexts.

4 Among the southern Betsileo, *ombiasa* (healers/diviners), heads of families and *hova* can perform cleansing rituals. The most powerful ones are believed to be those of *hova* (provided they have not married with *olompotsy*), followed by heads of families and then *ombiasa*. In an early version of the task I made the mistake of using an *ombiasa* in the story, but some friends in Beparasy advised me to refer to a *hova* instead, to make sure that the story seemed credible.

5 *Masina* is an adjective derived from the word *hasina*. *Hasina* has been a much-discussed issue in Malagasy scholarship and is often considered a central concept of Malagasy political thought. Evers argued that slave descendants are considered by the southern Betsileo as lacking *hasina* and possessing *hery*, i.e. according to her the negative 'energy' which causes 'infertility, illness and death' (Evers 2006: 424). My fieldwork did not

support these claims since nobody ever told me about slave descendants lacking *hasina*. When I asked questions aimed at prompting these issues in Beparasy I found that nobody really understood what I meant by these words or ideas. The local historian of noble descent mentioned in the previous chapter told me that *hasina* was a Merina concept rather than a southern Betsileo one, and that for the southern Betsileo 'things are much simpler' since only people of high status (e.g., *hova, andevohova*) were considered *masina*. This seems to be confirmed by Rainihifina (1975: 88–97) and is in accordance with Graeber's comment that *hasina* 'is first and foremost a way of talking about powers that no one fully understands' (Graeber and Sahlins 2017: 267).

6 In the experiments cited above (Rhodes, Leslie and Tworek 2012), both children and adults were given a picture book with lively characters. The novel category 'Zarpies' was therefore not an abstract concept for them, since they could map their conceptualisation on to concrete images of the people called 'Zarpies'. It is indeed hard to imagine that very young children could start essentialising a social category without being able to link this category to concrete examples (i.e., without visualising some members of the category).

Conclusion

In an afterword to a volume in Maurice Bloch's honour (Astuti, Parry and Stafford 2007), Jonathan Parry suggested that, over the years, Bloch's writings have shifted from an attention to history, political economy and 'differences' to an interest in cognition and the 'partial recurrences' observed across societies. Reflecting on Bloch's polemic lecture, 'Where did anthropology go?' (Bloch 2005), which championed the view that the investigation of human nature should be brought back to the centre of the discipline of anthropology, Parry concluded his essay with a warning: it would be a mistake to let the enquiry into the general properties of human nature eclipse the enquiry into political economy or the structure of society (Parry 2007: 360).

While I fully agree with Parry that it would, indeed, be a mistake to do so, it seems to me that this is not where Bloch's reflections on the relation between anthropology and cognitive science have led him, or will lead those who follow his path. As Astuti and Bloch (2012) have made very clear since then, it is only by continuing to do 'traditional' ethnographic fieldwork that anthropologists can make a significant contribution to cognitive science. Anthropologists simply cannot contribute to cognitive science without also addressing sociological questions like those concerning political economy and the structure of society.

In keeping a balance between my use of three different 'photographic lenses' – as explained in Chapter 2 – I have tried in this book to use a cognitive lens to address a social issue without falling into the pitfalls denounced by Parry: I have been careful not to let the cognitive part of my account eclipse its descriptive–interpretative and historical parts. On the contrary, I sought to integrate these different perspectives in what I hope has been a fruitful and insightful way.

On the basis of my ethnographic study of the Berosaiña, I have suggested that bilateral marriages with slave descendants in the

Betsileo southern highlands are avoided because descendants of *olom-potsy* (commoners), who form the majority of the southern Betsileo population, prefer to marry people of equal ancestry (*olo mitovy raza*) since they consider that entering hypergamous or hypogamous marriages will have the same outcome: the commoner descent side will become 'slaves'. This is because by marrying noble descendants they will be in an inferior position vis-à-vis the family of noble descent, while by marrying slave descendants they will have an unclean reputation and the offspring born from such marriage will be ascribed 'slave' status.

Looking for an explanation as to why slave descendants seemed to be 'locked' into their inferior status of 'unclean people', I have argued that commoner descendants think of them as people with a hidden essence (a deep uncleanliness) that makes them different 'in nature'. In order to best characterise my ethnographic data, I have borrowed the concept of psychological essentialism from cognitive psychology and have argued that commoner descendants essentialise the social category 'slaves'. They think that *andevo* have an unclean essence that cannot be changed and that this is passed on from parents to children, even in the case of mixed marriages, thus making it impossible to bury the children of such marriages in the ancestral tombs of free descendants.

Examining the idea that 'slaves' might have already been construed in this essentialist way in the pre-abolition era, I have suggested on the contrary that the entrenchment of the category is most probably a recent phenomenon. Colonisation and the abolition of slavery were crucial events in the causal story leading to this entrenchment, but it occurred in this particular form and at this particular moment among the southern Betsileo because it grew out of a set of pre-existing cultural practices – such as the investigations before marriage, the genealogical speeches at funerals and the sharing of the dead in the ancestral tombs – that made it easy for free descent people to enquire about the ancestry of recently freed slaves and very difficult for former slaves who had not been cleansed and reintegrated into a local descent group to be accepted as suitable marriage partners.

If it is the case, as I have argued, that social essentialism is a good lens through which to interpret the entrenchment of the category *andevo* following abolition and that the human cognitive disposition towards essentialism plays a causal role in the process by which present-day southern Betsileo children learn to essentialise slave descendants, then these issues should be of particular interest to scholars addressing post-slavery issues, not only in Madagascar but also in other contexts where former slaves and their descendants are confronted by similar difficulties. They should be equally important to policymakers, activists, NGOs and local communities, since only a clear understanding of the predicament of slave descendants might help these actors act efficiently on prejudice, discrimination and stigmatisation.

The predicament of the Berosaiña

When Rakamisy, a Berosaiña, arrived in the uninhabited region of Beparasy towards 1880, he was a former slave who had bought his freedom and volunteered to be among the handful of men who worked hard to clear the land from trees, build rice fields and grow rice in this peripheral area of the small polity of Ambatofotsy. As Chapter 4 showed, it is not clear whether Rakamisy first went to Beparasy because he was sent there by the *hova* of Ambatofotsy as an *andevo-hova* (as Randriatsoa explained), or whether he only became one later, possibly because he had replaced Rainibao's son when Merina occupiers raised an army in the region (as free descendants explained).

There is no doubt, however, that Rakamisy arrived in Beparasy as a free man and that he came before the abolition of slavery. Rakamisy had been a slave for part of his life but at some point he was able to buy his freedom and was legitimately freed by his master through legal and administrative proceedings. He had thus become a free man of commoner (*olompotsy*) status. Had he also been cleansed by a ritual? Apparently he had no free descent group into which he could have been reintegrated since, according to what Randriatsoa told me, the Berosaiña have no contact with their relatives in 'places of origins' before they arrived in Vinany, even though they recall the names of some villages. It seems very unlikely that Rakamisy had undergone a ritual cleansing performed to reintegrate him into a 'clean' descent group, as described by Isambo in Chapter 8. But I was told by elders that in the pre-abolition past the slaves who were freed were also cleansed by a ritual performed by their masters. Thus Rakamisy might well have been ritually cleansed when he was freed by his master in Vinany.

Whatever happened, it seems to me that the issue of Rakamisy's uncleanliness may have not been very important at that time, for two reasons. First, unlike Isambo's, Rakamisy's case was not that he came back to his region of origin and to his former free descent group. And as explained in the previous chapter, the purpose of the ritual of *manoza lela* was to reintegrate people who had been 'lost' for their kinsmen and had become 'unclean' because they had done things they should not have done according to their ancestors' customs. What this means, it seems, is that Isambo's ritual uncleanliness would have been a major problem above all for his kinsmen – those who had the same ancestors and were concerned about the reputation of the descent group – but a less important issue for people who were unrelated to him. Second, Rakamisy's freeing took place before the abolition of slavery. As I have explained, the category 'slaves' had not yet been entrenched, former slaves were not yet considered as irredeemably unclean persons and the issue of the uncleanliness of former slaves had not yet become a major concern for southern Betsileo commoners looking for spouses. Therefore I would argue that Rakamisy's free companions – in Beparasy or elsewhere – were, towards 1880, probably not sensitive (or, at least, not that sensitive) to the issue of his possible uncleanliness due to the fact that he may not have been ritually re-integrated into a descent group. What mattered most for them, at that time, was that Rakamisy had been legally freed by his noble master and had become an *olompotsy*. Only in this way can we understand that Rakamisy managed to become an *andevohova* in the short period between his manumission and the abolition of slavery.

We can imagine that, notwithstanding the status differences between the *andevohova* and the others, the relationships between these first settlers were rather egalitarian. When living together in the small for-tified village on Vatobe they must have relied heavily on mutual sup-port, because of the harsh living conditions and the constant threat of being raided. We can also imagine that, had things stayed as they were, Rakamisy's offspring would have married other commoners. Maybe some of them would have even married the children of another *ande-vohova*. Because of the prestige attached to the function of *andevohova* and the chance offered to start a new life in an uninhabited place, it seems likely that the story of Rakamisy's former enslavement, had it been known by his companions, would have soon been forgotten: as time went by, local people would have retained the figure of a founder and of a kind of 'ruler' (*mpanjaka*) – as Ramarcelline put it (Chapter 6) – rather than that of a 'slave'.

But things did not go that way and world history flipped the cards of Rakamisy's destiny. In 1895, only one or two decades after his arrival in Beparasy, the French invaded Madagascar and one year later they liberated all the slaves. In the Arindrano region, freed slaves did what migrants looking for new lands always did according to the local cus-toms: they asked the now former local rulers to give their blessing (that is, in this case, permission) to settle down and cultivate a plot of land

within their former fief. Thus, most probably, the freed slaves Rainihosy, Randriatsoakely and their 'mother' Rapitsarandro asked the
former ruler of Ambatofotsy if they could join their 'kinsman' Rakamisy in Beparasy. This must have been a formality, since the former
ruler had been left with very little power. Rakamisy welcomed them
and as a local *andevohova* he allocated them lands where they could
build rice fields.

Rakamisy's local status must have started to change at the very
moment of their arrival. While he had arrived as a free man and had
imposed himself as an *andevohova*, his 'brothers', Rainihosy and Randriatsoakely, and his mother Rapitsarandro arrived as slaves who had
just been liberated in a sudden and awkward fashion by the *vazaha*
(white foreigners) who had seized Madagascar. Needless to say, the
mother and 'brothers' had not been ritually cleansed. Thus when they
arrived in Beparasy immediately after 1896, villagers must have already
regarded them with suspicion, though presumably they did not essentialise them straightaway, because the entrenchment of the category
'slaves' and the new vigilance about former slaves' uncleanliness,
explained in the previous chapter, certainly took some time to take
hold in people's minds. Since Rakamisy and his relatives were identified
as a kin group – the Berosaiña – other people gradually started to
gossip about them being 'slaves' and 'unclean', in spite of Rakamisy's
andevohova status. In other words, although when Rakamisy arrived in
Beparasy he had the prospect of living the life of a free man and of a
powerful *andevohova*, the arrival of his liberated kinsmen severely
undermined his possibilities. From now on it would become very difficult for Rakamisy and his descendants to not be considered as 'unclean
people' in Beparasy. The local essentialisation of the Berosaiña had
begun.

Yet since Rakamisy was *andevohova*, his two 'brothers' obtained
particularly good and large lands. When shortly after their arrival the
fortified village on Vatobe was abandoned, the three 'brothers' established separate *vala* close to their respective rice fields. Then during the
French villagisation policy the three 'brothers' lived with commoner
descendants in larger villages: some families of commoner descent
joined the *vala* founded by the *andevohova* Rakamisy, where his
mother Rapitsarandro also lived (Mahasoa). Rainihosy founded with
other families the 'big village'. Rakamisy's young 'brother' Randriatsoakely lived with other families in yet another village. I suspect
that the ancestors of many of the families living in the *fokontany* of
Beparasy-I, which includes these three villages, were actually given
land by Rakamisy when they first arrived in Beparasy, because today's

fokontany of Beparasy seems to be roughly based on the territorial divisions that were administered by the four *andevohova*. But it is not surprising that these families prefer to keep silent about that aspect of their history. Ramarcel and some commoner descendants told me that, over the generations, the Berosaiña also gave parts of their land to people with whom they had good relations, especially to their *vakirà* kinsmen. This explains, once again, the ambivalent status of the Berosaiña that surprised me when I arrived in Beparasy: identified as 'slaves', they possessed good, centrally located lands and were acknowledged as important political figures.

On might surmise that, because of their relative wealth and the prestige derived from being the kinsmen of a former *andevohova*, the Berosaiña are not bothered by what their neighbours think of them and by the fact that they do not want to marry them. It does indeed seem that, to a certain extent, the Berosaiña put up with this situation. Or, at least, this is the conviction of commoner descendants, who tend to think that the Berosaiña are in good economic situations and that this is why they are not much affected by the existing prejudice against them. Commoner descendants are fully aware of this prejudice: several times I heard the sentence, 'They do not care, because they are rich'. Yet on a number of occasions I strongly felt that, on the contrary, the Berosaiña resented their situation deeply. When one day I asked Ramarcel whether his 'heart' (*fo*) was not sad because of the way people behaved towards his family, he replied: 'It's really very sad. These people should be our very close kinsmen, we should see each other on a daily basis. When there is a funeral they should send us an invitation. And they should know: "Ah, Ramarcel, he is our relative ..." But we are even afraid of trying to approach them.'

Ramarcel's conviction, I assume, was that Beparasy villagers should be grateful because many of them received their land from the Berosaiña. This, for Ramarcel, implied that people should treat them like close kinsmen and pay them regular visits, as kinsmen do. But it also implied that Beparasy people should accept the Berosaiña as suitable marriage partners. Yet Ramarcel found too few people show this kind of gratitude or respect for him and his relatives. As we have seen (Chapter 4), he is well aware, on the contrary, that they speak ill of them and refuse to marry them. 'They greet us at the market,' Ramarcel said, 'because it's an obligation for them, but they do not come to visit us and they do not invite us.' I do not know exactly what Ramarcel knows of what other people say about the Berosaiña – how would he know if people are so careful when they talk about these issues? But this remark shows that the Berosaiña strongly feel and experience that they are discriminated against and stigmatised because they are people with a history of slavery.

By way of conclusion, I would like to tell one last story about the Berosaiña which illustrates the awkwardness of their situation. The story concerns Vohangy's eldest son, who was born in Betroka. When his foster uncle, Redison, gave up priesthood and decided to come back to Beparasy (see Chapter 1), he and his wife Raely took the boy with them. They first fostered him in Redison's mother's village but, given the hostility of Redison's kinsmen, who did not like the idea of having a Berosaiña among them, the small household soon moved to the 'big village'. Later on, when the boy went to secondary school in Ambala-vao, Redison and Raely paid for his fees and his living expenses. Having passed his *baccalauréat*, the boy then went to university. This was a real achievement since very few people from Beparasy have the desire or opportunity to go to university, and, at the time of my stay, I was aware of only two such cases. For Vohangy's son, it had not been easy. Redison told me that the boy strongly desired to continue to study but that neither his mother nor Redison could bear the costs of his education in Toliara. In despair, the boy went on his own initiative to see one of Redison's cousins from Beparasy. This cousin's mother (Ramarcelline's sister) had married a policeman and had left Beparasy for Toliara a long time ago. Her son had found a good job in a maritime company transporting goods between Toliara and Réunion. When Vohangy's son came to see Redison's cousin, he asked him whether he could stay at his large and comfortable home in Toliara so that he could attend university at a lower cost to his mother, Vohangy. Redison's cousin was impressed by the teenager's determination and allocated him a room in his house.

The boy, a Berosaiña, was thus generously hosted by a close relative of the very people who so forcefully prevented Ramarcelline from marrying 'unclean' Rasamuel, who is no other than the boy's grand-father. The condition of the Berosaiña – whose harsh stigmatisation and discrimination are smoothened by a fiction of equality and strong practices of solidarity – is well captured by such an ironic story.

Appendix

Adoption story

Marcel and Hanitra are Betsileo. They come from a clean family. They have been married for a long time but they did not conceive children. One day Marcel found a baby abandoned in the forest. Marcel and Hanitra were happy to adopt the baby and they raised it until adulthood. The truth, however, is that the baby is the child of unclean people who abandoned it in the forest because of poverty.

Question: In your opinion, when it reaches adulthood, is the child still an unclean person or has it become a clean person?

Cleansing ritual

Mamy and Vao are Betsileo and live in the same village. They love each other but cannot marry because Mamy comes from an unclean family and Vao from a clean family. Mamy goes to see a 'noble really noble' (i.e., nobles who have not yet married commoners) and he asks him to perform a cleansing ritual so that he becomes a clean person and can marry Vao. The noble accepts. Mamy is bathed with silver water and *hazomanga*, a zebu is slaughtered, its blood is put on Mamy's forehead and the traditional speeches are made.

Question: In your opinion, after the cleansing, is Mamy still an unclean person or has he become a clean person?

Blood transfusion

Rakoto is Betsileo. He comes from a clean family that lives close to Fianarantsoa. One day he takes a bush-taxi to go to the city. An accident occurs on the road and he is seriously injured. He is brought to the hospital of Tambohobe (i.e., the hospital in Fianarantsoa).

He needs a blood transfusion since he has lost too much blood. For this transfusion the doctors use the blood of Ralaza, a man from an unclean family.

Question: In your opinion, after the transfusion, is Rakoto still clean or has he become unclean?

Additional sentences with reference to a consensus

At the end of the adoption story:

All the villagers agree that the baby has become a clean person because it was raised by clean parents.

At the end of the cleansing ritual story:

All the villagers agree that Mamy has become a clean person because he was cleansed by a 'noble really noble' (*hova tena hova*).

At the end of the blood transfusion story:

All the villagers have learned that Rakoto has received the blood of a slave descendant but they all agree he is still a clean person.

References

Acquier, J.-L. (1997). *Architectures de Madagascar*. Paris: Berger-Levrault/ Arthaud.

Allen, R. (2014). *European Slave Trading in the Indian Ocean, 1500–1850*. Athens, OH: Ohio University Press.

Allport, G. (1954). *The Nature of Prejudice*. Oxford: Addison-Wesley.

André, C. (1899). *De l'Esclavage à Madagascar*. Paris: Arthur Rousseau.

Astuti, R. (1995). *People of the Sea: Identity and Descent among the Vezo of Madagascar*. Cambridge, UK: Cambridge University Press.

Astuti, R. (2007). 'La moralité des conventions: Tabous ancestraux à Madagascar.' *Terrain* 48: 101–112.

Astuti, R. (2011). 'Death, Ancestors and the Living Dead: Learning Without Teaching in Madagascar.' In *Children's Understanding of Death: From Biological to Supernatural Conceptions*, edited by V. Talwar, P. Harris and M. Schleifer, 1–18. New York: Cambridge University Press.

Astuti, R. and M. Bloch (2012). 'Anthropologists as Cognitive Scientists.' *Topics in Cognitive Science* 4(3): 453–461.

Astuti, R., J. Parry and C. Stafford, eds. (2007). *Questions of Anthropology*. Oxford: Berg.

Astuti, R., G. Solomon and S. Carey (2004). 'Constraints on Conceptual Development: A Case Study in the Acquisition of Folkbiological and Folksociological Knowledge in Madagascar.' *Monographs of the Society for Research in Child Development* 69(3): 1–135.

Atran, S. (1990). *Cognitive Foundations of Natural History*. New York: Cambridge University Press.

Atran, S. (1998). 'Folk Biology and the Anthropology of Science: Cognitive Universals and Cultural Particulars.' *Behavioral & Brain Sciences* 21: 547–609.

Bales, K. (2004). *Disposable People: New Slavery in the Global Economy*. Berkeley, CA: University of California Press.

Bastian, B. and N. Haslam (2006). 'Psychological Essentialism and Stereotype Endorsement.' *Journal of Experimental Social Psychology* 42: 228–235.

Beaujard, P. (1983). *Princes et Paysans: Les Tanala de l'Ikongo.* Paris: L'Harmattan.

Beaujard, P. (1998). 'Esclavage et groupes sociaux en pays Tanala.' In *Formes Extrêmes de Dépendance: Contributions à l'Étude de l'Esclavage en Asie du Sud-Est,* edited by G. Condominas, 203–215. Paris: EHESS.

Beller, S., A. Bender and D. Medin, eds. (2012). 'Does cognitive science need anthropology?' *Topics in Cognitive Science* 4 (3). Special issue.

Besson, L. (1897). 'Etude ethnologique sur les Betsileo.' In *Notes, Reconnaissances et Explorations,* 538–552. Antananarivo: Imprimerie Officielle.

Birnbaum, D., I. Deeb, J. Segall, A. Ben-Eliyahn and G. Diesendruck (2010). 'The Development of Social Essentialism: The Case of Israeli Children's Inferences about Jews and Arabs.' *Child Development* 81(3): 757–777.

Bloch, M. (1968). 'Notes sur l'organisation sociale de l'Imerina avant le règne de Radama Ier.' *Annales de l'Université de Madagascar* 7: 119–132.

Bloch, M. (1971). *Placing the Dead: Tombs, Ancestral Villages, and Kinship Organisation in Madagascar.* London: Seminar Press.

Bloch, M. (1975). 'Introduction.' In *Political Language and Oratory in Traditional Society,* edited by M. Bloch, 1–28. London: Academic Press.

Bloch, M. (1977). 'The Past and the Present in the Present.' *Man* (n.s.) 12: 278–292.

Bloch, M. (1978). 'Marriage Amongst Equals: An Analysis of the Marriage Ceremony Among the Merina of Madagascar.' *Man* (n.s.) 13: 21–33.

Bloch, M. (1979). 'The Social Implications of Freedom for Merina and Zafimaniry Slaves.' In *Madagascar in History: Essays from the 1970s,* edited by R. Kent, 269–297. Albany, CA: Foundation for Malagasy Studies.

Bloch, M. (1980). 'Modes of Production and Slavery in Madagascar: Two Case Studies.' In *Asian and African Systems of Slavery,* edited by J. Watson, 100–134. Oxford: Blackwell.

Bloch, M. (1986). *From Blessing to Violence: History and Ideology in the Circumcision Ritual of the Merina of Madagascar.* Cambridge, UK: Cambridge University Press.

Bloch, M. (1991). 'Language, Anthropology and Cognitive Science.' *Man* (n.s.) 26: 183–198.

Bloch, M. (1993). 'Zafimaniry Birth and Kinship Theory.' *Social Anthropology/Anthropologie Sociale* 1(1b): 119–132.

Bloch, M. (1994). 'The Slaves, the King, and Mary in the Slums of Antananarivo.' In *Shamanism, History, and the State,* edited by N. Thomas and C. Humphrey, 133–145. Ann Arbor, MI: University of Michigan Press.

Bloch, M. (2005). 'Where Did Anthropology Go? Or the Need for 'Human Nature.' In *Essays on Cultural Transmission,* 1–20. Oxford: Berg.

Bloch, M. (2012). *Anthropology and the Cognitive Challenge.* Cambridge, UK: Cambridge University Press.

Bloch, M., G. Solomon and S. Carey (2001). 'Zafimaniry: An Understanding of What is Passed on from Parents to Children: A Cross-cultural Investigation.' *Journal of Cognition and Culture* 1(1): 43–68.

Boyer, P. (2001). *Religion Explained: The Evolutionary Origins of Religious Thought*. New York: Basic Books.

Boyer-Rossol, K. (2015). 'Entre les deux rives du Canal de Mozambique: Histoire et mémoires des Makoa de l'Ouest de Madagascar (XIXe–XXe siècles),' PhD thesis, Université Paris Diderot.

Brown, M. (2004). 'Reclaiming Lost Ancestors and Acknowledging Slave Descent: Insights from Madagascar.' *Comparative Studies in Society and History* 46: 616–645.

Campbell, G. (1998). 'Madagascar.' In *Macmillan Encyclopedia of World Slavery*, edited by P. Finkelman and J. Miller, 266–269. New York: Simon and Schuster Macmillan.

Campbell, G. (2005). *An Economic History of Imperial Madagascar, 1750–1895: The Rise and Fall of an Island Empire*. Cambridge, UK: Cambridge University Press.

Carol, J. (1898). *Chez les Hova (Au Pays Rouge)*. Paris: Ollendorff.

Carsten, J. (2011). 'Substance and Relationality: Blood in Contexts.' *Annual Review of Anthropology* 40: 19–35.

Cole, J. (1998). 'The Work of Memory in Madagascar.' *American Ethnologist* 25(4): 610–633.

Cole, J. (2001). *Forget Colonialism? Sacrifice and the Art of Memory in Madagascar*. Berkeley, CA: University of California.

Cole, J. (2010). *Sex and Salvation: Imagining the Future in Madagascar*. Chicago, IL: University of Chicago Press.

Condominas, G. (1961). *Fokon'olona et Collectivités Rurales en Imerina*. Paris: Berger-Levrault.

Cousins, W. (1896). 'The Abolition of Slavery in Madagascar, With Some Remarks on Malagasy Slavery Generally.' *Antananarivo Annual* 5(21): 446–450.

Demoulin, S., J.-P. Leyens and V. Yzerbyt (2006). 'Lay Theories of Essentialism.' *Group Processes & Intergroup Relations* 9(1): 25–42.

Deschamps, H. (1972). *Histoire de Madagascar*. Paris: Berger-Levrault.

Descola, P. (2005). *Par-delà Nature et Culture*. Paris: Gallimard.

Domenichini, J.-P. and B. Domenichini-Ramiaramanana (1982). 'Aspects de l'esclavage sous la monarchie merina.' *Omaly sy Anio* 15: 53–99.

Domenichini, J.-P. and B. Domenichini-Ramiaramanana (1998). 'L' "esclavage" dans la société malgache.' In *Formes Extrêmes de Dépendance: Contributions à l'Etude de l'Esclavage en Asie du Sud-Est*, edited by G. Condominas, 399–410. Paris: EHESS.

Domenichini-Ramiaramanana, B. and J.-P. Domenichini (2010). 'Sujétion royale et sujétion privée: Quelques aspects à Mananjary sous Ranavalona I.' *Tsingy* 12: 37–58.

Douglas, M. (1966). *Purity and Danger: An Analysis of Concepts of Pollution and Taboo*. London: Routledge and Kegan Paul.

Dubois, H. (1938). *Monographie des Betsileo*. Paris: Institut d'Ethnologie.

Dumont, L. (1970). *Homo Hierarchicus: Essai sur le Système des Castes*. Paris: Gallimard.

Durkheim, E. and M. Mauss (1903). 'De quelques formes de classification: Contribution à l'étude des représentations collectives.' *L'année sociologique* 6: 1–72.

Edholm, F. (1971). 'Royal Funerary Rituals Among the Betsileo of Madagascar,' MPhil thesis, University of London.

Ellen, R. (2006). *The Categorical Impulse: Essays in the Anthropology of Classifying Behaviour.* New York: Berghahn Books.

Ellis, S. (1985). *The Rising of the Red Shawls: A Revolt in Madagascar, 1895–1899.* Cambridge, UK: Cambridge University Press.

Elster, J. (2007). *Explaining Social Behavior: More Nuts and Bolts for the Social Sciences.* Cambridge, UK: Cambridge University Press.

Engelke, M. (2017). *Think Like an Anthropologist.* London: Pelican Books.

Evers, S. (2002). *Constructing History, Culture and Inequality: The Betsileo in the Extreme Southern Highlands of Madagascar.* Leiden: Brill.

Evers, S. (2006). 'Expropriated from the Hereafter: The fate of the landless in the southern highlands of Madagascar.' *Journal of Peasant Studies* 33(3): 413–444.

Feeley-Harnik, G. (1991). 'Finding Memories in Madagascar.' In *Images of Memory: On Remembering and Representation*, edited by S. Küchler and W. Melion, 121–140. Washington, DC: Smithsonian Institution Press.

Filliot, J.-M. (1974). *La Traite des Esclaves vers les Mascareignes au XVIIIe Siècle.* Paris: ORSTOM.

Freeman, L. (2001). 'Knowledge, Education and Social Differentiation Amongst the Betsileo of Fisakana, Highland Madagascar,' PhD thesis, University of London.

Freeman, L. (2013). 'Speech, Silence and Slave Descent in Highland Madagascar.' *Journal of the Royal Anthropological Institute* 19(3): 600–617.

Gardini, M. (2015). 'L'activisme politique des descendants d'esclaves à Antananarivo: Les héritages de Zoam.' *Politique africaine* 4: 23–40.

Gelman, S. (2003). *The Essential Child: Origins of Essentialism in Everyday Thought.* Oxford: Oxford University Press.

Gelman, S. (2004). 'Psychological Essentialism in Children.' *Trends in Cognitive Sciences* 8(9): 404–409.

Gelman, S. and C. Legare (2011). 'Concepts and Folk Theories.' *Annual Review of Anthropology* 40: 379–398.

Gerth, H. and C. Wright Mills, eds. (1948). *From Max Weber: Essays in Sociology.* London: Routledge and Kegan Paul.

Gil-White, F. (2001). 'Are Ethnic Groups Biological Species to the Human Brain? Essentialism in Our Cognition of Some Social Categories.' *Current Anthropology* 42: 515–515.

Graeber, D. (1995). 'Dancing with Corpses Reconsidered: An Interpretation of Famadihana (in Arivonimamo, Madagascar).' *American Ethnologist* 22(2): 258–278.

Graeber, D. (1997). 'Painful Memories.' *Journal of Religion in Africa* 27(4): 374–400.

Graeber, D. (2007). *Lost People: Magic and the Legacy of Slavery in Madagascar*. Bloomington, IN: Indiana University Press.

Graeber, D. and M. Sahlins (2017). *On Kings*. Chicago, IL: University of Chicago Press.

Grandidier, G. (1913). 'Le mariage à Madagascar.' *Bulletins et Mémoires de la Société d'Anthropologie de Paris* 4(1): 9–46.

Gueunier, N. (1974). 'Les monuments funéraires et commémoratifs de bois sculpté Betsileo (Madagascar),' PhD thesis, Université de Paris I.

Gueunier, N. (2012). 'L'évolution récente des noms de personnes à Madagascar.' In *Nomination et Organisation Sociale*, edited by S. Chave-Dartoen, C. Leguy and D. Monnerie, 181–208. Paris: Armand Colin.

Gueunier, N., F. Noiret and S. Raharinjanahary (2005). 'Esclavage et liberté sur les Hautes Terres à la fin du XIXe siècle: L'Histoire de l'asservissement et de la rédemption d'Isambo, ou Aogosta Herman Franke, 1877–1893, d'après les manuscrits Walen.' In *Hommage à Bruno Hübsch*: Volume II, edited by C. Ratongavao, 69–178. Lyon: Profac.

Haile, J. (1899). 'Betsileo Home-life.' *Antananarivo Annual* 23: 326–337.

Haile, J. (1900). 'Some Betsileo Ideas.' *Antananarivo Annual* 24: 1–16, 401–407.

Hale, T. (2015). 'A Non-essentialist Theory of Race: The Case of an Afro-indigenous Village in Northern Peru.' *Social Anthropology/Anthropologie Sociale* 23(2): 135–151.

Hanks, W. (2005). 'Explorations in the Deictic Field.' *Current Anthropology* 46(2): 191–220.

Haring, L. (1992). *Verbal Arts in Madagascar: Performance in Historical Perspective*. Philadelphia, PA: University of Pennsylvania Press.

Harris, M. and C. Kottak (1963). 'The Structural Significance of Brazilian Racial Categories.' *Sociologica* 25: 203–209.

Haslam, N. (2017). 'The Origins of Lay Theories: The Case of Essentialist Beliefs.' In *The Science of Lay Theories: How Beliefs Shape Our Cognition, Behaviour, and Health*, edited by C. Zedelius, B. Müller and J. Schooler, 3–16. New York: Springer.

Haslam, N. and M. Abou-Abdallah (2015). 'Essentialism.' In *International Encyclopedia of the Social & Behavioral Sciences*, Second Edition, Volume 8, edited by J. Wright, 13–15. Amsterdam: Elsevier.

Haslam, N., L. Rothschild and D. Ernst (2002). 'Are Essentialist Beliefs Associated with Prejudice?' *British Journal of Social Psychology* 41: 87–100.

Hébert, J.-C. (1965). 'La cosmologie malgache, suivie de l'énumération des points cardinaux et l'importance du nord-est.' *Taloha* 1: 84–149.

Hertz, R. (1907). 'Contribution à une étude sur la représentation collective de la mort.' *L'Année sociologique* X: 48–137.

Hirschfeld, L. (1996). *Race in the Making: Cognition, Culture, and the Child's Construction of Human Kinds*. Cambridge, MA: MIT Press.

Huntington, R. (1973). 'Religion and Social Organisation of the Bara People of Madagascar,' PhD thesis, Duke University.

168   *References*

Hurvitz, D. (1979). 'Anjoaty Cattle Ear Marks.' In *Madagascar in History: Essays from the 1970s*, edited by R. Kent, 42–101. Albany, CA: Foundation for Malagasy Studies.

Hutchins, E. (1995). *Cognition in the Wild*. Cambridge, MA: MIT Press.

Jackson, J. (2013). *Political Oratory and Cartooning: An Ethnography of Democratic Process in Madagascar*. Oxford: Wiley-Blackwell.

Jacob, G. (1997). 'L'abolition de l'esclavage à Madagascar: Les perspectives françaises.' In *L'Esclavage à Madagascar: Aspects Historiques et Résurgences Contemporaines*, edited by I. Rakoto, 259–271. Antananarivo: Institut de Civilisations-Musée d'Art et d'Archéologie.

Johnson, H. (1900). 'Betsileo, Past and Present, a Twenty Years Review.' *Antananarivo Annual* 24: 481–485.

Keller, E. (2005). *The Road to Clarity: Seventh-Day Adventism in Madagascar*. New York: Palgrave MacMillan.

Keller, E. (2008). 'The Banana Plant and the Moon: Conservation and the Malagasy Ethos of Life in Masoala, Madagascar.' *American Ethnologist* 35(4): 650–664.

Kopytoff, I. (1982). 'Slavery.' *Annual Review of Anthropology* 11: 207–230.

Kottak, C. (1971). 'Social Groups and Kinship Calculation Among the Southern Betsileo.' *American Anthropologist* 73(1): 178–193.

Kottak, C. (1977). 'The Process of State Formation in Madagascar.' *American Ethnologist* 4(1): 136–155.

Kottak, C. (1980). *The Past in the Present: History, Ecology, and Variation in Highland Madagascar*. Ann Arbor, MI: University of Michigan Press.

Kottak, C. (1986). 'Kinship Modeling: Adaptation, Fosterage, and Fictive Kinship Among the Betsileo.' In *Madagascar: Society and History*, edited by C. Kottak, J.-A. Rakotoarisoa, A. Southall and P. Vérin, 277–298. Durham, NC: Carolina Academic Press.

Lambek, M. (1992). 'Taboo as a Cultural Practice Among Malagasy Speakers.' *Man* 27: 19–42.

Lambek, M. (2002). *The Weight of the Past: Living with History in Mahajanga, Madagascar*. New York: Palgrave Macmillan.

Lambek, M. (2004). 'Revolted But Not Revolting: Reflections on the Sakalava Division of Labour and Forms of Subjectivation.' *Slavery and Abolition* 25(2): 108–119.

Larson, P. (1997). 'A Census of Slaves Exported From Central Madagascar to the Mascarenes Between 1775 and 1820.' In *L'Esclavage à Madagascar: Aspects Historiques et Résurgences Contemporaines*, edited by I. Rakoto, 121–145. Antananarivo: Institut de Civilisations-Musée d'Art et d'Archéologie.

Larson, P. (1999). 'Reconsidering Trauma, Identity, and the African Diaspora: Enslavement and Historical Memory in Nineteenth-century Highland Madagascar.' *The William and Mary Quarterly* 56(2): 335–362.

Larson, P. (2000). *History and Memory in the Age of Enslavement: Becoming Merina in Highland Madagascar, 1770–1822*. Oxford: James Currey.

Leach, R. (1961). *Rethinking Anthropology*. London: Athlone Press.

Legrip-Randriambelo, O. and D. Regnier (2014). 'The Place of Healers-diviners (ombiasa) in Betsileo Medical Pluralism.' *Health, Culture and Society* 7(1): 28–37.

Leslie, S. (2014). 'Carving Up the Social World with Generics.' *Oxford Studies in Experimental Philosophy* 1: 208–232.

Lévi-Strauss, C. (1963). *Totemism*. Translated from the French by R. Needham. Boston: Beacon Press.

Lyautey, 'Colonel' (1903). *Dans le Sud de Madagascar: Pénétration Militaire, Situation Politique et Economique, 1901–1902*. Paris: H.C. Lavauzelle.

Mack, J. (1986). *Madagascar, Island of the Ancestors*. London: British Museum.

Mahalingam, R. (1998). 'Essentialism, Power and Representation of Caste: A Developmental Study,' PhD thesis, University of Pittsburgh.

McIntosh, J. (2005). 'Language Essentialism and Social Hierarchies Among Giriama and Swahili.' *Journal of Pragmatics* 37(12): 1919–1944.

McIntosh, J. (2009). *The Edge of Islam: Power, Personhood, and Ethnoreligious Boundaries on the Kenya Coast*. Durham, NC: Duke University Press.

Medin, D. and A. Ortony (1989). 'Psychological Essentialism.' In *Similarity and Analogical Reasoning*, edited by S. Vosniadou and A. Ortony, 179–195. Cambridge, UK: Cambridge University Press.

Meillassoux, C. (1986). *Anthropologie de l'Esclavage: Le Ventre de Fer et d'Argent*. Paris: Presses Universitaires de France.

Metcalf, P. (2002). *They Lie, We Lie: Getting On With Anthropology*. London: Routledge.

Michel-Andrianarahinjaka, L. (1986). *Le Système Littéraire Betsileo*. Fianarantsoa: Ambozontany.

Miers, S. (2003). 'Slavery: A Question of Definition.' *Slavery & Abolition* 24(2): 1–16.

Miers, S. and I. Kopytoff, eds. (1977). *Slavery in Africa: Historical and Anthropological Perspectives*. Madison, WI: University of Wisconsin Press.

Moss, 'Mrs' (1900). 'Betsileo Funeral Customs. Translated From a Native Account.' *Antananarivo Annual* 24: 475–477.

Needham, R., ed. (1971). *Rethinking Kinship and Marriage*. London: Tavistock.

Ochs (Keenan), E. (1973). 'A Sliding Sense of Obligatoriness: The Polystructure of Malagasy Oratory.' *Language in Society* 2: 225–243.

Ochs (Keenan), E. (1974a). 'Conversation and Oratory in Vakinankaratra, Madagascar,' PhD thesis, University of Pennsylvania.

Ochs (Keenan), E. (1974b). 'Norm-makers, Norm-breakers: Uses of Speech by Men and Women in a Malagasy Community.' In *Ethnography of Communication*, edited by R. Bauman and J. Sherzer, 125–143. Cambridge, UK: Cambridge University Press.

Osterhoudt, S. (2016). 'Written with Seeds: The Political Ecology of Memory in Madagascar.' *Journal of Political Ecology* 23: 263–278.

170   *References*

Parker Pearson, M. and D. Regnier (2018). 'Collective and Single Burial in Madagascar.' In *Gathered in Death: Archaeological and Ethnological Perspectives on Collective Burial and Social Organisation*, edited by A. Schmitt, S. Déderix and I. Crevecoeur, 41–62. Louvain-La-Neuve: Presses Universitaires de Louvain.

Parry, J. (2007). 'Afterword.' In *Questions of Anthropology*, edited by R. Astuti, J. Parry and C. Stafford, 337–363. Oxford: Berg.

Piolet, J. (1896). 'De l'esclavage à Madagascar.' *Le Correspondant*, 10 February: 447–480.

Portais, M. (1974). *Le Bassin d'Ambalavao: Influence Urbaine et Évolution des Campagnes (Sud Betsileo, Madagascar)*. Paris: ORSTOM.

Prenctice, D. and D. Miller (2007). 'Psychological Essentialism of Human Categories.' *Current Directions in Psychological Science* 16(4): 202–206.

Rafidinarivo, C. (2000). 'Le référent de l'esclavage dans les représentations transactionnelles marchandes à Madagascar.' *Journal des africanistes* 70(1–2): 123–144.

Rahamefy, A. (1997). *Le Roi ne Meurt pas: Rites Funéraires Princiers du Betsileo, Madagascar*. Paris: L'Harmattan.

Raherisoanjato, D. (1982a). 'Les vazimba dans le Sud Betsileo.' *Omaly sy Anio* 15: 7–19.

Raherisoanjato, D. (1982b). 'Christianisme et religion traditionnelle (l'exemple de l'Arindrano).' *Taloha* 9: 25–33.

Raherisoanjato, D. (1984a). *Origines et Évolution du Royaume de l'Arindrano jusqu'au XIXe siècle: Contribution à l'Histoire Régionale de Madagascar*. Antananarivo: Musée d'Art et d'Archéologie.

Raherisoanjato, D. (1984b). 'Les Hova Zafimahafanandriana de l'Arindrano dans le Sud Betsileo.' In *Ny razana tsy mba maty: Cultures traditionnelles malgaches*, edited by J.-P. Domenichini, J. Poirier and D. Raherisoanjato, 205–233. Antananarivo: Librairie de Madagascar.

Raherisoanjato, D. (1988). 'Le vala du pays Betsileo (XVIIIe-XXe siècle).' *Omaly sy Anio* 27: 93–101.

Rainihifina, J. (1956). *Lovantsaina I: Tantara Betsileo*. Fianarantsoa: Ambozontany.

Rainihifina, J. (1975). *Lovantsaina II: Fomba Betsileo*. Fianarantsoa: Ambozontany.

Rajaonarimanana, N. (1979). 'Achèvement de funérailles et offrandes de linceuls: Rites funéraires et commémoratifs du Betsileo de Manandriana.' In *Les Hommes et la Mort: Rites Funéraires à Travers le Monde*, edited by J. Guiart, 180–193. Paris: Le Sycomore.

Rajaonarimanana, N. (1996). 'Les 7 pilons de fer: Traditions orales du Manandriana.' *Études Océan indien* 20: 1–160.

Rakoto, I., ed. (1997). *L'Esclavage à Madagascar: Aspects Historiques et Résurgences Contemporaines*. Antananarivo: Institut de Civilisations-Musée d'Art et Archéologie.

Rakoto, I. and E. Mangalaza, eds. (2000). *La route des Esclaves: Système Servile et Traite d'Esclaves dans l'Est Malgache*. Paris: L'Harmattan.

Rakotomalala, M. and C. Razafimbelo (1985). 'Le problème d'intégration sociale chez les Makoa de l'Antsihanaka.' *Omaly sy Anio* 21–22: 93–113.

Ralaikoa, A. (1987). *Fiscalité, Administration et Pressions Coloniales dans le Sud Betsileo (1895–1918)*. Antananarivo: Université de Madagascar.

Ramamonjisoa, J. (1984). '"Blancs" et "noirs", les dimensions de l'inégalité sociale.' *Cahiers des Sciences Sociales* 1: 39–77.

Randrianja, S. and S. Ellis (2009). *Madagascar: A Short History*. London: Hurst and Company.

Rantoandro, G. (1997). 'Après l'abolition de l'esclavage à Madagascar: Le devenir immédiat des esclaves émancipés.' In *L'Esclavage à Madagascar: Aspects Historiques et Résurgences Contemporaines*, edited by I. Rakoto, 273–288. Antananarivo: Institut de Civilisations-Musée d'Art et d'Archéologie.

Rantoandro, G. (2005). 'L'esclavage comme enjeu de la mémoire à Madagascar.' In *Le Monde Créole, Peuplement, Sociétés et Condition Humaine (17e-20e)*, edited by J. Weber, 369–383. Paris: Les Indes Savantes.

Rasamoelina, H. (2007). *Madagascar: État, Communautés Villageoises et Banditisme Rural*. Paris: L'Harmattan.

Rasoamampionona, C. (2000). 'La survivance d'inégalités dans les castes betsileo.' In *L'Extraordinaire et le Quotidien: Variations Anthropologiques. Hommage au Professeur Pierre Vérin*, edited by P. Vérin, C. Allibert and N. Rajaonarimanana, 369–375. Paris: Karthala.

Raveloson, G. (1956). 'La levée des troupes en Betsileo.' *Bulletin de l'Académie malgache* 34: 107–109.

Razafiarivony, M. (2005). 'Les descendants des anciens esclaves importés d'Afrique à Madagascar: Tradition et réalité.' *Journal of Asian and African Studies* 70: 63–80.

Razafindralambo, L. (2003). 'La notion d'esclave en Imerina (Madagascar): Ancienne servitude et aspects actuels de la dépendance,' PhD thesis, Université de Paris Ouest Nanterre La Défense.

Razafindralambo, L. (2005). 'Inégalité, exclusion, représentation sur les hautes terres centrales de Madagascar.' *Cahiers d'études africaines* 3(179–180): 879–904.

Razafindralambo, L. (2008). 'Les statuts sociaux dans les hautes terres malgaches à la lumière des archives missionnaires norvégiennes.' *Ateliers du LESC* 32. Available online at: http://journals.openedition.org/ateliers/2122; doi:10.4000/ateliers.2122 (accessed 17 January 2019)

Razafindralambo, L. (2014). 'Esclavages et inégalités: Entre constructions sociales et différences "naturelles".' In *Esclavage et Libération à Madagascar*, edited by I. Rakoto and S. Urfer, 95–106. Paris: Karthala.

Razafintsalama, A. (1983). 'Les funérailles royales en Isandra, d'après les sources du XIXème siècle.' In *Les Souverains de Madagascar: L'Histoire Royale et ses Résurgences Contemporaines*, edited by F. Raison-Jourde, 193–209. Paris: Karthala.

Regnier, D. (2012). 'Why Not Marry Them? History, Essentialism and the Condition of Slave Descendants Among the Southern Betsileo (Madagascar),' PhD thesis, London School of Economics and Political Science.

Regnier, D. (2014a). 'Pourquoi ne pas les épouser? L'évitement du mariage avec les descendants d'esclaves dans le Sud Betsileo (Madagascar).' *Études rurales* 194: 103–122.

Regnier, D. (2014b). 'Les esclaves morts et leur invocation dans les rituels du Sud Betsileo.' *Études Océan indien* 51–52: 253–276.

Regnier, D. (2015a). 'Clean People, Unclean People: The Essentialisation of 'Slaves' Among the Southern Betsileo of Madagascar.' *Social Anthropology/Anthropologie Sociale* 23(2): 152–168.

Regnier, D. (2015b). 'Tombes ancestrales et super mariages chez les Betsileo de Madagascar.' In *Le Funéraire: Mémoire, Protocoles, Monuments*, edited by G. Delaplace and F. Valentin, 117–124. Paris: Éditions de Boccard.

Regnier, D. (2016). 'Naming and Name Changing in Postcolonial Madagascar.' *Pacific Studies* 39(1–2): 201–215.

Regnier, D. (2017). 'La fondation d'une nouvelle terre ancestrale dans le Sud Betsileo (Madagascar): Dilemme, transformation, rupture.' In *(Re)Fonder: Les Modalités du (Re)Commencement dans le Temps et l'Espace*, edited by P. Gervais-Lambony, F. Hurlet and I. Rivoal, 121–128. Paris: Éditions de Boccard.

Regnier, D. (2019). 'Forever Slaves? Inequality, Uncleanliness and Vigilance About Origins in the Southern Highlands of Madagascar.' *Anthropological Forum: A Journal of Social Anthropology and Comparative Sociology* 29(3): 249–266.

Regnier, D. and R. Astuti (2015a). 'Introduction: Taking Up the Cognitive Challenge.' *Social Anthropology/Anthropologie Sociale* 23(2): 131–134.

Regnier, D. and R. Astuti, eds. (2015b). 'The Cognitive Challenge.' *Social Anthropologie/Anthropologie Sociale* 23(2). Special issue.

Regnier, D. and D. Somda (2019). 'Slavery and Post-slavery in Madagascar: An Overview.' In *African Islands: Leading Edges of Empire and Globalization*, edited by T. Falola, D. Porter-Sanchez and J. Parrott, 345–369. Rochester, NY: University of Rochester Press.

Rhodes, M. and S. Gelman (2009). 'A Developmental Examination of the Conceptual Structure of Animal, Artifact, and Human Social Categories Across Two Cultural Contexts.' *Cognitive Psychology* 59: 244–274.

Rhodes, M., S. Leslie and C. Tworek (2012). 'Cultural Transmission of Social Essentialism.' Proceedings of the *National Academy of Sciences* 109: 13526–13531.

Rhodes, M. and T. Mandalaywala (2017). 'The Development and Developmental Consequences of Social Essentialism.' *Wiley Interdisciplinary Reviews: Cognitive Science*. https://doi.org/10.1002/wcs.1437.

Richardson, J. (1875). 'Remarkable Burial Customs Among the Betsileo.' *Antananarivo Annual* 1: 70–75.

Richardson, J. (1885). *A New Malagasy–English Dictionary*. Antananarivo: London Missionary Society.

Rossi, B. (2009). 'Introduction: Rethinking slavery in West Africa.' In *Reconfiguring Slavery: West African Trajectories*, edited by B. Rossi, 1–25. Liverpool, UK: Liverpool University Press.

Rothbart, M. and M. Taylor (1992). 'Category Labels and Social Reality: Do We View Social Categories as Natural Kinds?' In *Language, Interaction and Social Cognition*, edited by G. Semin and K. Fiedler, 11–36. Thousand Oaks, CA: Sage.

Ruud, J. (1960). *Taboo: A Study of Malagasy Customs and Beliefs*. Oslo: Oslo University Press.

Sage, J. and L. Kasten (2008). *Enslaved: True Stories of Modern Day Slavery*. New York: Palgrave Macmillan.

Salomon, G. (1993). 'No Distribution Without Individual's Cognition: A Dynamic Interactional View.' In *Distributed Cognitions: Psychological and Educational Considerations*, edited by G. Salomon, 111–138. Cambridge, UK: Cambridge University Press.

Sayer, A. (1997). 'Essentialism, Social Constructionism, and Beyond'. *The Sociological Review* 45(3): 453–487.

Sharp, L. (1993). *The Possessed and the Dispossessed: Spirits, Identity, and Power in a Madagascar Migrant Town*. Berkeley, CA: University of California Press.

Sharp, L. (2002). *The Sacrificed Generation: Youth, History, and the Colonised Mind in Madagascar*. Berkeley, CA: University of California Press.

Shaw, G. (1877). 'The Betsileo: Country and people.' *Antananarivo Annual* 3: 73–85.

Shaw, G. (1878). 'The Betsileo: Religious and Social Customs.' *Antananarivo Annual* 4: 312–334.

Shore, B. (1996). *Culture in Mind: Cognition, Culture and the Problem of Meaning*. New York: Oxford University Press.

Sibree, J. (1870). *Madagascar and Its People*. London: The Religious Tract Society.

Sibree, J. (1898). 'Remarkable Ceremonial at the Decease and Burial of a Betsileo Prince, Translated from an Account Written by an Unnamed Informant.' *Antananarivo Annual* 22: 195–208.

Sodikoff, G. (2012). *Forest and Labor in Madagascar: From Colonial Concession to Global Biosphere*. Bloomington, IN: Indiana University Press.

Solondraibe, T. (1994). 'Communautés de base et pouvoirs politiques dans le Lalangina et le Vohibato (Sud-Betsileo) du XVIe au début du XXe siècle.' *Omaly sy Anio* 33–36: 15–46.

Somda, D. (2009). 'Et le réel serait passé: Le secret de l'esclavage et l'imagination de la société (Anôsy, sud de Madagascar),' PhD thesis, Université de Paris Ouest Nanterre La Défense.

Somda, D. (2014). 'De la pierre à la croix: Interprétation d'un paysage commémoratif (Anôsy, sud-est de Madagascar).' *Études rurales* 194: 79–102.

Southall, A. (1986). 'Common Themes in Malagasy Culture.' In *Madagascar: Society and History*, edited by C. Kottak, J.-A. Rakotoarisoa, A. Southall and P. Vérin, 411–426. Durham, NC: Carolina Academic Press.

Sperber, D. (1996). *Explaining Culture: A Naturalistic Account*. London: Blackwell.

Sperber, D. and H. Mercier (2012). 'Reasoning as a Social Competence.' In *Collective Wisdom: Principles and Mechanisms*, edited by H. Landemore and J. Elster, 368–392. Cambridge, UK: Cambridge University Press.

Stépanoff, C. (2014). *Chamanisme, Rituel et Cognition chez les Touvas (Sibérie du Sud)*. Paris: Éditions de la Maison des Sciences de l'Homme.

Stépanoff, C. (2015). 'Transsingularities: The Cognitive Foundations of Shamanism in Northern Asia.' *Social Anthropology/Anthropologie Sociale* 23(2): 169–185.

Strauss, C. and Quinn, N. (1997). *A Cognitive Theory of Cultural Meaning*. Cambridge, UK: Cambridge University Press.

Testart, A. (1998). 'L'esclavage comme institution.' *L'Homme* 38(145): 31–69.

Thomas, P. (2006). 'The Water That Blesses, the River That Flows: Place and the Ritual Imagination Among the Temanambondro of Southeast Madagascar.' In *The Poetic Power of Place: Comparative Perspectives on Austronesian Ideas of Locality*, edited by J. Fox, 23–41. Canberra: Australian National University Press. First published 1997.

Valensky, C. (1995). *Le Soldat Occulté: Les Malgaches de l'Armée Française*. Paris: L'Harmattan.

Van Gennep, A. (1904). *Tabou et Totémisme à Madagascar*. Paris: Ernest Leroux.

Walsh, Andrew (2001). 'When Origins Matter: The Politics of Commemoration in Northern Madagascar.' *Ethnohistory* 48(1–2): 237–256.

Walsh, A. (2002). 'Responsibility, Taboos and "the Freedom to do Otherwise" in Ankarana, Northern Madagascar.' *Journal of the Royal Anthropological Institute* 8: 451–468.

Whitehouse, H. and R. McCauley (2005). *Mind and Religion: Psychological and Cognitive Foundations of Religion*. Walnut Creek, CA: Altamira Press.

Yzerbyt, V., O. Corneille and C. Estrada (2001). 'The Interplay of Subjective Essentialism and Entitativity in the Formation of Stereotypes.' *Personality and Social Psychology Review* 5(2): 141–155.

Yzerbyt, V., C. Judd and O. Corneille, eds. (2004). *The Psychology of Group Perception: Perceived Variability, Entitativity, and Essentialism*. New York: Psychology Press.

Index

184   *Index*

Betsileo polities around the *mpanjaka* (ruler) 4, 97; the present-day descendants of 5; the residence of noble families in Ambatofotsy and Ambalamasina 124n3; the ritual powers of 134, 142, 152n4, 161, 162; the slave owning practices of the, 40–41, 43, 61, 64–65, 90, 106n5, 134, 157; the tomb incident at Imerina 124–125n4; the vulnerability to attacks and enslavement during certain historical periods 136

hovavao (slave descendants) 59, 67n8, 83, 109, 144, 146, 147

Imerina (region) 1–2, 124–125n4, 141, 152n1

interviews and discussions: with a free descent elder and daughter regarding marriage between commoners and slave descendants 109–110; with a mother and son regarding the uncleanness of slave descendants 145–148; conducted in the Malagasy language, 19, 21; difficult and failed 54, 60, 107–108; discussion with a free descent woman 83; experiments 132–133; the orchestration required for some, 54, 55; with Rakoto Jeannot 59–60, 60–63; with Ramarcel 50–54; with Ramarcelline, 95–101; with Randriatsoa 47–48, 54–58, 65, 67n5, 83–84, 124n1; *see also* fieldwork

Isambo (noble enslaved as a child) 137–139, 141, 156–157

Ivohibe (region) 31, 36–37, 101, 106n4

kinship: the Betsileo system 112; commoner investigations of links 120–121; *fehim-poñena* ('tying of kinship') 73, 76, 77, 80, 84n5, 87–88, 94; the *fianakaviana* (family) 31, 105; *fombandrazana* (ancestral customs) that bond alliances 80; the function of the *tandra vady* to strengthen alliances between

families 84n4; *havana* (kinsmen) 11–12, 48, 49–50, 75, 79, 122; marriage and the establishment of between families 82, 84nn4–5, 87–88; the *vakirà* (blood bond) ritual as a means of establishing links 82–83, 105, 131–132

lamba, lamba arindrano, and *lamba-hoany* (cloth, wrap) 47, 50, 51, 55, 67n4, 151

land: the allocations of for settlement through an *andevohova* 3, 7, 42, 58–65, 69, 97–98, 158; ancestral land (*tanindrazana*) 31, 36, 37, 38, 42–43, 44n7, 112, 122, 141, 142; Berosaiña claims to Beparasy lands occupied by free-descent families 13–14, 52–53, 67n5, 122, 158–159; Berosaiña possession of good, well-located 11, 25, 28, 43, 52–53, 159; conflicts (*ady tany,* land conflicts) mediated by *andevohova* 15n12, 47, 59; cultivation and cultivation rights in Beparasy 5, 7, 37, 141; descent group ownership of (*fañahia* status) 30, 36–37, 42, 61, 93, 142–143, 157–158; *farihy* (wet rice lands) 29, 158; the inability to identify one's ancestral as an indicator of enslavement 130–131, 142; the land of origin as a social signifier 57, 90; landowner ('master of the land') *tompontany* 13, 27, 43, 108; Raboba's ownership, 13, 28–32, 67n5, 101; Randrianja Albert's 35–37; recordkeeping of descent ownership by local *andevohova* 15n12, 57, 59; Redison's ownership, 8, 10, 13; the settlement of new, cultivable in Beparasy 5, 42, 58–59, 63, 66, 141–142, 157–158; taboos that can be linked to descent group, 30, 38; tombs as evidence of a claim on 37, 40, 43–44, 67n5; transactions 13, 15n12, 30, 101; *see also* migration and settlement

stigmatisation; psychological essentialism; slavery and slave descent

vadipaisa (ceremony for the transport of ancestral bones to a new tomb): as a means of securing land claims 37; the attendance and duration of 33, 69, 89, 91, 108, 122; the multiple shifts of the bones of Rakamisy and his descendants via 39–40; as the product of kinship disputes 39–40, 68–69, 100–101, 102; the sponsored by Randrianja Albert, 37; the that moved the bones of Rainihosy and his descendants 35
vakirà (blood bond): as an excuse to prevent marriages between commoners and slave descendants 104–5; as the basis for agreements between rulers 5; on the *Bible*, 83; as the means of establishing kinship (*mpivakira*) between free- and slave-descended individuals 6, 82–84, 105, 159; the of Randriatsoa with five free descendants of Beparasy 83; the ritual establishing 82–83, 132; the socially integrative potential of 83–84, 105
Vaofara (free descent) 9, 11
Vatobe hill 6–7, 15n11, 39–40, 49–50, 63, 157, 158
vazaha (white foreigner) 12, 20, 28, 47–48, 55–56, 64, 158
villages and hamlets: the Berosaiña call for total equality within mixed 49–50; descent groups in 8; early fortified hilltop *vala* 2–5, 7, 157; early hilltop *afo* (fire) 7; the economies of Beparasy 19; as elements of an individual's identity 48, 71, 89, 91, 115, 118–123, 147; the establishment of new hearths in through marriage, 75–77; the French *politique de villagisation* ('villagisation' policy) 8, 28, 158; the interrelationships among villagers of different, 10, 48, 68–69, 71–74, 77–78, 92, 95, 101–104, 106n3; itinerant workers 71; Merina-era

40–41; mixed 8, 36, 44n1, 44n4, 48, 157–158; population and distribution in southern Betsileo 2, 5, 8, 15n11, 118, 150–151; prejudice, discrimination, and ostracism within 42–43, 48–49, 54, 56, 66, 67n11, 71, 89–92, 111, 117–118, 123–124, 147–149, 151–152, 159–160; the proximity of most to rice fields 2–3, 7, 43, 151; relationships between free- and slave-descent co-villagers 44n5, 46, 48–49, 157, 159; the settlement of new 58; slave descent, 41, 44n8, 66, 69, 90, 101, 122–123; the suspicion toward strangers among villagers 19–21, 158; *vala* (cattle pen, hamlets organised around their cattle pens) 3, 7–8, 14n4, 44n1, 125n9, 150–151, 158; village councils (*fokonolo*) 53, 94, 103, 107, 116
Vinany (Vinanimalaza or Mahasoabe [early Betsileo capital]) 61, 63, 66, 98, 99, 156
Vohangy (Berosaiña): the biological daughter of Rasamuel and the foster daughter of Ramarcelline, 37–38, 102; the catering business of 37–39, 46; the classificatory sister of Randriatsoa 39; the experiences of the eldest son of 160; her business damaged by arson 38–39; her children 37; her sales of food at the Ambalavao market as a taboo violation 38–39; the sister of Redison 37; the tomb controversy among her matrilineal kin 68–69

war: Berosaiña participants in World War I 28, 29, 32, 33, 44n2; the French pacification campaign 15n10; inter-polity in pre-eighteenth century Betsileo 2, 4; massacres and enslavement during the of Merina King Radama I 5, 41, 52, 136–137; Merina conflicts with the French, 63; other Malagasy soldiers in World War I 44n2, 66,